Yale Romanic Studies, Second Series, 7

Revised Edition

# MODERN FRENCH THEATRE

from Giraudoux to Genet

by JACQUES GUICHARNAUD

in collaboration with June Guicharnaud

New Haven and London, Yale University Press, 1967

*To Louisa, Marc, and Willie—again*

# PREFACE

This book is not intended to be a systematic study of contemporary French theatre. All the facts and dates are not included, although the most important can be found in the Appendixes. The following chapters deal primarily with those playwrights who have proved to be or show promise of becoming first-rate and describe in general terms the dramatic universe of each. If neither Sacha Guitry, nor Madame Simone, nor Maurice Rostand, nor André Roussin are considered, the reasons for omitting them will soon become apparent; and if Supervielle, Georges Neveux, André Obey, and Marcel Achard are barely mentioned (or not mentioned at all), it is only because they unfortunately wrote at the same time as others greater than they.

From Jean Giraudoux to Ionesco and Beckett, French theatre has exploited a marked and powerful trend that began with the revolution of 1890, and works outside the trend now seem insignificant. For the last thirty years it has been a theatre of exploration. Its objective has not been to offer ready-made solutions on the level of either form or substance: it does not give reassuring answers to everyday problems, nor does it flatter the public's aesthetic lethargy with established forms. Each writer, rather than just tell a story in more or less dramatic form, has tried to express the human condition metaphorically. In comparing American and French theatre of the fifties Robert Brustein has remarked:

> While we are trying to come to terms with human condition-
> ing, the French are trying to explore the boundaries of human
> limitation; while we are seeking security, ease, and happiness
> within the social unit, the French are seeking metaphysical
> freedom outside of human institutions; while our key words
> are *adjustment* and *affirmation,* the key words in France are
> alienation and negation.*

Not all the playwrights treated in this book are necessarily nihilistic. But all have tried to define man in metaphysical terms and
outside of human institutions. Giraudoux's universe or Claudel's is
no easier to live in than Sartre's or Beckett's: man is defined in
terms of his agony, and the universe itself is seen as being fundamentally in a state of conflict. Giraudoux's search for harmony is
not situated "within the social unit"; Claudel's religion is hardly
concerned with accepted ethics. On the whole, the hero of modern
French theatre is a character who refuses to play the game of "ad-
justment" but rather tries to find himself through a higher game,
if only that of theatre itself. According to the playwright's degree
of optimism or pessimism, souls are saved or man is brought back
to man. Whichever the case, the basic conflict is a vertical one in
which man is not limited to socio-psychological tensions easily
resolved through what Brustein calls "pious pronouncements."

Nor is the anecdote ever separate from the form. Each vision
of the world is not only dramatic but theatrical, whether it be the
spectacle God has created for himself, as in Claudel, or Beckett's
life-farce. The hero of such theatre is not only constantly torn
apart and situated beyond himself; he is also an actor who struggles
with his own masks. The universe presented onstage is given not
as the real universe but rather as a metaphor of it. Everything is in
fact unreal. The spectator is asked to put himself in the state of
consciousness in which he both accepts and rejects the reality of

*"Nihilism on Broadway," *The New Republic* (February 29, 1960).

what unfolds before his eyes. Everything onstage happens "as if
. . . ," implying that in life, also, everything happens "as if . . .".
Reality is always elsewhere. Life and theatre are but approxima-
tions of it, images, reflections. And in the past few years the reflections have evolved more and more distinctly toward reflections
of nothing.

Whether or not his humor is as "dark" as that of the French
theatre today, Henri Peyre's lively encouragement and perceptive
advice in the writing of this book were, as always, inspirational.
We should also like to thank Edwin Stein for his sharply critical
eye and Benjamin F. Houston for seeing the manuscript through
to its final stages.

J.G.<br>J.B.

*October 1960*

Since the publication of *Modern French Theatre* some six years
ago, the "new theatre" of the fifties developed to such a degree
and in so many directions that a reevaluation of it seemed in order.
What was originally Part III has therefore been completely revised and expanded into the present Parts III and IV, in which
much new material has been added, changing perspectives considered, and promising new playwrights introduced. This new edition has, of course, given us the opportunity to make minor cor-
rections both of fact and of style, to bring the Appendixes and
Bibliography up to date, and to give Anouilh and Salacrou each
the chapter he deserves. There has been no change, however, in
the general spirit and method of the original volume.

For his very able assistance in preparing this revised version
we should like to thank Wayland W. Schmitt, whose enthusiasm
for the subject matter was, to say the least, provocative, but whose
eye remained resolutely sober.

J.G.<br>J.G.

*April 1967*

# CONTENTS

*. . . and if these powers and possibilities
are dark, it is the fault, not of the plague,
nor of the theatre, but of life.*

Antonin Artaud, *Le Théâtre et la Peste*

# INTRODUCTION

## THEATRE RESURGENT

The representational arts are most particularly open to prostitution. Poets and novelists can always dream about the love or recognition that their works provoke in their readers—even in one single reader—but they rarely witness it. The playwright or the author of a film script hides in the theatre and takes part in a mass phenomenon. One reader's letter overjoys a poet; one satisfied spectator in a hostile audience does little more than emphasize the failure of a play or film. Outbursts of enthusiasm, laughter, tears, and applause are collective. They are addressed, beyond the performed work, to the author and have meaning only in terms of quantity. Success in the theatre is concrete, sensual. It is communicated through calls for the author, facial expressions that penetrate beyond the footlights, and the roar of bravos. At that level, it is often difficult to evaluate the quality of the emotion provoked.

"The great art is to please," said Molière—an ambiguous statement of principle which leaves the door open to all interpretations. The question is: What in the spectator does one aim to please?

"They like it," says the complacent writer or director who has been reproached with turning out degrading theatre. Obviously "they like it!" The audience is almost always ready to be satisfied with little. But the audience is almost always open to quality as well. The charms of quality may work slowly and sometimes require subtle strategy, for the audience, long accustomed to mediocrity, has ultimately been corrupted. The public can easily allow itself to be dragged down because of a quite natural human penchant for the facile. How relatively little it takes to entertain! And since entertainment is an important dimension of art, the two are easily confused. We are indulgent, we succumb to flattery, and in utter bad faith we give purely entertaining works an aesthetic value.

An audience is made up of people who are perpetually concerned with the problems of their everyday lives and are therefore infinitely more amused by what reassures and upholds them in their own realms than by any offer of an opening onto something else. Their realms consist of the ready-made vision each one has of himself and of life, as well as the conception, also ready-made, of the art forms which express that vision.

Asking the playwright to present the bourgeoisie with a show representing the bourgeoisie, as Diderot did, was not only to go from classical realism (which aimed at the reality of universal man) to postrevolutionary realism (which aimed at man in relation to his milieu) but also to lay the first stone in the foundation of a theatre of complacency. The tradesman who spent his time developing commerce, or avoiding bankruptcy, or simply arranging a good marriage for his daughter, did not like the fact that the contrast of Phèdre's passion or Polyeucte's martyrdom relegated his particular values to the background. The merchant who attended a performance of *Phèdre* was in great danger of wondering whether his trading was worth quite so much effort and of questioning the meaning of his life—in short, of suffering.

Diderot and Beaumarchais were the originators—at least in their theoretical works—of a theatre of reassurance. In the second half of the nineteenth century, when their conceptions were picked up and extended by writers in the service of triumphant merchants, there resulted a whole doctrine of systematic indolence in the theatre. *Vaudeville,* comedy, and bourgeois drama seemed to join forces in order to give the maximum of good conscience to the ruling bourgeoisie, both in their virtues and their vices. Each performance persuaded the audience that man, life, and reality were no more than what they believed them to be. The public and its art closed in upon each other. Their agreement was so perfect that the theatre presented the audience with an image not of what it was but of what it wished to be—hence the innumerable basic conventions that had almost become an institution. Everything took place as if the self-satisfied performance of mediocrity ennobled that mediocrity and as if the closed doors of the bourgeois drawing room, on which the curtain usually went up, symbolized the sanctification by art of the limitations of the bourgeois' intellectual, spiritual, and moral horizons.

An image of what the public believed itself to be was presented in forms that were thought to be the only forms possible. Late nineteenth-century theatre, derived from the "well-made" play, reduced the Aristotelian notion of action to its most superficial level. Made up of proven stage tricks and conventions of dialogue and staging, the plays never questioned the idea of theatre itself, nor did they ever suggest a universal Drama. They always recalled something that already existed, both in the technique of detail and in their basic conception.

As soon as the rules of an art cease being thought and felt, they are simply applied and imitation sets in. The French theatre of 1840–80 is not a unique example: eighteenth-century pseudo-classical tragedy, the French Boulevard theatre of today (often spoken of as "Boulevard recipes"), and a great part of the American naturalistic theatre of the forties and fifties are cases in point. The result in the late nineteenth century was a progressive disbelief in dramatic art. Those who studied the theatre in the light of their own philosophies signed its death warrant. Auguste Comte went so far as to say that the very institution of theatre had no meaning in modern society. Barbey d'Aurevilly spoke of the "fundamental inferiority" of theatre as a genre. Mallarmé dreamt of a theatre-Mass, but one assimilated to his universal "Book," and emphasized the absolute degradation of the theatre of his time. (Jacques Copeau used the following lines of Mallarmé as an epigraph for the programs of the Vieux Colombier: "Do you go to theatre?— No, almost never.—Well! neither do I.")

The last years of the century brought about an awakening both of the theatrical world in general and of the playwright. Almost simultaneously, the attempted reform took two divergent directions: Antoine's Théâtre Libre, founded in 1887, became the champion of realism and naturalism, and Paul Fort's Théâtre d'Art, 1891, champion of the so-called poetic theatre. In fact, this was but the prelude to a revolution. The Théâtre d'Art was held up to ridicule; the Théâtre Libre failed with the decline of the naturalist vogue. Yet both experiments were carried on in other forms. They were but the first manifestations of a reform which sought to formulate its program and its doctrine. There was a general reaction against clichés, conventionalism, and tricks that corresponded to no reality, outer or inner, and were neither the fruit nor the seed of any truly aesthetic experience. Not that conventionally mediocre and vulgar plays were eliminated—even today they continue to fill Parisian theatres—but by around 1890 true theatre began to take back its rights.

Although they agreed on a negative program, the two camps were radically opposed when it came to defining positively the art of theatre, one claiming that theatre should be an imitation of the real, the other defining it as a poetic interpretation of that same reality, as the creation of an independent universe, or even as an almost mystical experience.

A detailed analysis of the origins of the two tendencies would be more involved than this study will allow.[1] The various forms

1. See John Gassner, *Form and Idea in Modern Theatre.* (*Note:* Full bibliographical data for works referred to in the footnotes may be found in the Selected Bibliography, below, pp. 355-71.)

of bourgeois drama originated in Romantic theatre, but the Romantic theatre and its manifestos were also at the root of the principles of both realism and symbolic theatre. Behind the dual orientation lie the examples of Shakespeare, Aeschylus, and, in some ways, the ambiguity of Aristotle's formula, according to which a dramatic work is "the imitation of an action." It would be necessary to go back to Aristotle and show how different styles, schools, and cultures have interpreted the formula, both analytically (What is imitation? What is action?) and synthetically. Would one be faithful to nature (What nature?), cultivate the natural, paint a tableau of life, reveal the essence of man, represent the Idea or the Spirit which *is* reality, reconstruct the true definition of man? Were the human drama to be restricted to the phenomena of psychological and social behavior that we perceive directly in daily life, the imitation of that drama would consist in reconstructing onstage, with the fidelity of a documentary film, the very behavior we observe around us. Here the definition of action necessarily involves that of imitation—that is, a way of writing, directing, and acting the play. It would seem today that certain American writers and directors have become masters of this style. If one puts aside the meaning of the play and the juggling tricks involved in the denouement, the verism of the slices of life is almost too convincing. On the other hand, if we situate truth above, below, or beside daily perceptible phenomena, the arts of theatre have in fact nothing to imitate. They interpret or they reveal or they invent. Or, if they imitate, it is no longer the real such as we perceive it but rather the alleged image of a reality situated beyond the perceived universe.

Since 1890 it has become more and more fashionable to disparage realistic theatre: the style never leaves the ground; it lacks grandeur. The slice of life is "dull," to use Diderot's adjective describing a valet played "naturally."[2] And it is dull for two

---

2. "If a valet speaks on stage as he would in society, he is dull; if he speaks in any other way, he is false" was the way Diderot formulized the main dangers of realism and antirealism. (Diderot, "Entretiens sur *Le Fils naturel*," *Œuvres* [Paris, Gallimard, 1946], p. 1276.)

reasons. First, as a reaction against artificial gaiety or moral optimism, realism has been directed toward a portrayal of the commonplace, the mediocre, the boring; secondly, by its very definition, total realism is unable to break away from psychology and sociology. By excluding any transcendency (religious, mythical, or ontological) and explaining directly in psychological or sociological terms, realism and its offshoot, naturalism, do not transfigure our participation in human misery or human happiness; they merely repeat it. If a vague transfiguration does take place, it is because the work has departed from its principles. The irony of the *comédie rosse,* "miserabilism," or elements of satire are actually distortions of reality. As for *epic* realism (Brecht), the term itself implies a synthesis.

However, realism in the theatre—that "renaissance in reverse," as it was called by Jean Hort[3]—in addition to giving the French stage a welcome and thorough cleaning, restored a human quality to the art of theatre. "Realism," according to John Gassner, "gave [man] the recognizable features of a functioning human being."[4] And the Théâtre Libre reaffirmed a professional conscience, the notion of the production as a coordinated and unified whole, and the idea of harmony between the character and his surroundings (just as valid for fantastic or abstract surroundings as for the piece by piece reconstruction of a shoddy hotel room). Since the Théâtre Libre, the famous actor's number has been replaced by an attempt to convince the spectator of the real, sensual presence of the character and the play's universe.

To that extent at least, all great theatre profited from the demands of the Théâtre Libre. Although the antinaturalists' reaction was to go beyond its limitations, they had every intention of keeping the basic tenets. But extremes provoke extremes, and an absolute aestheticism took the place of the sordid boredom of certain slices of life. As a result, theatre was in danger of being completely dehumanized and even negated. Obviously neither the German

3. Jean Hort, *Les Théâtres du Cartel.*
4. *Form and Idea,* p. 93.

set-designers nor Gordon Craig went quite so far. In 1891, however, the Théâtre d'Art planned to end its production "by putting an unknown painting on stage," with musical accompaniment and wafts of perfume sprayed throughout the theatre.[5] While a fear of superficial anecdotes led to the suppression of all action, a fear of psychologism transformed the character into an entity: the danger of symbolist theatre was that of becoming a play of static shadows. An intense search for hidden meanings of the "modern" world often resulted in a mechanical stylization, beautiful perhaps, but cold and inhuman. The aesthetic value of these attempts is undeniable, but are they truly theatre? Drama consists not in the ghosts of man but in the relations between man and his ghosts; it consists not in mechanized man but in the search for the man within the mechanized man. In short, antirealism can be just as limited as realism: the highest plane, if only a plane, is as desperately flat as any other. The realistic and naturalistic universe is often suffocating, but it is just as easy to die of asphyxiation at heights where the air is unbreathable.

Despite its dangers, antinaturalism did restore theatre to its real possibilities. It affirmed that man is not defined solely by psychology and his material and social environment: he is also a metaphysical and poetic being. By the same token, antinaturalism made it possible for theatre once again to become a fund of ideas and realized images. It gave the word "action" its full meaning by reestablishing various forms of the transcendency without which there is no tragic dimension, only laws and chance.

Today realism has been conquered; it has only to be perfected. A good naturalistic drama, with real wine in a real bottle, no longer surprises anyone. Add a bit of psychoanalysis, a few moral and current political ideas, or the savor of a detective story and the spectator feels that he is in the presence of an honest and solid work. Any true effort at inventiveness and discovery consists in going beyond the solid foundation. Since 1890, theatre in general,

5. See Jacques Robichez, *Le Symbolisme au théâtre: Lugné-Poe et les débuts de l'Œuvre,* p. 112.

and French theatre in particular, has been searching for its own special poetry. The definitive step forward came a little before 1930, when four great directors joined together to form a group called *le Cartel des quatre* (1927),[6] and Jean Giraudoux had his first play produced (1928). In other words, behind the new spirit was a solid organization and a really great writer.

From 1890 to 1930 the most active agents of the reform were directors and theorists, whose most important conceptions can be found in Appendix I, below. After the somewhat chaotic experiences early in the century, Jacques Copeau—the revolution's master hand—finally established the idea of total renovation by demanding "a bare stage" to start with. That accomplished, new staging, both simplified and imaginative, gave back dramatic energy, poetry, and meaning to great works of the past, with the result that the Greeks, Shakespeare, Racine, Molière, and others were successfully reinterpreted.

The program had another point, however: that of creating a truly modern theatre with the help of living playwrights. There the work was slower. The reform of the written text was hardly comparable to the activity of theorists and directors. Directors were the first to complain. Where were they to find good modern plays corresponding to the new principles of theatre? The realist revolution did eliminate a good many absurd conventions even from commercial theatre. But although certain playwrights gave up being entertainers to become authentic dramatic writers, the form of the written play was not as completely revolutionized—at least not until the last few years—as were the forms of staging, and, quantitatively, there were more modern or revolutionary stagings than truly new texts.

The idle indulgence, even the admiration of many critics for the Boulevard "masters," along with the official respect surrounding the "thinkers" and "psychologists" of the Third Republic,

6. See below, Appendix I, pp. 307-13.

saved from oblivion by traditionalists and textbooks, can hardly be said to have clarified the situation. There is no need to take into account all the works or even all the dramatic currents of those years. More than a hundred playwrights were relatively much talked about from 1900 to 1930, but few really contributed to the development and modernization of theatre.

Certain names—even "great" names—would today seem like survivals of a dead past that is better forgotten. Porto-Riche, Maurice Donnay, François de Curel, Paul Hervieu, Eugène Brieux, and even more contemporary playwrights such as Bernstein and Bataille had less to say and were of less value to the theatre than, for instance, Dumas père. We no longer consider the creation in 1919 of François de Curel's *L'Ame en folie* as an important event, but we do remember that of Lenormand's *Le Temps est un songe* in the same year. The opening of Henri Bataille's *Le Scandale* (1909) had best be forgotten, but how can one forget the arrival of the Ballets Russes in Paris, also in 1909. In other words, one *Ubu Roi* (1896) by Jarry is worth ten *Amants* (1895) by Maurice Donnay.

To borrow a word from André Gide, we judge "discourteously" everything that caused the theatre to mark time or set it on the wrong track. Many poets wrote for the theatre, of course, hoping to save it from mediocrity. But whether ignored or praised by the public at large, they were most often behind the times: Edmond Rostand, Saint-Georges de Bouhélier, François Porché, and even Paul Fort, who began his dramatic writing far too late. When successful, their success only showed the public's appetite for what was missing from commercial theatre or limited realism; it was no gauge of poetic maturity. Often their success was no more than the sign of a prudish reaction to the immorality of the naturalists. The pure and simple rejection of realism's limitations had meaning only when the realms explored beyond its limitations were new. A return to superficial Romanticism and the conventional exploitation of certain symbolist tricks represented no more than false revolutions.

What, then, is worth remembering? In the tradition of naturalism, either foretelling or following the principles of the Théâtre Libre: Henri Becque's *Les Corbeaux* (produced in 1882), Courteline's *Boubouroche* (1893), Jules Renard's *Le Pain de ménage* (1898) and *Poil de Carotte* (1900), Octave Mirbeau's *Les Affaires sont les affaires* (1903). Obviously there can be no absolutely realistic work: all of the above plays contain a commentary, even a judgment on life. In other fundamentally naturalistic works the commentary takes the foreground and directs the play beyond an imitation of everyday reality toward a more or less poetic universe. Such is the case of Charles Vildrac's *Paquebot Tenacity* (1920) and Simon Gantillon's semi-expressionistic *Maya* (1924).

Such is also the case of the plays of Henri-René Lenormand, the most important playwright of the years 1919–30. Doubtless Lenormand took a strong position against the restrictions of dramatic realism by his very collaboration with Pitoëff, for whom the minutiae of realism consisted in "hiding souls under false beards"—even when the false beards were made of real hair. Lenormand's works, however, are constructed upon a solid naturalistic foundation. Although he rises above it, he does so through exoticism (*Simoun*, 1920) or through the use of Freudian mysteries (*Le Mangeur de rêves,* 1922). On the whole, Lenormand's poetry consists more in the evocation of outer and inner "atmosphere," permeated with the unknown, than in an actual inquiry into that unknown.

The historical genre—in the broadest sense of the word—inherited from the Romantics and dehydrated, asepticized, and carefully wrapped up by Scribe and Sardou, gave rise to innumerable pseudo-Romantic works. Only two writers of this genre are worth considering, and then with reservations: Edmond Fleg (*Le Juif du Pape*, 1925) and Romain Rolland (certain scenes in *Le Théâtre de la Révolution,* 1898–1938), although the feeling of collective belonging is more successfully created by other means in Jules Romains' *Cromedeyre-le-Vieil* (1920).

As for truly poetic theatre, the symbolists and their successors produced little that is still performable or even readable apart from Maeterlinck's *Pelléas et Mélisande* (1893). The systematic experiments with fantasy, "unrealism," or surrealism, due to a contempt for traditional forms, offer a richer and more lively production. Despite the purely militant nature of their boldness, and often because of it, two plays count among the most significant acts in the theatrical revolution and remain living examples for theatre today: Jarry's *Ubu Roi* (1896) and Apollinaire's *Les Mamelles de Tirésias* (1917). Further, Roger Vitrac, with the help of Antonin Artaud, tried to replace somnolent theatre with a theatre of shock (*Victor ou Les Enfants au pouvoir*, 1928), and Jean-Victor Pellerin's *Intimité* (1922) and *Têtes de rechange* (1926), although now obsolete, represent still another interesting experiment in theatrical allegory. Of course, Claudel and Cocteau were the most important contributors, but their really mature works were written or extensively performed after 1930.

Comedy in modern form can be found in the works of Jarry and Vitrac and, in more traditional form, in Crommelynck's grating farce *Le Cocu magnifique* (1921). Representative also, in a facile and often low genre, is Georges Feydeau (*L'Hôtel du Libre-Echange*, 1894), who, in applying the rules of *vaudeville* with the intransigence of a mathematician, arrived at a kind of formal perfection—a theatricalism that places him far above his predecessors, his contemporaries, and particularly his successors. Among the more recent writers Marcel Achard, although lax in form and mediocre in message, could be mentioned for his *Voulez-Vous Jouer avec Moâ?* (1923).

A good anthology of the French theatre from 1880 to 1930 would be made up of such plays—a subjective choice in some ways and, as such, perhaps somewhat unfair. But it does not claim to be representative: except for Feydeau, the enormous production of the Boulevard is excluded. It is based not on statistics but on considerations of value, inventiveness, and real dramatic intuition.

We know that directors continued to complain about the small number of good or great texts written by modern playwrights.

Too many plays, not enough good plays, they said. Therefore almost all of them produced reinterpretations of old masterpieces, almost all experimented and compromised with their own principles, all went out in search of new writers and produced their works even when certain of courting failure with the public, and almost all accustomed France to great modern writers of other countries: Ibsen, Strindberg, Chekhov, Pirandello, Shaw. Although the theatrical reform was clearly turned toward the present and the future, it was not iconoclastic and proved to be even less chauvinistic.

One tendency seems to dominate the French theatre of today: a clear movement toward antirealism and its growing acceptance by the public. During the last years French critics have frequently found fault with the "naturalism" of American plays produced in Paris—that is, the "return to Antoine and the Théâtre Libre." Detailed photography of the perceived real or purely psycho-sociological visions are without doubt capable of getting an emotional response from the spectator, but not the dual experience of recognition and theatricalist ambiguity.

The mask of nonrealistic theatre is ambiguous: it presents the true and the false at the same time. With antirealism, theatre stops being documentary, but it is only art when it provokes a dual state of consciousness in the spectator, who at once believes and disbelieves. When the suspension of disbelief is total, the aesthetic experience is nil. When disbelief is not suspended, the play remains an outer object and aestheticism is void of all human content. In the simultaneity of the two states of consciousness lies the state of grace which is precisely that of a complete dramatic experience.

Modern French theatre is increasingly oriented toward a search for that simultaneity. Antirealist but also suspicious of pure aestheticism, French playwrights and directors have tried to synthesize a concrete equivalence of their creation and the world in which we live *and* the constant reminder of theatre's unreality.

Identification is meant to take place not with the surface anecdote, itself a fiction, a masquerade, a poet's lie, but with the deep drama underlying it. Spectators and characters, each in his own way, wear masks, no one of which has more reality than any other. The characters' masks are simply more obviously illusory *and* more revealing.[7]

The play of masks leads to questions about life, theatre, and their reciprocal relations. It is not the creation of a new art but the return, with the help of new forms, to a simple and ancient conception, outside of which there is no theatre, only entertainment. Writers and directors have obviously gone back to the source, whether it be Greek or Shakespearean, and have directly or indirectly been influenced by foreign contemporary theatre, chiefly that of Pirandello. However, the following chapters are less studies of sources and influences than portraits, descriptions of the principal masks presented to the French public, from Giraudoux to Genet, each one seen in its fundamental ambiguity.

7. Theatricalist ambiguity is of course not the privilege of nonrealistic theatre. John Gassner points out, in *Form and Idea in Modern Theatre,* that in the presence of a realistic work the spectator quickly becomes sensitive to its theatricality and that, when viewing an "imaginative" production, he ends by accepting the characters and decor as real. Yet theatrical disbelief, in the first case, often takes place in spite of the playwright's and the director's intentions.

# PART I

# A THEATRE OF THE SUPERNATURAL

# CHAPTER 1

# THEATRE AS PROPOSITION:
## JEAN GIRAUDOUX

When novelist Jean Giraudoux's first play, *Siegfried,* was produced by Louis Jouvet at the Comédie des Champs Elysées on May 2, 1928, the then fashionable playwrights suddenly seemed quite definitely second-rate. Giraudoux had created an original universe, corresponding to most of the demands for "true" theatre. Indeed, his was the first coherent and satisfying form of modern theatre presented to a general public, and his plays dominated the French stage all during the thirties and early forties—a time which might be called the Age of Giraudoux.

Although not one of his best plays, *Siegfried* does contain all the indications of what Giraudoux was to become and of the scenic universe he was to create and enrich from play to play. Clearly, he would use simple individual conflicts as metaphors of conflicts between great universal themes: the story of Siegfried, a German political hero who lost his memory during the first World War and discovers that he is in fact Jacques, a French soldier, is but the pretext for an allegorical dialogue between France and Germany, each country being considered in its atmosphere, its culture, its poetry. And clearly, by simplifying the terms of the conflict, Giraudoux would bring out the subtlety of their relations and play freely with the element of surprise in unexpected reversals: at the end of the play Geneviève, having helped bring the French Jacques out from the depths of the German Siegfried, lets herself be charmed by Germany, and at the very moment Siegfried has become Jacques, she cries out, "Siegfried, I love you."

But, above all, he would "write" his plays, and through the writing itself, on every level of style and composition, both Giraudoux's universe and his true originality are revealed. One of his most apparent devices is the presentation of stylized debates in which the characters embody the great themes in question. One particular scene in *Siegfried* serves as a model or pattern of such precisely defined staging, structure, and composition that it seems like a beautifully chiseled nail hammered right into the heart of the play, intended to hold down that delicately embroidered stuff, often so light that it would seem to fly offstage: the scene in Act III in which Siegfried's anguished struggle is exteriorized, represented, or acted almost allegorically by Geneviève and Eva, both throwing concrete and opposing arguments into the the scale of a balance which is tipped in their favor, until finally the two women throw the conflict back within Siegfried.

Almost all of Giraudoux's works are organized around analogous debates: between war and peace in *La Guerre de Troie,* the love of a young man and the love of an old man in *Cantique des cantiques,* the human and the supernatural in *Ondine* and *Intermezzo,* English morality and natural amorality in *Supplément au Voyage de Cook,* sensual love and saintliness in *Judith,* man and woman in *Sodome et Gomorrhe.* Each play leads the spectator toward a solution of the conflict by means of great contrasts and sudden reversals, as in *Siegfried.*

Within the debates themselves Giraudoux would clearly use language to provide the most specific and unexpected images. Often the characters, in explaining themselves, make use of details that are comical in the contrast between their apparent insignificance and the importance of their function. In *Siegfried* Zelten explains that he was unable to bring about his counterrevolution for want of arms but also, and most importantly, for want of glue to stick up his manifestos. Similarly, in *Electre* Clytemnestra explains that much of her hate for Agamemnon stems from the way in which he always, in no matter what circumstances, held his little finger up in the air.

An elaborately wrought language, the reversal of situations, and great stylized debates accompanied by the most whimsical and singular details are unchanging in Giraudoux's works, in the masterpieces as well as in his less successful plays. His universe is created more through the fixed elements of his theatrical vision than through the choice and evolution of certain themes and ideas, so often catalogued and analyzed.

Essentially a theatre of language, Giraudoux's works relate to a strong tradition which has characterized the French stage since the Renaissance. From Garnier to Montherlant, Sartre, and Genet, French playwrights have been garrulous. Doubtless the reasons for this recourse to language are varied: plays written more to be read than performed; material conditions of staging (in the classical period, for example), reducing physical action to a minimum; and the pride of poets. The fundamental reason, however, would seem to be always the same: a belief in the magic and power of words and combinations of words.

Characters on Giraudoux's stage talk more than they move. The greater part of certain scenes, even of certain plays, can be performed sitting down, for the drama can best be expressed through conversation or verbal debate. The characters reveal their inner struggles through the shock of words and phrases, or, as bearers of contrary truths, they oppose one another like lawyers in court before judges (the gods) and a jury (the spectators). Language, the weapon of poets and diplomats, is the primary instrument of poet-diplomat Jean Giraudoux.

The use of language in Giraudoux's theatre is the result not only
of a particular temperament but also of a deliberate choice. In his
article "Le Metteur en scène,"[1] where he compares German and
French theatre, Giraudoux defines French theatre in terms of the
sovereignty of language. When the German public, just before
the advent of Hitler, was reveling in Max Reinhardt's great
spectacles or participating in Piscator's "fire-arms" theatre, the
Frenchman remained faithful to his traditions.[2] According to
Giraudoux, "the true dramatic effect for him is not the clamor of
two hundred extras, but the ironic nuance given to a phrase of the
hero or heroine," for the Frenchman believes that the "great debates of the heart" are settled "by conversation":

> He persists in considering dialogue as the supreme form of
> the duel for the creature gifted with words. What he likes
> to experience is the power of that dialogue, its effectiveness,
> its form, hence the purely literary merits of the text. For him,
> theatrical action consists, not in submitting to a frantic mas-
> sage of almost physical vision and emotion, from which he
> leaves exhausted, as from a Turkish bath, but in hanging his
> worries and the conflicts of his life and personal imagination
> on a model dialogue which can elucidate them.

A model dialogue: such would seem to be Giraudoux's definition of theatre. Every drama would be one of the spectator's conflicts—conflicts in his life and in his imagination—put into model
language. The words that never come, the vital discussions that
daily life does not allow, the clarification by category of the soul's
and heart's confusion—that is what the spectator would hear
onstage. Language would become a prism in which the whitish,
monotonous, and imperfect light of life is decomposed into basic
and dazzling colors.

---

1. In Jean Giraudoux, *Littérature* (Paris, Grasset, 1941).
2. During the same period in France, Antonin Artaud was fighting for
quite a different conception. See below, Conclusion, pp. 283–90.

It would be easy, of course, to hold the conception up to ridicule. Do you have a great inexpressible love for peace? Go and see your love take shape in Hector's long speeches in *La Guerre de Troie n'aura pas lieu*. If you can't explain why your husband irritates you and why and how you have been unfaithful to him or killed him, go and listen to Agathe and Clytemnestra in *Electre*. If you are a minor civil servant and are unsuccessful in persuading the romantic young girl you're in love with to marry you, go and hear the Supervisor in *Intermezzo*. Or if you happen to be the young girl, listen to Isabelle in the same play. Yet there is no doubt that the characters' model speeches do more than replace political editorials in the newspapers or the correspondence of Miss Lonelyhearts.

The principle, confirmed by Giraudoux's theoretical writings and immediately apparent as a presupposition of his entire theatre, is that no reality can withstand human language. Giraudoux was a humanist, and doubly so: he not only based his conception of theatre on his knowledge and interpretation of European culture, but he had complete confidence in the human logic of language as a means of accounting for the universe. Language is the spider's web, spun by intelligence, in which reality, surreality, and the supernatural are caught. The end of *Sodome et Gomorrhe* is the end of the world, but despite God's wrath, the war of the sexes will continue *ad saecula saeculorum*. It was characteristic of Giraudoux to have chosen as an image the voices of man and woman, continuing their discussion all the same:

> *The Archangel:* Are they never going to be quiet! Are they never going to die!
> *The Angel:* They are dead.
> *The Archangel:* Who is speaking then?
> *The Angel:* They are. Death was not enough. The scene continues.

Language, even with no support, perseveres in its existence. It lives on independent of the men who use it, just as for a believer the soul survives the body.

Although it does not necessarily create its objects, language does confer a privileged existence upon them, next to which their *unspoken* existence seems less important. In Giraudoux not only does it give a different reality to the spectator's life ("the style smooths out wrinkled souls," *L'Impromptu de Paris*), but each character plays with the reality of his own universe through words: Ondine makes Hans' love exist by telling it, while another language, that of the Undines, gives a reality to treason in love; in *Judith* the heroine, in her duel with Holophernes, counted not on poison but on words; and through an ironic contrast Lucile's silence in the first act of *Pour Lucrèce* is what brings about the horrible drama that follows. Language does have the power of ordering the universe, either by defining situations in an intelligible manner or by imposing a direction on the course of events. The importance of its function justifies all the adornments—sentences wrapped in ceremonial robes, as it were—and all the rites, hence the privileged situation of the long speech in Giraudoux's theatre.

Reintroducing the monologue and the *tirade* was not simply the coquetry of a man of letters who wanted to show his originality by returning to outdated techniques. It is a form of theatricalism, the modern spectator being conscious of the unreality of the tirade or monologue. What he hears is not a dialogue of everyday life but a reorganization of it. Giraudoux insists on such theatricalism by emphasizing the artificiality of the process. Characters and spectators are warned so that they can create suitable attitudes— the spectators within themselves, the others through their positions onstage.

Giraudoux used the monologue time and again. Whether the gardener's *lamento* in *Electre* or Mercury's monologue in the second act of *Amphitryon 38,* the speech is situated somewhat outside the action as an interlude addressed to the spectator, establishing the bridge between the play's universe and his own. It thus creates a higher complicity with the play, making the spectator into a kind of god, while reassuring him as to the humanity of the drama.

The so-called tirade is just as literary and artificial. During scenes in which the drama is in full swing, there is suddenly a stop, to give the protagonist of the moment an opportunity to clarify the terms of the conflict he represents. This is true not only of Hector's prayer for the war dead in *La Guerre de Troie,* which is a ceremony in any case, but of long speeches situated in the heart of a debate. Moreover, Giraudoux's construction is such that the director is compelled to clear the stage or to arrange the other characters in secondary positions, just as the chorus in an opera is grouped around the tenor.

In Corneille the tirade is an explanation through reasoning or a justification a posteriori; in Racine it is generally a narrative which results in the actual situation and which, by its very sequence, emphasizes the situation's inevitability; and for the Romantics it was a poetic or pseudo-philosophical digression around a situation. In Giraudoux it is neither a digression nor a minor slackening off of the situation nor a step ahead. In the flow of the drama it is a snapshot taken of all the tensions of a particular moment, catching the scenic athlete in mid-air and making it possible for us to examine it with care. It actualizes Lamartine's wish, "O Time, suspend your flight."

The spectator is warned about every stop in the movement by a key word, which carries within itself one of the basic elements of a particular tension. "My language," "my violence!" says Judith at the beginnings of two speeches addressed to Suzanne. "Yes, I hated him!" shouts Clytemnestra in *Electre.* The word "control" is the basis for Armand's speech about the proofs of his wife's fidelity in *Pour Lucrèce.* Giraudoux organized his speeches around a key word, just as in Wallace Stevens' poem *Anecdote of the Jar* Tennessee takes shape around the jar that was placed upon a hill. In other cases the spectator is warned by a character who catches his breath, saying something like "Understand me," or by be-

ginning with an inadequate response to the preceding line. It is rare
for a character, having "answered back," as it were, to give the impression of continuing to speak without having given advance
warning as to the length of his inspiration. The characters carry
within themselves, in advance, the completed structure of their
remarks. And here we are at the antipodes of naturalistic theatre,
with its language at the mercy of all stimuli, which determine its
successive forms and abundance.

The tirade constructed in such a way would seem to imply a
conception of reality in which form precedes content. Sartre's
article on Giraudoux's Aristotelianism[3] and the discussion taken
up by Claude-Edmonde Magny in *Précieux Giraudoux* poses the
problem of Giraudoux's philosophy: Is he Aristotelian? Is he
Platonic? There is no need here to go into the debate in detail,
but it is worth noting that Giraudoux, like the courtly poet or
the *précieux,* played on both sides. The characters in the plays
and the plays themselves offer a Platonic vision of the world, in
which the Idea precedes life. There is an Idea of love, an Idea of
Electra, an Idea of Isabelle, an Idea of peace, an Idea of treason, an
Idea of the couple situated in the heavens of the drama. The
heroes and situations are the closest possible concrete expression of
perfection. The universe itself, however, is not that of the spectator
or the poet. For them Ideas, of which they are the imperfect
realization, do not exist. The poet expresses the Forms toward
which our reality would seem to tend through images. The Forms
exist only through the extrapolation of intelligence or the imagination. They are posterior to reality and invented by man in
order to make his universe intelligible.

Giraudoux's "model dialogue" is the proposition of a poet. It
implies a twofold movement in literary creation: the reduction of
the real to a diagram, in which the intelligence is capable of
establishing the continuity of interrupted lines and introducing
symmetries, and the act of bringing concrete content to the per-

fected diagram. Ronald Peacock described it as a "myth-allegory" form,[4] and the process is in fact very close to allegorization. Yet it avoids allegory in that there is a reduction not to separate abstract qualities but to essences, whose totality Giraudoux preserves. The scenes of debate are the most characteristic. Whether domestic quarrels or the disputes of diplomats, they are illusory reconstructions, dreams of the intelligence, a fictional universe in which there is no break between the perceived real and the almost mathematical structure the mind seems to have discovered in it.

A product of the intelligence, Giraudoux's fictional universe is satisfying to the mind because it is made up of all the relations that the mind establishes between the things of the world, and the network of so-called précieux metaphors establishes its coherence. One of the characteristics of the précieux metaphor is the intellectuality of the bond that unites the two terms. Claude-Edmonde Magny points out that it begins with forms very close to the pun and results in a whole complicated reasoning in which contraries are united. It has nothing to do with any analogy imposed by illuminations of the subconscious, nor does it spring from an intuition of the real: it gives form to the real from the outside. In Giraudoux it is part of a process of reconstruction: it adds secondary structures to the basic diagram and contributes to the creation of an imaginary world in which the mind is always satisfied. In *Cantique des cantiques* the President asks Florence, apropos of Jérome, "Where did you find him?"

> *Florence:* We bumped straight into each other on the boulevard. He was running with all his might . . . He hurt me.
>
> *The President:* He was coming from far away. He was given a start twenty years ago . . .
>
> *Florence:* Twenty-one . . . He hurt me . . . I still can't make up my mind whether the exhaustion within me is love or stiffness.

4. *The Art of Drama* (London, Routledge and Kegan Paul, 1957), p. 205.

The basic diagram here is formed by a belief in the fatality of
a meeting, but Giraudoux also brought in the comic note of a
small accident. A purely intellectual liaison establishes a link
between the destiny of the lovers and the accident, between what
is already an image (the race of life) and Jérome's real race.
Then the metaphor is extended and the consequences remain an
intellectual proposition. The link of the metaphor is expressed
by the word "exhaustion," but the two parts remain separate, in
the forms of "love" and "stiffness."

Helen of Troy rubbing men against her "like great cakes of
soap" to purify herself, Lia reinventing the *carte du Tendre* in her
dialogue with the Angel, and the Beggar advising Electra to
"start from dawn" offer so many suggestive metaphors of a world
in which the slightest glance of the mind sees the possibility of
creating a web of analogies and correspondences.

Through language Giraudoux has tried to create a universe
which is not that of just a dream but that of a dream of the intelligence. Claudel's theological universe, Audiberti's poetic universe, Montherlant's ethical universe, Sartre's phenomenological
and idéological universe, and Genet's dreamlike universe also
claim to give concrete metaphors of the essence of reality, the
metaphor being situated very precisely in a certain beyond, in
certain depths of consciousness, or at a certain level of being. In
Giraudoux the essence is *proposed* by the intelligence. The question is not one of discovering the meaning of God's work but of
actualizing, through art, what the man gifted with reason would
have created had he been God. It means rejecting Leibnitz' postulate according to which this world is the only possible world, and
showing that with the same materials a more intelligible world
might be conceived.

Germany and France, war and peace, phantom and Supervisor,
man and woman, virtue and vice, the President and Jérome,
England and the South Sea Islands: Giraudoux's drama is based
on simple conflicts. The conflicts are all the more intense in that

Giraudoux, in his creation of an intelligible universe, starts out with particularly clear and distinct ideas: Germany is everything that France is not, the President is everything that Jérome is not, Andromache is everything that Helen is not. The drama somehow springs naturally from the clarity with which the essences are defined. The major bond between them, the field of conflict, is the hero or heroine—and here Giraudoux goes back to a classical conception of drama: Hector participates in both peace and war, Ondine is caught between man and the supernatural, and Outourou finds himself at the junction between all the mysteries of Polynesia and Anglo-Saxon ethics, just as Siegfried carried within himself the definitions of both France and Germany. In Giraudoux's theatre the hero or protagonist straddles two essences and either believes he can participate in both at the same time or is forced or asked to participate in them.

Giraudoux's hero is also unique in that he carries his universe about with him. In Greek tragedy the plague was rampant in Thebes *because* of Oedipus' crimes; the series of contaminations, like the series of murders in Atreus' family, was causal. Giraudoux's hero walks about with a world that copies his definition or corresponds to it, just as at the end of *Electre* Aegisthus walks about with a vulture over his head. While the Greek hero provokes events by his acts, Giraudoux's protagonist, like Wallace Stevens' jar, makes the surrounding world take part in his own being. Giraudoux has been reproached for his color-print landscapes, comparable to the illustrations in primary school textbooks: the France of *Siegfried,* the Bethulia of *Judith,* and the Greece of *Amphitryon* or *Electre* are as naïve as pictures in a geography book and at the same time like a modern primitive dream à la Grandma Moses. What is important is the stylization—the structure brought to the landscape by the character's language and its transformation by his very presence. Indeed, the entire universe of the play is transformed: the elements of the landscape change from masculine to feminine, valets begin to speak in verse, villages are seized with poetic delirium, adulterers start to tremble.

The hero or heroine is the agent of a metamorphosis of the world or an attempted metamorphosis, for the world sometimes resists and may win out. In *Judith* Giraudoux painted a stylized portrait of the biblical world, with its mythology, its own necessity, and a structure whose evolution is known in advance—in other words, the essence of the Old Testament world as corrected and simplified by Giraudoux. According to its laws, Judith is destined to be the saintly heroine who saves her people by sacrificing herself. Giraudoux's Judith, however, embodies less the idea of sacrifice than an idea of the young girl. A virgin, she gives herself to Holophernes and then kills him. But she does not kill him to save her people: she kills him because she loves him and wants, through his death, to preserve the perfection of the night she had just spent with him. For Judith's world is not the same as that of the other characters, even in the most concrete details brought out by the dialogue: her description of the battlefield is quite the contrary of her guardian angel's, and her description of her night with Holophernes is also quite the contrary of her guardian angel's. Were the soldiers on the ground dead or asleep? Did Judith caress Holophernes' body because she loved him or was she disgustedly locating the spot she would strike? Which is the truth? In fact, through language the play presents a kind of double truth: two worlds, or two essences of the world, coexist at the same moment, in the same place—Judith's and that of the angels and the God of the Old Testament. "A question of lighting," says the angel, and what we are asked to accept at the end of the play is the simultaneity of both lightings. The subject of the play is more the hesitation between two truths than the discussion of a problem of religious metaphysics, as André Gide had thought.[5]

For Giraudoux's theatre is not a theatre of ideas in Gide's sense of the term. His plays are in the form of debates, but the debates are not really discussions: they are an aesthetic equilibrium between contrary definitions. There are no problems concerning

5. See André Gide's *Journal,* November 12, 1931.

political ideas in *La Guerre de Troie:* there is a conflict between a definition of peace and a definition of war. Giraudoux's characters do not reason; they describe. In *Sodome et Gomorrhe,* when Jean says that the weather is fine in Sodom, Lia answers that the weather is frightful. What directs the drama toward the victory of one essence or another is the weight of a particular description, of a particular definition. Often a definition or description grows richer by stealing, so to speak, from another and ends by conquering it through absorption: in *Intermezzo* Isabelle gives up her phantom, but only because the Supervisor managed to constitute the universe of civil servants as an equivalent of the specter's romantic world.

There are of course irreconcilable definitions, and then the "strongest" wins: war in *La Guerre de Troie,* the young man's love in *Cantique des cantiques.* But it would be vain to separate Giraudoux's plays into those in which contrary definitions are reconciled through facile satire, a feat of God, or a complicity between gods and men intended to satisfy them both, and those in which the reconciliation never takes place. It would mean putting too great an emphasis on the message or lesson contained in each play (we love peace but war is inevitable; shame on the mean capitalists who destroy the poetry of the French landscape; and so on), reducing works whose subject is hesitation to some positive thesis. The subject of *La Guerre de Troie* is not the arrival of war but the hesitation of the world between war and peace; the subject of *Judith* is not a secret formula for making saints (what Gide perhaps wanted to find in it) but the oscillation between the lover and the saint; and it is hardly important, at the end of *Cantique des cantiques,* that Florence chooses Jérome: the subject is the simultaneous presence of two faces of love. What is important in *Sodome et Gomorrhe* is not the weather and not even knowing whether Jean or Lia is right; nor is it to have the right one win: it is their disagreement, it is the fact that two incompatible universes occupy the same space, that the weather is fine and bad at the same time at the same point in the sky, that there is an essence

of man and an essence of woman. Here Giraudoux's desire coincides with God's: there should be an essence of the couple. Lia
and Jean are opposed, and that duality is opposed to a desire for
unity. Such is the play of perpendicular tensions underlying the
drama.

The drama's intensity is in direct proportion to the range of
difference between conflicting definitions. Through his choice of
details and images Giraudoux often increases the intensity to such
a point that the spectator has the impression of an absolute impasse. Yet his plays present satisfying solutions. When the curtain
goes down, the world is in order.

The denouement is partly determined by Giraudoux's précieux
attitude. A work characterized as *précieux* generally ends with a
usual or well-known solution or one related to a familiar genre—
the final conceit of an intellectual reconstruction of the world.
For example, a sonnet of Voiture is resolved by a final conceit of
an already known genre (the *concetto* or Petrarchan antithesis),
and its value lies in the ingenuity of its twists. In the same way,
the denouement of a Giraudoux play is one familiar to the
spectator, after he has been led to expect almost anything else.
Such acrobatics of intelligence and imagination are not a simple
game. They represent a challenge. By means of perspective, the
writer puts himself on a level with God, thus becoming His rival.
He shows that one can achieve the same result with more clarity—
that in accentuating the contrasts and in multiplying the relations
of things, even the horrors of the universe can satisfy the mind.

The denouements are also determined by the play's genre,
somewhat in the manner of the seventeenth century, when every
play with more or less ridiculous bourgeois characters had to have
a happy ending and every play with noble heroes had to end in a
catastrophe or with spectacular acts of high generosity. Giraudoux's genres are personal and varied, but they always evoke a
familiar literary horizon. In the historical plays, despite liberties
taken with the story itself, the denouement comes from history. In
spite of all the contortions, the Trojan War does take place,

Hercules will be born, Judith does become a holy figure, Sodom is destroyed. Despite German influences, Giraudoux would have had Joan of Arc die on the stake in Rouen and not, like Schiller's, on a battlefield. The play's finality comes from the already known denouement. Yet during the plays themselves we realize that the Trojan War might have been avoided, that Judith could have sent Suzanne in her place, that her night of love with Holophernes is perhaps just a virgin's first night of love, and that although Jupiter did sleep with Alcmene, it does not count. The denouement is faithful to history less because the plot leads to it than because the work must conform to an idea of the legend.

In the plays with invented subjects it is the tone of the whole, their background of popular anecdote, which leads to suicide, separation, or a victory for the young man. In *Cantique des cantiques* Giraudoux applied his method no longer to Greek myth or to a biblical or Germanic legend but to an edifying, popular, romantic story. Therefore the young man had to win out over the old. In *Supplément au Voyage de Cook* Outourou's last speech is determined not by the play itself but by anti-Christian eighteenth-century irony, which had originally furnished the idea for the situation. The Ubuesque character of the solution in *La Folle de Chaillot* is a final exaggeration of a secondary aspect of the play, revealing the cultural background of the play's universe: the melodramatic, romantic, and movie world of the mysteries of great cities. The underground chasm into which the pimps disappear is an exaggeration of the sewers in *Les Misérables* or the dens of Eugène Sue's characters, just as in the rest of the play the young lovers, the ragman, and the madwomen are very masked reminders of the fauna in that kind of literature.

In short, Giraudoux did not invent the denouements of the perfect dramas he proposed. Reality and myth or tradition took back their rights. Surprises comparable to the final pistol shots in Salacrou's *Histoire de rire* or in Montherlant's *Brocéliande* are unimaginable in his works. A higher form is superimposed on the drama, a form forged from an idea of tragedy, comedy, melodrama,

fairy tale, history, sentimental anecdote, and so on. The end of a
Giraudoux play is not only the resolution of a conflict proposed
during the play by the subject itself; it is also, and sometimes
principally, the aesthetic resolution of the distance between the
subject and the genre to which it belongs.

The characters Giraudoux has put onstage are in full possession
of their natures. Their degree of humanity depends largely on just
how complex that nature is, as well as on their rank in the drama.
If the pattern is simple, they seem like puppets or personified
entities. When they are neither heroes nor protagonists, they are
too exceptional for their dramatic situations and seem to be
ornaments more than characters. But they all contribute to giving
the play's universe its style and specifying its definition. On the
whole, we must accept the fact that the world proposed to us by
Giraudoux is peopled only by rare creatures. Little girls too intelligent for their ages, café waiter-poets, and précieux soldiers are
exceptional only in relation to the spectator; they are quite
naturally in their places within the play's universe: its form requires such fauna. The play demands, however, that we consider
them as metaphors of ordinary humanity, caught up, of course,
in a drama played out by heroes. The unreality of the secondary
characters predominates, and the spectator's pleasure lies in his
recognition of the writer's fantasy, not in the kind of participation
or complicity provoked by Greek choruses, the confidants of
French classical tragedy, or the sensible characters in Molière's
comedy.

We must also accept the very *idea* of Giraudoux's theatre: a
play of the reincarnation of perfected essences. Each character is
therefore complete in himself and is nothing more than what he
says and what Giraudoux tells us. When he expresses himself in
clichés and hasty generalizations, he himself is a cliché or a gen-
eralization. In more naturalistic theatre a character can be represented by traits which suggest a whole psychology and behavior,
the postulate of such theatre being that each trait is a product, an

effect within a whole determined system. A sketchy character, for example, is comparable to those studies of certain great painters in which a detailed nose is enough to suggest the rest of the face and reveal a soul. When Giraudoux draws only a nose, it means that the character is nothing more than a nose; or rather, the sketch of a face by Giraudoux would not consist in the suggestion of it by a study of one of its parts: he would draw a complete circle. Even when individualized to the extreme, Giraudoux's sketchy character will always give the impression of being an archetype—if only of himself—because in fact he is always complete. The same lighting falls on the hero as on the gardener or soldier; the structure of the main character is just more complex. And that is the basis for his hierarchy of characters.

Giraudoux's theatre gives rise, therefore, to a very special impression, quite the contrary of that ordinarily provoked by ambitious plays: the hero, who rises above the common mortals, seems more human than the minor characters, who as a rule represent a world nearer to that of the spectator. In the same way that Siegfried, Eva, and Geneviève are more real than the German officers or the customs officials, Judith is more real than the rabbis or Holophernes' officers, Ondine more real than the members of the Court, and the Madwoman of Chaillot more real than the little people around her. What happens is that we accept the hero as exceptional and find it more normal to hear a hero accumulate metaphors than a soldier or café waiter. Given Giraudoux's method, only through actual excess can life be re-created—or at least an equivalent of the richness, complexity, and struggle of life. While the secondary characters are often prisoners of simple attitudes that completely define them, the hero, through an accumulation of details and retouching, assumes flesh, a personal history, and an illusion of humanity distinctive of the dramatic character. Everything happens as if the process of adding details and colors to an anatomical diagram of the human body were to give it the quivering equivalent of a particular living human body.

Much of the severe criticism directed at Giraudoux's theatre

is based on a judgment of his method, not on the works themselves. For the critic the method is easily discernible. It implies
an essentialist position, and it has been decreed in advance that
a work which begins from abstactions (ideas, essences, and forms)
must necessarily be abstract or, at the very least, will always remain
this side of the illusion of reality. It is précieux or formal.

Giraudoux's works are, of course, those of a man of letters—
works in which the writer seems to be both present and outside,
since he always gives the impression of knowing more than his
characters. His tragedy, comedy, and criticism were all conceived
in the same fashion. He knew in advance that after *Phèdre* Racine
would not write again, that the Trojan War would take place, that
Judith would be a sanctified heroine, and that Sodom and Go-
morrah would be destroyed, with the result that the spectator may
feel like both a god and Micromegas. The mathematical patterns
of life, grasped directly in all their complexity, in time and in
space, make life seem like a piece of ingenious machinery in
which the observer knows everything but "lives" nothing. Yet
beyond all the intellectualized movements directing the characters
and the plays themselves, there is an élan which dominates the
whole, creating a movement not only from one form to another
or from one level of form to another, but from form to matter.

"Theatre," says little Véra in *L'Impromptu de Paris,* "is being
real in the unreal." Giraudoux's ambition is just that elementary
and just that unbounded. His universe is deliberately unreal. At
the same time, what upholds it and makes it vibrate is an intense
effort toward reality. Starting from form at its most extreme (an
almost medieval conception of essence), he tries to arrive at the
closest approximation of reality: the flesh-and-blood individual on
a dramatic stage. Instead of just remaining the respectful tran-
scriber or explorer of the Creature, Giraudoux tries to repeat the
process of Creation, the passage from the plan to the act, and
become the rival of that Architect whose image, as Albérès has
shown, constantly recurs in his works.[6]

6. See R.-M. Albérès, *Esthétique et morale chez Giraudoux.*

Yet he always refuses to give the illusion of reality by using trickery, which, in his case as in that of any antinaturalistic playwright, would consist in introducing, at a given point, certain traits or remarks taken from life—what Anouilh did not hesitate to do, for example, in his *Antigone.* In Giraudoux the Greek hero speaking about his carriage or Judith talking like a fashionable young girl of the thirties is pure burlesque; that is to say, naturalistic or realistic details are introduced not for themselves, nor to give everyday reality to the play's universe, but for a pleasant effect of pure literary virtuosity.

An explanation of the life' of Giraudoux's universe lies not in the comic absurdities of its anachronisms but rather in the synthesis, made by the spectator, of all the concrete elements accumulated by the writer. Just as Giraudoux asks the actress in *L'Impromptu de Paris* to recall her own emotions of the day in order to give life to Agnès' line in Molière's *L'Ecole des femmes,* "the little cat is dead," so the spectator feels that Giraudoux's characters live through the presence, within himself, of his own life. Giraudoux's theatre is one of collaboration—a rather different notion from the more fashionable one of participation, but not foreign to it, simply more active. Like reformers such as Jouvet and the Cartel, he wanted his audience to be ready for action. He could be accused of illusions or of living in the dream of a world where ideal plays would be applauded by an ideal audience, had he not shown that he was perfectly aware of the sluggishness of his times *(L'Impromptu de Paris).* Like the reformers, he wrote neither for the real public nor for an ideal public but for the potential in the real public.

While in the American "living newspaper" of the twenties, actors were mixed in with the audience so that the shouts on either side of a spectator would lead him to recognize the political entities onstage as living symbols of man's destiny on earth, Giraudoux waits for the shout to come spontaneously from within the spectator and assumes that his emotion would give the play its finishing touch—life. At that point the spectator is truly a god, for he is observer and creator at the same time. There is no great theatre without the spectator's recognition, that last spark in the creation of a play.

At a time when theatre demands no more than immobility from a spectator so that it can painlessly graze him, Giraudoux demands cooperation, the presence of heart and imagination—hence the "difficulty" of his plays. His importance in the history of modern French theatre is both to have demanded a very active collaboration on the part of the spectator and to have given back to the theatre its function of elucidating the world in fundamental terms. Certain types of plays may force the spectator to use his mind so as to understand a particularly rare and complex problem; others may pick up the notions of destiny, death, or love and feed them to the passive spectator. Giraudoux's theatre is made neither for those in search of intellectual rarities nor for the passive but for a "normal" audience—the norm being defined as the audience of Greek tragedy, of the Spanish theatre of the *Siglo de Oro,* of Shakespeare, of French Classicism. "Those who want to understand in the theatre do not understand theatre . . . The theatre is not a theorem, but a spectacle, not a lesson, but a philter. It should enter your imagination and your senses more than your mind," say the actors in *L'Impromptu de Paris.* Moreover, in *Visitations* Giraudoux wrote that theatre must reveal to the spectator

> these surprising truths: that the living must live, that the living must die, that autumn follows after summer, spring after winter, that there are the four elements, and happiness, and billions of catastrophes, that life is a reality, that it is a dream, that man lives by peace, that man lives by blood, in brief, what they will never know.[7]

Such affirmations may seem in contradiction with the judgment of many critics for whom Giraudoux's theatre consists of works of the mind, their revelations far indeed from the commonplaces

7. Giraudoux, *Visitations* (Neuchâtel and Paris, Ides et Calendes, 1947), trans. Bert M.-P. Leefmans, in *The Kenyon Review,* 1954.

of the last quotation. Actually, the misunderstanding about Giraudoux that reigned during the thirties can be reduced to the following: since his method is complicated and baffling, the idea expressed must itself be difficult to understand. In fact, quite the
contrary is true. Giraudoux's theatre is presented as an initiation
into simplicity—in other words, a reevaluation of simplicity
through the detours that must be made in order to rediscover it.
The objective is to exasperate the mind by an accumulation of
intellectual subtleties, to the point that an emotional adhesion
beyond all comprehension will spring from the network of multiple lines that the intelligence has been following.

Knowledge of a certain order can be acquired only through
the delirium of an inferior order. In certain religions the individual
must subject his body to the most extreme violations in order to
attain mysticism. Giraudoux's postulate seems to be that a manifest
truth can be reached and experienced beyond intellection, through
a paroxysm of the intelligence. Preciosity, burlesque, humanist
rationalism, and Aristotelian rationalism are actually means of
making the mind so dizzy that it bows to the unchallengeable and
striking fact of life. The spectator of good faith is expected to
relive the adventure of creation—that of the writer at the time
of composition, as well as that of the director, from the blocking
on paper to the performance—in other words, the movement from
ideas, form, or essences to the synthetic emotion of the human adventure.

In *La Guerre de Troie n'aura pas lieu* peace, represented both
mythically and negatively by the title and the first line of the
play (immediately challenged by the second—hence the drama):

> *Andromache:*   There will be no Trojan War, Cassandra.
> *Cassandra:*   I'll take that bet, Andromache.

is specified in the very first scene, then becomes "happiness," then
"beauty"—all abstract notions—then the "sun" of that day, then
evocative expressions like a "fisherman's house" and the "murmur
of seashells," and is finally, through a double ambiguity, embodied

in a character, Hector. We thus move from what is most abstract
in peace (its negative definition: the absence of war) to one man
who will take its defense.

The concrete images remain vague enough for each spectator
to give peace the face of his choice. The "fisherman's house," the
"murmur of seashells," and the sun that spreads its "mother of
pearl" over the unspecified landscape all indicate a Mediterranean
universe without particularizing it, merely suggesting its essence,
from which the spectator can imagine his own fisherman's house,
murmur, sun. Owl, station, train, birch tree, cat, silk, fur, hand,
armor—Giraudoux's glossary always directs the spectator toward
a certain concrete category, concrete feeling, or concrete landscape.
He never individualizes it; he is satisfied to emphasize its dominant
feature. It is up to the spectator to bring about the final individ-
ualization. The Germany and France of *Siegfried* are deliberately
clichés of the two countries, posters of the French or German
railways; the fashionable young girl Judith is hardly more than
a literary convention before she takes on the dimension of
tragedy; the married life of Clytemnestra and Agamemnon is
evoked by a "curly beard" and a raised little finger. There is
nothing more concrete than those notations, yet nothing more
open to all imaginations. In sparking his text with words that
grammarians call concrete but which, in context, are no more than
generic terms, Giraudoux launches the spectator out in the direction of a specific, even individual image. He never actually imposes it, however; he lets the audience discover its own.

Once again in Giraudoux's works we have the inversion of a
habitual approach. Where others impose a particular image from
which the spectator is expected to extract generalizations, Giraudoux first affirms the general and demands not that the spectator
imagine an illustration of that generality—the play itself fulfills
that function—but that he provide some living correlative. In this
respect, Giraudoux's theatre is one of the first complete or total
theatres of the French stage. If the playwright devotes himself
entirely to his text, the spectator must devote himself to the per-

formance. In other words, this theatre excludes both passive auditors and unimaginative readers. It is not paradoxical to say that Giraudoux's plays are among those that are the most misunderstood when simply read. They are composed and "written" texts, similar to poems in dialogue but meant to be spoken, performed, acted—texts which are, and were intended to be, the drama's fundamental means of expression and consequently incorporate all of its structure, symbols, and ideas. But they become dramas, theatrical works, only when supported by the play of the flesh-and-blood actor and appropriate staging. Indeed, the most "written" plays are those which are truly grasped only when performed or imagined as performed. And that, Louis Jouvet understood.

Giraudoux claimed to have had two muses: "Thalia before, and Jouvet after."[8] His theatre is a theatre of language—but of spoken and acted language—and Jouvet was known as anything but an unobtrusive director. Although a student of Copeau, and as respectful of the text as he, Jouvet used all the pomp of the scenic spectacle to make it live. A director who at the end of his career would make a special tableau of Sganarelle's last line in *Dom Juan,* or add the majestic spectacle of a tribunal at the end of *Tartuffe,* believed in the importance of scenery and staging for reinforcing and adding life to the text. He did justice to Giraudoux's texts when he called on set designers such as Guillaume Monin *(Electre),* Léon Leyritz *(Intermezzo),* Pavel Tchelitchev *(Ondine),* or Christian Bérard *(La Folle de Chaillot)*—all otherwise designers of ballets or operas. When in his article on the director and in *L'Impromptu de Paris* Giraudoux himself rose up against "staging," he meant to protest against the systems and theories of pure spectacle in which the text is sacrificed. In the texts of his plays, however, he constantly indicated the recourse to stage devices and machines, their power of enchantment, and his belief in the actor and the audience.

Therefore, when Clytemnestra delivers her well-known speech

8. "Le Metteur en scène," *Littérature.*

on Agamemnon's little finger and curly beard, it must be *heard,*
while her dress, the tension of her body, the pillar she leans against,
the grouping of the other characters, and Electra's isolation must
be *seen.* When reading *Intermezzo,* the phantom gives the impression of being merely a voice within Isabelle. When performed,
his existence must be believed, for he is really standing up behind
Isabelle, draped in his cape, in the semidarkness of a Limousin
evening.

Such is the difference beween Giraudoux's plays and other
theatres of language (some of the dialogue in George Bernard
Shaw's political plays, for example), which are self-sufficient nondramatic debates that have no need of staging. Actors, scenery, and
staging are indispensable in Giraudoux. The text gives the fundamental drama, which is complete only when the three collaborators—the written text, the spectator, and the actual performance
—are united. The meeting of all three is necessary to the incarnation of the symbol.

From *Siegfried* to *Pour Lucrèce* a definite evolution can be seen
in Giraudoux's art and thought. It was sensed from year to year
by drama critics such as Robert Kemp and Pierre Brisson and has
been the object of many academic studies. While the thematic
content of the plays oscillates from man to the supernatural and
from Anglo-Saxon or Germanic culture to Mediterranean culture
(after *Siegfried* came *Amphitryon 38;* after the adaptation of
*Tessa, La Guerre de Troie;* after *Electre, Ondine*), an orientation
of the whole shows Giraudoux to have discovered tragedy, expressed it through myths and the intervention of various forms
of divinity, hesitating all the while between the supernatural and
the preternatural, and then let a particular theme invade his works
—the war of the sexes, last expressed as completely humanized.

But one idea dominates his evolution: the idea that man will
never live in peace because he is not alone, that God or the gods,
social or psychological forces, and members of the other sex all
set definitions before him which are different from his own and

which attract and repel him at the same time. There is no judgment on Giraudoux's part; there are merely choices and ambiguities determined by the nature of each play. It is probably exaggerated to say with Jacques Houlet[9] that all Giraudoux's characters win our sympathy in some way or other. For actually, in the combat that takes place onstage between man and the gods, between man and woman, between France and Germany, between Hector and Ulysses, between Lia and Jean, our sympathies are not with either side but with the struggle itself as symbolized by the combat. So that beyond more or less individual definitions or essences, dividing and wrangling over the play's universe, a radically dramatic definition of man's condition is posed. Comedy springs from the triumph of human definitions (and, as Georges May pointed out, "Giraudoux's men are expert at beating the gods");[10] tragedy, from the triumph of forces that refuse man peace.

Critics have put great emphasis on the fine formulas scattered throughout his fantasies and plays concerned with God or the gods. Holophernes, for example, describes the universe as a place infested by the gods: "From Greece to India, from North to South, there isn't a country which doesn't swarm with them, each with his vices, his odors . . . The atmosphere of the world, for anyone who likes to breathe, is that of a barrack of gods." Here a pagan is speaking. For Judith and her people Jehovah and his messengers alone "infest" the universe. Just as each hero carries his universe about with him, so each period, each culture, and each genre carries its own gods about—those that can be touched as well as abstractions—in other words, symbols of that which transcends the individual and attempts to snatch away his privilege of giving order and form to his own world: for a knight of the courtly novel, spirits and enchanters; for the inhabitants of Sodom, a proliferation of angels; for the French bourgeois of the Second Empire, imperatives of the bourgeoisie's vices and virtues. A secularization of the conflicts does not change the vision of the world and destiny

9. *Le Théâtre de Jean Giraudoux.*
10. "Jean Giraudoux: Diplomacy and Dramaturgy."

underlying Giraudoux's plays. Metaphors and masks of man's condition vary, but both the situation of man and the poetic vision
remain the same.

For in a world expressly constructed to satisfy the mind, there is
no break between things and their essences, and the separation
between essences leads to the exteriority of things. Worlds can be
superimposed on the world; two worlds can occupy the same space
at the same time, in the boldest desire of the mind—contradiction.
For the individual who is well defined within his own nature, a
bearer of his own universe, everything occupying that same space
would thus seem supernatural. Woman is a monster for man, man
a monster for woman. There is clearly a hierarchy of characters,
from the literal-minded, who are willing to see only their own
essence and universe, to the "elect," who plainly see the super-
position and separation of universes and accept it so as to be able
to combat it, surmount it, or communicate with those other worlds
denied or rejected by their fellowmen.

Destiny is the directing force of the election which places such
and such character at a junction and gives him the lucidity to see
in both directions: Florence between the President and Jérome,
Judith between love and sanctity, Isabelle between the phantom
and the Supervisor, Ondine between humanity and nature, Siegfried between France and Germany. Destiny gives the elect just
enough freedom to be in agony. Whatever the situation and world
in which a man lives, there is always a transcendency—puzzling,
repelling, or attractive—and it is represented by Giraudoux as a
concrete and present universe, mixed in with the so-called normal
universe but separated from it, like two faces superimposed on a
photograph, yet always distinct.

According to Giraudoux,[11] the Frenchman, in a kind of moral
and metaphysical Bonapartism, delegates tragedy to tragic heroes
and does not identify with it. All of Giraudoux's characters are
more or less delegates: his gardeners and soldiers are delegates of

11. "La Tragédie et Bellac," *Littérature*.

our gardeners and soldiers; his waiters delegates of our waiters. Above them are the great ambassadors, who treat with the supernatural as equals and reveal its dangers, its charms, its grandeurs. Giraudoux's theatre is definitely a diplomatic operation, an open diplomacy—a machine intended to make men conscious of a destiny concerning them and transcending them at the same time, and to rid them of the debate by taking it on in their places.

Giraudoux treats man's condition in the same way as Talleyrand treated Europe: the hand that played with the destiny of nations was the hand of an artist. And if a lesson exists, it is a lesson of artistic perspective. Laurent Lesage[12] interprets the ironic distance established by Giraudoux as an inheritance of German Romantic stoicism. It can also be seen as a lesson for man in how to dominate his own condition, a metaphor of Pascal's thinking reed, of the feeble creature constantly threatened by the supernatural, in danger of being crushed by the universe, but always superior to that universe to the extent that he is capable of "thinking" his own oppression and making it an object of diversion by means of the mind and art. As a result, Giraudoux's theatre has often been reproached with coldness and a lack of pity. Yet through the "delegation" and the perspective furnished by intelligence, Giraudoux succeeded in avoiding that self-pity so easily confused, in the theatre, with participation.

Despite the value of other methods and other results, Giraudoux has taken a privileged place in the history of the French stage. By avoiding purely psychological identification, too easily and superficially offered by the realistic play, he was the first French playwright to respond to the demands of modern theatre and reach a large public at the same time. He transformed theatre into a feast, comparable to the passing of a Prince, surrounded by his pomp and ceremony, prisoner of his legend, and both separated from his people and bearer of their destiny.

12. "Jean Giraudoux, Surrealism and the German Romantic Ideal."

# CHAPTER 2

# THE DOUBLE GAME: JEAN COCTEAU

The ease created by Giraudoux's presence on the French stage during the last years of the Third Republic was countered by an uneasiness produced by Jean Cocteau. Just as Gide's scandals contrasted with Valéry's order, so in the theatre Cocteau's scandals offset Giraudoux's order. Giraudoux arrived on the twentieth-century French stage at precisely the time it was ready to receive him, as Racine did in the seventeenth century. Cocteau, however, began to write for the theatre in 1916, when the battle for reform was at its most acute. He started as a revolutionary and continued as a revolutionary, finding any immobility or rigidity distasteful. If his works often give more the impression of a great to-do and confusion than of revolution, it is because, mixed in with his desire for complete change, was an unquestionable narcissism.

Added to the conflicts and struggles of Cocteau's subjects and themes are the unexpected contrasts of the works as a whole. His theatre would seem to have covered all possible genres, from the avant-garde spectacle to commercial cinema, everything that could be represented or played by actors of every type—ballet: *Parade, La Dame à la licorne;* farce: *Les Mariés de la Tour Eiffel;* opera: *Le Pauvre Matelot, Oedipus-Rex;* fairy tale: *Les Chevaliers de la Table Ronde;* film: *La Belle et la Bête;* pseudo-classical tragedy: *Renaud et Armide;* transposition of classical myth: *La Machine infernale;* naturalistic dramas: *Les Monstres sacrés, La Machine à écrire, Les Parents terribles;* and Romantic dramas: *L'Aigle à deux têtes, Bacchus.* Such diversity of means gives Cocteau's works a disparate appearance, a sort of jack-of-all-trades or amateur aspect that makes him seem rather like Georges in *Les Parents terribles.* Cocteau tried to perfect already existing genres and make them more effective, just as Georges, having tried other experiments, wants to perfect the spear gun and make it shoot bullets.

With each work Cocteau plays the game he has chosen to play. In theatre he plays at being a playwright. He accomplishes the necessary rites: advance interviews in the newspapers and, at publication, explanatory prefaces or analyses. The preface to *Les Parents terribles* reveals that the play was written in a hotel room in Montargis and that the objective was to produce a play "which, far from serving as a pretext for staging, would serve as a pretext for great actors." His prefaces often give the impression that the work is an exercise in style, imposed by outer circumstances. The "idea" of theatre comes first and varies according to the period, the year, the month. Every play is an example or a model or an illustration. Indeed, Cocteau's works are presented as a group of occasional plays—to enhance actors or actresses, to satisfy a request from the Vicomte de Noailles, or to scandalize a certain public.

Once he has decided that a particular circumstance is in need of an ad hoc poet, Cocteau starts to work as if the genre of the play he is writing were the only one possible. In fact, he is more actor than playwright. He identifies with his role, with every role that circumstances have led him to play in the world of letters, and he is an actor who gives himself completely and honestly to the role of the moment. For Cocteau is a writer who lives in the literary moment, whether it be called *La Machine à écrire, Renaud et Armide,* or *Bacchus.* If Victor Hugo, according to Cocteau, was a madman who thought he was Victor Hugo, Jean Cocteau is an actor who identifies himself successively with the fictional ideal playwrights that the particular period would seem to demand. While he plays minor as well as leading roles, according to the need of the times, he is an understudy of genius. When there is a comedy lacking on the French stage, Cocteau is ready to stop up the hole. He provides an avant-garde spectacle when needed. To the Boulevard, which complained about the exhaustion of its great suppliers, he gave *Les Parents terribles, La Machine à écrire,* and *Les Monstres sacrés,* just as for the Comédie Française he produced the new play in verse that no one any longer dared write, *Renaud et Armide.* He became Edwige Feuillère's Rostand with *L'Aigle à deux têtes,* just as with *La Machine infernale* he was the first of his generation, even before Giraudoux, to reinterpret Greek tragedy because the new era needed a Racine. The general impression is that Cocteau has always something to do, if not always something to say. The problems he would seem to pose are of an aesthetic and even technical nature, for he is more interested in the secrets of workmanship than in the actual material of the product.

If there is an evolution in Cocteau's works, it is based on a twofold movement: he wanted both to create fashions and to revive them. In most of his prefaces he affirms the necessity of saying No to whatever is established, as soon as it is established. One must never become immobilized in a game. Once the rules are fixed, "the rules must be changed."[1] His is indeed the psychology of a great dress designer, and in his perpetual invention of new rules Cocteau constantly refers back to a certain past—now a lost naïveté, that of primitive theatre or childhood, now the bygone age of the theatre of actors, the sacred monsters: the ancient tunic is made old-fashioned by knight's armor, the suit by Second Empire uniforms. Just as Antoine was right to have imposed "real quarters

1. See Prefaces to *Les Mariés de la Tour Eiffel,* 1922; *Les Parents terribles,* 1938; and *L'Aigle à deux têtes,* 1946.

of meat and a fountain" on a public used to painted objects, Cocteau was to consider it his duty as an artist to impose painted canvas on a public accustomed to real quarters of meat or to reinvent the Boulevard for a public that had come to demand modernist theatre.[2] He created the fashion by reintroducing his grandmother's and great-grandmother's dresses. The objective of such an operation is to keep the public's aesthetic consciousness in a state of alert. However, a multiplicity of changes ends by resembling constancy, and in spite of the unexpected and the novelty, every one of Cocteau's plays can be recognized by a group of permanent features that constitute his signature.

Indeed, Cocteau has more of a signature than a style. The handwriting is always the same, while the style changes. To whatever genre it may belong, a Cocteau play can be recognized by certain words, certain formulas, certain images, just as in some families, despite a difference in sex, age, physical appearance, and temperament, each member has a beauty mark on his left shoulder. The words "wonder" and "witchery," "charms" and "enchantment," "miracles" and "magic," each a part of the very flesh of his fantasies such as *Les Chevaliers de la Table Ronde,* somehow or other work their way into the more or less realistic plays like *La Machine à écrire* and *Les Parents terribles.* Every situation that is out of the ordinary becomes "a dream" for the characters—a comparison that stems from a cliché, but one that Cocteau accentuates by extension. The characters ask to be awakened or not to be awakened, or they compare themselves to the dreams of someone else, as in *L'Aigle à deux têtes.* Moreover, symbols reappear: the thread (*Orphée, La Machine infernale, Renaud et Armide*) and the mirror, either actualized (*Orphée,* the film *Le Sang d'un poète*) or used as a metaphor (the lake of the Queen's death in *Les Chevaliers*). These are but a few examples of the vocabulary and passkey devices which constitute the superficial signature of Cocteau's works, just as a little star signs his drawings.

2. See Preface to *Les Parents terribles.*

On another level we find that the milieu of nearly all Cocteau's plays is the family—including not only an idea of the couple in the manner of Giraudoux but also the idea of a household: the households of Orpheus, King Arthur, Jocasta, Yvonne, and Esther, all characterized by a feeling of bedroom slippers and slammed doors never found in those of Giraudoux's Alcmene, Clytemnestra, Lia, or Lucile. The novel *Les Enfants terribles* and the play *Les Parents terribles* have fixed the theme of family promiscuity at the center of Cocteau's works—a promiscuity of people (mother-son, sister-brother) and also of intimate objects. But even in the deliberately antinaturalistic plays Cocteau introduces a realism of intimacy through pieces of clothing, physical contact, and childish quarrels. In *La Machine infernale* Jocasta promiscuously touching the young soldier in Act I; Jocasta and Oedipus, wearied by ceremonies, "letting themselves go" in the bridal chamber of the third act; Jocasta beginning to undress Oedipus; her dialogue with him on their wedding night—all suggest, beyond the play's tragic ambiguity and symbols, a whole universe of contact, underclothes, whispering, shut-in household scenes, and family secrets. Therefore it is hardly surprising that the man who wrote *La Machine infernale* also wrote *La Machine à écrire*. In *Les Chevaliers de la Table Ronde,* another "family" play, the great halls of King Arthur's and Merlin's castles change in the third act to the Queen's own room, where Guinevere appears in a nightgown, ready for a jealous scene that suggests Chrestien de Troyes as modified by Henri Bataille.

Those constantly reappearing rooms in Cocteau's theatre—rooms of the Queen, the wife, the mother—might well be reminiscent of Gertrude's room in *Hamlet,* while the bed, the chair, the disorder of intimacy, and its somewhat sickening tepidness would appear to constitute for Cocteau the ideal place where love appears in all its dimensions: physical contact, incest, hate, the minute of truth. In any case, bedroom atmosphere is obviously one of his signatures, the other being a reference to magic, witchcraft, and miracles. Here again a comparison can be made with the signature of his drawings. The handwriting of the "Jean Cocteau" or quite simply "Jean" is soft and childish. It evokes the warmth of the breast; it is Oedipus crying "Mother!" The star accompanying it is a sign of the higher and occult powers mixed in with that intimacy and directing it toward the glory of catastrophe.

Intimacy and witchcraft often have a meeting point in the object—more or less ordinary—that lies about, goes astray, or behaves in unexpected ways. "Even the familiar objects have something suspicious about them," wrote Cocteau in his description of the stage set for *Orphée*. The objects that furnish his stage are therefore intimate or ordinary, but also magical. While in *Les Mariés de la Tour Eiffel* the phonograph and camera are magical (the camera produces an ostrich and a lion that eats generals), the rest of his works are strewn with object-witnesses, which are apparently most ordinary and become suddenly gifted wtih supernatural powers: in *Orphée* the horse (demoniac) and mirror (the door to death), in *Les Chevaliers* a flower pot (the flower speaks) and a bat (a carrier pigeon), in *Les Parents terribles* a bourgeois apartment (a gypsy caravan), in *La Machine infernale* Jocasta's scarf and brooch (weapons of fate), in *La Voix humaine* the telephone (a new weapon with which to kill women). The object's mystery or secret is accentuated either by language or by its physical appearance, in a kind of expressionism rare on the French stage until Adamov and Ionesco.

The objects often acquire their powers from disorder. Out of their usual places they seem stripped of their usual functions, diverted from their roles in this world, and free therefore to assume new functions. The incongruity of an object not in its proper place creates an uneasiness in the spectator which comes from the consciousness of pure unjustified being. The transcendency of being that emerges when being is stripped of the habitual relationships established with it becomes magic in the hands of a poet—the sign of, or a door opening onto, the supernatural. Through not belonging, the being of things becomes strange. The point at which consciousness comes up against an impenetrable transcendency—a fact or an exceptional or monstrous relationship—is the point at which the poet, by an act of faith, affirms that *there* the world of poetry begins and that the imagination, the poet's "deep night," is called upon to give perceptible content to the ensuing uneasiness. If need be, the poet gives the finishing touch that makes the strange seem stranger still. But he also takes refuge behind analogies. For the talking flower in *Les Chevaliers,* he recalls that a plant which sends forth waves has been discovered in Florida; for the automobile that dictates his poems to Orpheus in the film *Orphée,* he evokes the car radios that transmitted B.B.C. code messages during the Nazi occupation.

An object that is not in its place can be poetic: a lion on the Eiffel Tower, theatrical costumes in a bourgeois house, even a stray shoe under an armchair. The same holds true for the characters. Cocteau tries to poetize them by isolating them, displacing them, or making them somewhat foreign. On the simplest level he does it by a disparity of class: Stanislas in the Queen's room *(L'Aigle à deux têtes);* Hans, the poor mad peasant, chosen as king for a week *(Bacchus);* the situation in *Ruy Blas* (Cocteau's film adaptation). In a more visual way he disguises or masks the character in a decisive scene: Margo, in *La Machine à écrire,* is dressed up like Lucrezia Borgia during most of the first act; Esther, in *Les Monstres sacrés,* completely covers her face with cold cream when Liane confronts her with cruel facts. The displacement is complete in *La Machine infernale,* in which Jocasta speaks and gesticulates like a foreigner. Cocteau used the device not only to justify the speech of Elvire Popesco[3] but, as in the other cases, to isolate the character by an accidental peculiarity—or at least seemingly accidental.

In the same way, Cocteau hoped for revelations from certain coincidences or unexpected encounters. Just as Elvire Popesco was to give a more staggering meaning—unpredictable but hoped

3. A famous Boulevard actress of Roumanian origin for whom Cocteau wrote the part. She did not play it, however, until the revival of *La Machine infernale* in 1954.

for—to the myth of Oedipus, so the music of Bach as background to the film *Les Enfants terribles* was to furnish "accidental synchronisms" out of which the most original beauty would spring. At the beginning of every Cocteau play a certain amount of chance, coincidence, and accident must be accepted in addition to the usual dramatic conventions: Orpheus' poetry dictated by a horse, his guardian angel in the form of a glazier, Jocasta's Roumanian accent, Stanislas as the image of the dead King. The process is similar to a combination of fairy-tale illusion and surrealist experiment. Cocteau's world is made up of disparate beings and elements, each one generally familiar, but isolated from its context, whirling about in a vacuum, fastening on to one another as if by chance, and thus perhaps creating poetry. Cocteau has said that the great writer is he whose "aim is straight." He himself gives the impression of hoping to aim straight while closing his eyes, like the characters of certain comic films who haphazardly shoot in the air and out of the sky falls a duck or a balloon, although Cocteau hopes to shoot down the bluebird.

More than a vision of the world, this is a device—one which can lead to every extravagance and which is legitimate to the extent that the incongruity of the combined elements is a protestation against the superficial coherence of psychological theatre or the theatre of ideas, as well as against the traditions surrounding myth and certain great subjects. The poetry of *Les Mariés de la Tour Eiffel,* for example, consists in replacing traditional coherence by an inner chance that is quite contrary to the logic of everyday reality. "The scenes fit together like the words of a poem," says Cocteau in his preface. Here the poem would be a surrealist divertissement or, more explicitly, a collage. Its interest lies both in its amusing absurdity and its challenge to accepted forms of poetry or painting. Cocteau counts on "the part that belongs to God" to make the symbol emerge, just as a chemist's apprentice might haphazardly choose two substances, mix them together in a test tube, and hope for an explosion. There is of course the danger of his obtaining no more than a bit of smoke and a change in color. Underlying that kind of operation is the hope that the audience will ask two questions, for which the answers are all prepared: Why? —Why not?, and What will come of it? —We shall see.

Cocteau's experiment in *Les Mariés* in 1921 might seem old-fashioned today, for it is essentially a document, a polemic argument that took place during a quarrel now established in history. It does not have the weight of either Jarry's *Ubu Roi* or Apollinaire's *Les Mamelles de Tirésias,* in which the revolution in form was accompanied by a true theme. Yet *Les Mariés,* in the intransigency of its conception, is still a call to order every time a resurgence of naturalism in the theatre begins to exercise its charms. It remains a warning against psychologism, earnestness, and want of imagination.

The plays that follow, from *Orphée* to *Bacchus,* and whatever the genre, reaffirm the poet's right to search for a synchronism of chance between elements drawn from the familiar world and the most exalted forms of myth or art. The Parisian vulgarity and banter of the demon Jinnifer in *Les Chevaliers,* the duality of Jocasta and the Sphinx in *La Machine infernale,* the great themes of incest and death embodied in Boulevard characters in *Les Parents terribles* are most striking examples of it. But do the shocks thus provoked have real dramatic value? There is no doubt that they create a tension between the play and the audience (surprise, indignation, irritation). The determining factor, however, is largely "the part that belongs to God," with the result that the juxtaposition of disparate elements may be rich in living tensions or turn out to be sterile, the spectator's interest being caught up in the play's ingeniousness or absurdity rather than in the drama itself.

A theatre of exorcism, Cocteau's works drive the demon out so effectively that there is hardly time to see him. The spectator is usually too busy watching the exorciser's pirouettes and incantations to think about the person possessed—whence the clear divi-

sion of public and critics into raving admirers and rabid disparagers, into those who see Cocteau's works as the reflection of a
deep and intense drama and those who see Cocteau as the enter-
tainer of a certain high society with a taste for anarchy.

> Three managers organize the publicity. In their terrifying
> language, they tell each other that the crowd takes the parade
> for the inner spectacle, and they grossly try to make the crowd
> understand it.

> No one enters. . . .

> The Chinaman, the acrobats, and the little girl come out
> of the empty theatre. Seeing the managers' supreme effort
> and failure, they try, in turn, to explain that the spectacle is
> given inside.

Such, in general, is the scenario of the ballet *Parade,* produced in
collaboration with Picasso, Erik Satie, Diaghilev, and Leonide
Massine. Besides its value as a manifesto, it has a theme that
might serve as a symbol for the whole of Cocteau's works: Cocteau
keeps his public outside. The true spectacle of the inner circus remains forbidden, despite the poet's innumerable invitations to
enter, and perhaps that inner circus is no more than an absolute
vacuum, as Eric Bentley has suggested.[4]

Yet beyond the parade, beyond the enormous differences of style
and tone that are so many theatrical variations of an outer
ceremony, there is the suggestion of a real drama, if not its total
realization. Almost all of Cocteau's plays lead toward the same
resolution. They are often directed toward a violent death, and
the hero generally appears more like a victim of the drama than
the tragic master of his fate. Victims of either magic spells or
very special circumstances, Cocteau's heroes submit to action
more than they direct it. In *Les Parents terribles* it is not Yvonne
who is responsible for Madeleine's lie, but Georges and Léo; in

4. *In Search of Theatre.*

*Les Chevaliers* many of the characters are replaced by a demon who takes on their appearances; and particularly in *La Machine infernale* such stress is put on the caprices of the gods and destiny that Oedipus' heroism disappears. Oedipus did not solve the Sphinx' riddle: she gave him the answer out of love; and although he puts out his eyes at the end, it is not so much his own act as it is in Sophocles' version.[5] During Cocteau's play the weapons themselves (Jocasta's brooch and scarf), from the very beginning, are impatient to put out Oedipus' eyes and strangle Jocasta. Moreover in the third act there is a kind of rehearsal of Oedipus becoming blind when he looks into Tiresias' eyes and thinks he is blinded by pepper. In short, Cocteau emphasized Oedipus' mechanical victimization more than his tragic heroism.

Here Cocteau is eminently representative of modern drama, which draws as near to tragedy as possible, yet most often remains on this side of it. Tragic heroism for the Greeks consisted in going all the way through an ordeal, to the point of giving any final acceptance the value of a challenge and finding true grandeur in the catastrophe itself. Today this conception is replaced by a taste for victimization that is still colored by Romanticism.

Cocteau uses the basic elements of tragedy in his dramas: the misunderstanding, a source of tragic irony, and the play of supernatural forces or obscure powers. Yvonne is mistaken about the meaning of her love for Mik, just as Oedipus is mistaken about the oracle and the encounters in his life, while the interiorization of fate and its expression in psychological terms detract nothing from its transcendency. But either the characters, following in the path of fate, stop just on the edge of the revelation that might have elevated them (Yvonne, in *Les Parents terribles,* dies without having really got to know herself), or the development of the action remains outside the character, who is victimized and then liberated, without having had any determining effect on the drama

5. "As for the hand that struck my eyes, it was mine and no one else's" (*Oedipus Rex,* line 1330). See Bernard Knox, *Oedipus at Thebes* (New Haven, 1957).

(King Arthur, in *Les Chevaliers,* does no more than talk about the forces that "intoxicate" and then "disintoxicate" him), or, as is most frequently the case, the characters accelerate the final movement and precipitate their own deaths in gestures that are more evasive than fulfilling (Solange's suicide in *La Machine à écrire,* the anticipation of Hans, who kills himself, in *Bacchus*).

Although the precipitated denouements are far from classical tragedy, they have two great merits. First of all, their theatricalism is effective. The foreshortening, the elements of spectacle, and the effects of surprise and shock do create an unquestionable climate of finality. The spectacle is carried away by an increasingly rapid whirlpool of scenic movements and at the end death is imposed, so to speak, on the spectator's nerves. Secondly they suggest a conception of freedom which is Cocteau's own. In the preface to *Les Mariés de la Tour Eiffel,* he wrote:

> One of the photographer's lines could be used on the title page: *Since these mysteries are beyond us, let's pretend to be their organizer.* It is our line par excellence. The conceited man always finds refuge in responsibility. Thus, for example, he prolongs a war after the phenomenon that had been its deciding factor is over.

Freedom would then be shown in the acceleration or slowing down of the necessary developments, in their foreshortening or extension. Freedom is Cocteau's "pretense" and the others' "conceit." And Cocteau has no illusions about his own characters. When at the end of *Bacchus* Hans cries out, "Free . . . ," his way of dying should be seen not as "tragic death par excellence, both fated and chosen,"[6] but as a pretense, a voluntary illusion. Hans' final freedom is in fact abstract. It consists only in anticipating an already determined event. Similarly, the Queen's command, "Say that I wanted it," in the third act of *L'Aigle à deux têtes* seems merely a verbal claim, for Stanislas' suicide—the very reason for her own—was not part of her plans.

6. Pierre Dubourg, *Dramaturgie de Jean Cocteau,* p. 157.

What Cocteau's plays reveal, then, is not a traditional tragic vision but a particular conception of destiny very near to fatalism, wherein the best man can do is to live "as if" he were capable of controlling his fate. That "as if" can be found in all the eloquent affirmations, costumes, grand gestures, and, at the extreme limit, art itself. In *La Machine à écrire* many inhabitants of the city claim, at one point or another, to have written the anonymous letters. The play explains that in making the claim they hope to escape from the mediocrity in which they are imprisoned. They want to be recognized even in crime, and their desire is so powerful that they end by believing their own lies. Actually, their mythomania picks up the "pretense" and "conceit" of the preface to *Les Mariés*. Caught in a development of events that is beyond them and for which they are not responsible, they want to have themselves put in prison so that everything will happen *as if* the scandal was their own work. In short, the only escape from fate is in the lie, and the game of lying must be played to the very end—that is, until total illusion is achieved, until the mask of freedom is seen as the very flesh of man—for man's only recourse is to deceive himself and others.

Death by suicide, in Cocteau's works, is the highest form of human pretense. By precipitating death, it often appears as an escape. The character disappears before the last illuminations of his ordeal. He wants to testify before it is too late and thus makes himself the martyr of certain values (poetry, love, grandeur, humanity) at the very moment that those values may be shown as impossible. As soon as the character realizes that the world has tricked him, he answers with the definitive trickery of suicide. He neither triumphs nor makes his peace: he retires. The deep and despairing cry of Cocteau's works is in the agitation of man who is caught and either ignores the fact or succeeds only in reconstructing a higher ignorance in the form of illusion. But although gilded by language and adorned with all the devices of mind and imagination, the trap remains merciless. By means of theatrical devices Cocteau has invented a masked ball, and he is the first to proclaim its vanity.

Cocteau's heroes—pure, still not disillusioned, and preys to circumstance—are victims of chance, of a *fatalitas* often similar to that of melodrama. They believe that they benefit from it until, having gone too far in the game, they are seized with an unbearable mistrust which leads to a voluntary illusion. Cocteau's universe is one not of tragedy but of danger. The cosmos surrounding the characters is not that of a great moral order in the Greek manner, in conflict with man's affirmation of himself; it is a Coney Island contraption, a layout of pitfalls: in *Les Chevaliers* the characters are deceived by a demon who takes on the appearances of several of them, and the Grail that appears is a false Grail; in *Les Parents terribles* mother love hides incest; in *La Machine infernale* everything is a trap or a threat, from Jocasta's scarf to the young girl who is a mask of the Sphinx. Those who fall into the traps—and who are marked out for them—are the naïve and the pure in heart: poets, idealized adolescents, dewy-eyed revolutionaries—whence the melodramatic aspect of Cocteau's theatre.

Parallel to the hero of Byronic gloom or the fated Romantic, his hero can be recognized by a sign, a coincidence, or phrases with double meanings that he utters without quite knowing their significance. One might cry out *Fatalitas!* during *La Machine infernale,* in which ghosts and ambiguous dialogue transform the *Tyrannos,* caught by Sophocles at the height of his glory, into the hero of an adventure novel; or when during a storm in *L'Aigle* a young revolutionary, who just happens to be the dead King's double, takes refuge in the Queen's room; or during *Les Parents terribles,* when Mik, a good son and good lover, finds himself not only the object of incestuous love but his own father's rival. Characterized by adolescence—a state of both grace and malediction, and a combination of impulsive acts, ignorance, purity, disorder, and youth—Cocteau's heroes are to a certain extent "going forces" in the Romantic manner, and they are "going" in a treacherous universe filled with every danger. Actually, "Romantic" does somehow describe Cocteau's works. The variety of forms, the aesthetic debates surrounding the plays, and the justifying abstractions of the subject matter (poetry, youth, impure order, pure disorder) only partially disguise the underlying theme of isolation—an isolation of the individual destined for better and for worse.

In *Scandal and Parade* Neal Oxenhandler emphasizes the theme of the *poète maudit* found throughout all of Cocteau's works. The ambiguity of benediction-malediction, generally identified with adolescence, is also, directly or indirectly, identified with the situation of the poet. Orpheus is a poète maudit, as are Stanislas and Galahad (at the end of *Les Chevaliers* when the birds sing "Pay, pay!"). They are poets like Ruy Blas (it was no accident that Cocteau adapted Victor Hugo's *Ruy Blas* for the screen) or Hernani, with a slight touch of Rimbaud. Doubtless society has cursed these poets, but so have the supernatural powers that play with the poet, giving him privileges in order to deceive or trap him more successfully.

Further, the poet constantly feels himself in danger of death. Cocteau, accused by Mauriac of having dragged the Catholic Church in the mud with *Bacchus,* answered that such accusations could only come from a man who belonged to the race of those "who kill poets."[7] Yet whatever Mauriac's bad faith in attacking him, he was not aiming at Cocteau the poet. He only meant to protect the Church from any scratch, however slight. Cocteau's vigilance was of the same order as his characters' mistrust. For him Mauriac became identified with Hans' accusers, with Orpheus' Bacchantes, with "impure order." The same motives pushed him into taking Jean Genet's defense in the courts. Cocteau was a man perpetually on trial, either by himself, through the poets of his time, or through his characters. He undoubtedly exaggerated the trial; after all, he was elected to the French Academy. But, in

7. See *Théâtre de France,* No. 2 (Paris, 1952), p. 32.

fact, any feeling of being hunted, any individual anguish can become a model for a more universal anguish. It would seem that Cocteau came to a stop between the rather Romantic individual complaint and universalization, which he replaced in part by all the surface effects of his contradictory aesthetics.

The problem of the cursed protagonist is complicated by the fact that the young hero in each of his works, often played by Jean Marais, cannot be considered individually. Cocteau also counted on Yvonne de Bray, Elvire Popesco, or Edwige Feuillère. The female role (mother, sister, queen) is just as important in Cocteau's plays as the leading male role, except perhaps for Eurydice in *Orphée*, who is a bit pale and simpleminded.[8] Because of a kind of allegorical redistribution of qualities that somehow recall Tennessee Williams and, in certain cases, Jean Genet, Cocteau's hero can only be truly understood as part of the couple, young man–older woman. The poet-martyr's identification with his persecuted or rebel hero is obvious, but so is his identification with the feminine mask. "*I* am Yvonne," Cocteau might have said, paraphrasing Flaubert's "*I* am Madame Bovary." All more or less Jocastas, Cocteau's women are not only incarnations of the poet's feelings with regard to the young hero but also women-obstacles, now an outer obstacle (mother, wife, lover), now an inner one (the Fantôme de Marseille in *Théâtre de Poche*).

The comparison with Tennessee Williams seems even more apt when we consider that Cocteau chose to adapt *A Streetcar Named Desire* for the French stage and that Tennessee Williams attempted an adaptation of the Orpheus myth in *Orpheus Descending*. Obviously the heavy sexual atmosphere of Williams' works is foreign to Cocteau's or at least considerably relieved in the major plays. Yet the general pattern—the duos, even the trios—are analogous. The unity of the couples reveals that they are but two faces of one basic individual—an eagle with two heads or with two sexes, as it were. In minor works such as *Le Fantôme de Marseille*

8. In the film *Orphée* Death was the strong feminine mask, fundamental to all of Cocteau's drama.

the hero remains undivided by also playing the part of a female impersonator. In fact, the hero in Cocteau's dramas and certain of Tennessee Williams' plays is not one character but a couple, a divided hermaphrodite who tries to possess himself—an often impossible and always tormenting desire.

The idea of the hermaphrodite can be seen in the complicity of intimacy so characteristic of Cocteau's atmosphere: the complicity of Yvonne and Mik, Jocasta and Oedipus, Maxime and Margot, Maxime and Solange, the Queen and Stanislas, Hans and Christine, or Guinevere and Lancelot, parallel to that of King Arthur and the false Gawain. In Cocteau's theatre there are always at least two who are marked out—for poetry, grandeur, disorder, or love. Even the fairies or the Sphinx want somehow to absorb the young hero, who is as beautiful as an angel or, in Swedenborgian terms, as half an angel.

Cocteau does everything he can to set up obstacles between the two poles of the divided hermaphrodite, making the union either criminal or impossible. In *L'Aigle à deux têtes* and *Bacchus* the distance is established in the form of social or political incompatibility in a given civilization. In *Les Parents terribles* and *La Machine infernale* it consists in a difference in ages but chiefly in a mother-son relationship, making any attempt at union monstrous incest. When one of the poles is part of the supernatural (Renaud and the fairy Armide, or Orpheus and Death, particularly in the film), there is what might be called a metaphysical incompatibility. Indeed, the hermaphrodite might well be a metaphor of the "difficulty of being" in a universe where the traps of nature are mixed with social taboos. The key to the agony is given in a short scene, generally cut, of the film *Le Sang d'un poète,* in which the hermaphrodite uncovers the lower part of his body and discovers a sign reading: "Danger of Death."

That monstrous touch of fate serves as an archetype for the metaphors of danger and universal fatality which constitute the unchanging hidden drama in Cocteau's works. Each story consists in the search for union, realization, or equilibrium, until the very last scene, when an unexpected meaning breaks through in the form of catastrophe, a price to pay, or a fatal incompatibility. The rest is surface effect. By means of a kind of baroque or rococo disproportion, the surface effects conceal the drama's underlying structure and are in fact taken for it—an obtrusive "parade," intentionally created by Cocteau, who, through the diversity and exuberance of his talents, wanted both to disclose *and* to mask the danger in order to give a true equivalent of man's condition.

In *Les Chevaliers de la Table Ronde* the demon Jinnifer is never seen. He can be perceived only by his "signature" (a certain vulgarity of language and humor) and by his fundamental malevolence. Between the two there stretches the whole domain of physical appearance, situation, and roles to be played. The same is true for Cocteau's plays themselves, in which the most superficial and the most profound are the only constants. Danger, like Jinnifer, plays the most diverse parts. In the same way that the Knights feel uneasy in the presence of the false Gawain and the false Queen, so the spectator is disturbed and apprehensive when confronted by Cocteau's apparent dramas. Metaphors of destiny's traps, his plays themselves are traps. The spectator should be seized with the same mistrust in their presence as Cocteau was in the face of life.

Mistrust is characteristic of Cocteau's sensibility[9] and creates a primitive and somehow pretragic terror in his works. He never intellectualized his fear but preserved it in its integrity and its extreme discomfort. Theatre, for him, was one of man's maneuvers to appease a threatening nature or supernature—but an illusory maneuver, since, despite embellishments and digressions, the universe can be portrayed only as implacable. Whereas Giraudoux resolved the problem of tragedy through intelligence, Cocteau,

9. In the weekly French paper *Arts* of November 19–25, 1958, Cocteau wrote: "Ink has become dangerous in a period when the slightest sign might well be misconstrued. That is why I am taking refuge . . . in a manual craft [pottery] which demands nothing more than a piece of work well done."

completely involved in a world for which the time of brilliant solutions was past or yet to come, did the dance of a man who is condemned to death, with no appeal possible. His masquerade was a staggering metaphor of the hesitation of a consciousness before its condemnation. If man innocently proclaims his freedom or his realization of certain values, desperately clinging to those desires yet masking their inevitable defeat by a voluntary illusion, so, in a parallel way, the playwright played an analogous double game: he put all his effort into raising the exalting or blinding illusion to the rank of reality, while preserving enough illusionism to keep the reality from ever being achieved.

Success—a synthesis of the hermaphrodite, the triumph of poets or lovers, the realization of a total and happy equilibrium, excluding all hazards or perils—is not of this world. It is in a beyond where Orpheus and Eurydice, Guinevere and Lancelot, Patrice and Nathalie (the Tristan and Isolde of the film *L'Eternel Retour*) are reunited. The price for union is death. And even then an entire staircase separates the dead bodies of Stanislas and the Queen; Yvonne dies without Mik; Maxime abandons Solange. In this world everything must be paid for, and the deal is transacted above man and without his consent: Galahad is condemned always to leave what he loves in order to keep the purity that makes it possible for him to chase out Merlin.

A grim and anguished theatre, full of surface glitter that is no more than an illusion of aesthetic satisfaction, Cocteau's plays are outwardly like entertainments of the twenties and thirties. He has used all the devices of the entertainment, from avant-garde forms to the Boulevard, in order to express the meeting between the illusionism of that time and the personal and sincere perception of a basic dimension of man's condition. Cocteau searched the present and a recent past for all the masks imaginable. Clowns, music-hall stars, and the favorite actors of the bourgeoisie and other classes are all buffoons in a masquerade addressed as much to the Prince de Beaumont as to the masses who attended vaudeville theatres during the time of the Popular Front. Indeed, what gives Cocteau's theatre its value is its cry of warning addressed, whatever may be said, to all men.

Added to that is his fidelity to an uncompromising idea of theatre. He is a modernist not only when he concretizes psychological or metaphysical phenomena onstage, with the freedom of today's poets, but also in his "Boulevard" plays. Even *La Machine à écrire,* generally considered his worst play and one that he himself repudiated, is infinitely superior to works of the same genre in that, while continuing to play the Boulevard game to the very end, Cocteau goes beyond the document on life in the provinces and succeeds, through dialogue and action, to actualize a theme of pure theatre: that of illusion as both mask and instrument of the inexorable destructibility of man.

Cocteau has a love of the theatre which is evident from his general declarations, but which can also be found in the conception of his plays themselves. A metaphor of illusion, theatre should be presented with all the signs of illusion. At certain moments the reality of what unfolds onstage must be forgotten so that the spectator may once again become conscious of the actor's number. The acting of Jean Marais, who was trained by Dullin but chiefly by Cocteau, does not ring true because it should not ring true, for he must constantly maintain that distance which is the very definition of theatre and makes it possible for the spectator both to believe and not believe. The same can be said for the stage sets (often designed by Christian Bérard) and the texts themselves. In *Les Parents terribles* the characters constantly remind us that they are acting out a play—vaudeville, drama, or tragedy, depending on the moment and situation. Allusions to dreams and magic, now represented by living beings or objects, now evoked by metaphors of language, should also be interpreted in the sense of a diversion from the real. What happens onstage is never absolutely true, despite appearances. Each play is presented as a trance or comedy, involving man in a story that is fictional or dreamed up by some god.

A Protean theatre, it is the faithful image of a Protean universe.

The number of forms that the traps of the universe can take is infinite; so are the forms taken by man's illusory defenses. The meaning of reality is finally lost in the game of lies and counter-lies. By means of an intransigence recalling the Baudelairean dandy, Cocteau, as the only possible affirmation of his identity, succeeded in immobilizing two elements of the confusion: theatre and the emotion of fear. His double game is tragic even though, individually, his plays are not. It is a recognition, a voluntary act. For Cocteau, writing a play is taking man's part—but he takes it in all lucidity, for by resorting to devices and deliberate illusion, he affirms that he defends a lost cause.

# CHAPTER 3

# THE UNIVERSE AS PARABLE:
# PAUL CLAUDEL

Paul Claudel's dramatic works are certainly the most ambitious of all French theatre. As an attempt to embrace time and space, they can be compared only to one other gigantic work, Victor Hugo's nondramatic *La Légende des siècles*. Both poets wanted to synthesize man's past and bring out its meaning. But while Hugo, the Romantic, tried to respect historical time and crowned his vision with humanitarian dreams, Claudel cast over our history the eye of an eternal God capable of telescoping time, and once he grasped the globe as a unit, he set up the Cross. This epic work is an accounting of the world and its history, with history being explained in terms of destiny. The supernatural is not localized: it informs the whole. A meaning is not revealed through time: it is given in advance. The one great symbol of all symbols is that of the Christian Cross.

We are very far indeed from the magic of *Les Chevaliers de la Table Ronde*, the room in *Les Parents terribles*, the columns of

*Electre,* even the sky of *Sodome et Gomorrhe.* The plays of Cocteau or Giraudoux are sufficient unto themselves. Claudel's theatre is not. It takes on its complete meaning only when integrated into an infinitely vaster drama, that of the Christian universe. In some ways Claudel's works are made up of fragments of *the* Drama par excellence and in that respect are forever incomplete.

In his preface to Paul Claudel's *Théâtre* Jacques Madaule shows how the place of Claudel's works, in relation to a dying civilization in the first half of the twentieth century, is similar to that of the works of Homer, Virgil, and Dante in relation to their own times. Claudel is the poet who sings of a world in which a cycle of history has come to an end. *Le Soulier de satin* and the trilogy of the Turelure-Coûfontaines—*L'Otage, Le Pain dur,* and *Le Père humilié*—mark Europe's material and spiritual supremacy over the world. The twentieth century marks the beginning of another conjunction of forces, another civilization. The order of the world under the Cross at the end of the nineteenth century is comparable to the order of Dante. It has its Paradise, its Purgatory, its Hell. Everything is clearly in its respective place: popes, kings, antichrists, sacrifice, lust, politics, and materialism. Claudel was the poet of the end of a world. Born at the height of Europe's power, a witness to the upheavals at the beginning of the twentieth century, conscious of European grandeur as well as its vices, he tried, as it were, to evaluate that enormous fragment of history. On the threshold of a new world he stopped to sing and devoted himself to meditations on the Bible. His dramatic works as a whole are an answer to Valéry's well-known formula: "We civilizations know now that we are mortal." Claudel became the Bossuet of one of those civilizations. He eloquently stylized its most significant moments and gave them eternal meaning guaranteed by the Catholic God; that is to say, a civilization is planned by God, its realization on earth is transitory, but because of its figurative value it participates in eternity.

From the very beginning, from the minute the curtain goes

up on a Claudel play, the poet's dogmatic and uncompromising position must be accepted, for to the merest detail it dominates his vision of man and history. Claudel was a Roman Catholic, and a fervent one, ever since his profound mystical upheaval in 1886. Doubtless Giraudoux's essentialism and Cocteau's contrived universe must also be accepted. But their works were not meant to illustrate their "philosophies," which merely provided the drama's inner structure. In Claudel anecdote and drama are deliberate illustrations of a doctrine. His works are didactic—not demonstrations but pure and simple affirmations, for faith does not allow of discussion. Every one of Claudel's plays is a parable meant to illustrate concretely a lesson given in advance.

To be sure, his works would necessarily have two publics. A Catholic and a non-Catholic audience would see the plays in different ways. For the first the plays' explanation of the world is the only true explanation; for the second it is the metaphor of a possible explanation. For the first the analogies are *real;* for the second they are concrete content given to the general feeling for analogism or to the mind's and heart's need to discover an illusion of intelligibility in the universe. There is no doubt that a wholly and deeply Catholic audience at a Claudel play would actualize the dream of today's playwrights: a union of theatre and religion comparable to that of Aeschylus' time—the drama expressing the destiny of a collectivity in terms of the belief which is the very flesh of that collectivity. But our epoch is characterized by a dispersal of beliefs. Claudel's audience—that of the Théâtre de L'Œuvre, the Comédie Française, the Théâtre Marigny, or the Théâtre de France—is necessarily mixed. To certain spectators Claudel's drama presents truth itself, embellished by poetry; to others, and in the same way as any poetic theatre, it is a very beautiful metaphorical hypothesis. For some it is history clarified, for others a fantasy. Because of its intention and didacticism, Claudel's drama divides the spectators into believers and aesthetes.

Yet his theatre exists beyond its intentions. Many of Claudel's admirers are non-Catholics, and their appreciation is somewhat

similar to Renan's of the life of Jesus. For Christianity, with its
dialectic of salvation, is essentially dramatic. Beyond the doctrine
itself the drama may be considered as one of the best Western
metaphors of man's condition, and Claudel's theatre brings it to
light.

The whole of Claudel's work has a structure which makes it into
a kind of "Divine Comedy," with the principal plays grouped
almost chronologically into three cycles.

The first is "L'Arbre," or "The Tree," a collection of the first
or second versions of his first plays, written between 1894 and
1898 and including *Tête d'or, La Ville, La Jeune Fille Violaine,
L'Echange,* and *Le Repos du septième jour.* Related to that cycle
are *Partage de midi* (1905) and *L'Annonce faite à Marie* (1910),
which is the last version of *La Jeune Fille Violaine.* A trilogy
follows: *L'Otage* (1909), *Le Pain dur* (1914), and *Le Père humilié*
(1916). The last cycle consists in *Le Soulier de satin,* completed in
1924. The title "L'Arbre" would actually be suitable for Claudel's
works as a whole, for the group of plays just mentioned might
be considered a trunk to which numerous branches are attached.
For example, a dramatized narrative like *Le Livre de Christophe
Colomb* (1927) belongs to the cycle of *Le Soulier de satin* but
constitutes, along with *Jeanne au bûcher* (1935), a lyrical and
allegorical meditation on an exemplary destiny, just as *L'Histoire
de Tobie et de Sara* (1942) is on a book of the Bible. Similarly the
earthy comic vein which comes through in most of the plays, particularly in *Le Soulier de satin,* is exploited for itself in the farces
*Protée* (1926) and *L'Ours et la lune* (1917).

In Claudel's evolution as a playwright the dominant movement
is that of an increasingly clear and specific incarnation of the Idea
at a given moment of history. The use of history is inherent to the
Christian doctrine, which is based on events and dogmas expressed
in a chronicle. Every moment of the chronicle is eternal as well.
In his plays Claudel wanted not only to bring out a universal
Meaning and show how that Meaning is embodied in possible

anecdotes, but to incorporate it in the actual past of the collectivity to which it belongs.

The first part of Claudel's works, "L'Arbre" and connected plays, establishes the basic themes, occasionally linking them to a moment in history but chiefly treating them for themselves: the themes of conquest and pride *(Tête d'or)*, government and faith *(La Ville, Le Repos du septième jour)*, Grace through evil in the adventure of the couple *(L'Echange, Partage de midi)*, sacrifice and miracle *(La Jeune Fille Violaine)*.

In such plays his characters are one with a universal inner category and practically admit, themselves, that they are symbols. Thus Claudel avoided the particularizing so dear to naturalistic and realistic theatre, but sometimes at the price of an absence of life never quite filled by either picturesque settings or the concrete vigor of certain images. This is especially flagrant in *La Ville,* in which the great scenes harden into stylized debates between Poetry, Disbelief, Femininity, and so on—abstractions that are hardly concealed by the characters' names and masks. By means of true allegorization, the poet tried to escape from his subjectivity by translating his inner conflict into the most general terms, objectifying it through the great commonplaces of the intellectual crisis at the end of the nineteenth century.

Even in *Partage de midi* the metaphorical ballet danced by De Ciz, Mesa, and Amalric around the Woman, Ysé, is a result of that method. In *L'Annonce faite à Marie* as well, the two couples, Pierre/Jacques and Violaine/Mara, dominated by the figure of Anne Vercors, all settled down in the shadow of Monsanvierge, give the anecdote the value of an allegory, in which each character coincides with a vocation, the vocations obviously arranged by the poet in order to illustrate a truth given in advance.

Yet the two plays transcend hyperbolic allegories like *La Ville.* By referring to history, they avoid abstraction. There Claudel recognized Christianity's historicity, the fact that every epoch has its specific forms of incarnation. The miracle of a child's resurrection, reproducing the birth of Jesus on Christmas night *(L'Annonce faite à Marie),* is situated precisely at a time when that miracle would be acceptable—the Middle Ages—whereas the first version of the same theme took place at a rather vague moment somewhere between the Renaissance and today. In the same way, the modern circumstances in *Partage de midi* give life to the drama of the couple, torn between the spirit and the flesh.

With the Turelure-Coûfontaine trilogy Claudel used actual historical events as the subject of his plays. The great themes are not merely stated but embodied in a given moment of history—the fifty-odd years between Pope Pius VII's abduction to Fontainebleau (1813) and the unification of Italy (1860–71). The vicissitudes of the papacy and the Church dominate the plays, and Napoleon's fall, Louis XVIII's return, the colonization of Algeria, the division of Poland, the Italian War, and general social upheaval are all determining events and dependent for their ultimate meanings on the fate of the Church. Thus the protagonists are not only participants but truly makers of history.

In these dramas Claudel has almost completely refused to indulge in the usual tricks of the historical genre. At no time did he ever claim to present a faithful reconstruction of events. The characters who play with the fate of the world, aside from the popes and kings, are imaginary beings with fanciful names. Between 1815 and 1870 everything happened *as if* a family called Turelure-Coûfontaine had played a determining role. True, the Baron Toussaint Turelure was probably patterned after Joseph Fouché. But Turelure is a poetic creation based on certain of Fouché's fundamental characteristics, developed or simplified. Turelure is the ideal agent of a particular policy that had been imperfectly embodied in figures of the Revolution and the Empire such as Fouché. Indeed, Claudel deals with early nineteenth-century history in the same way as the writer of *La Chanson de Roland* dealt with an episode of the wars of Charlemagne.

The trilogy, then, represents an attempt to give the French stage a "historical tragedy." The meaning of the events is the reality, the events themselves only a sign. And the meaning justifies all the distortions of so-called historical truth.[1] Since the meaning here is the Catholic Mystery, the tragedy would be more comparable to Spanish drama than to Aeschylus or Shakespeare.

By actually using Spanish drama as a source of inspiration, Claudel reached the high point in his art with *Le Soulier de satin*. There he used the method with infinitely more breadth and audacity and with greater success as well. Since the period was remote, Claudel was able to modify historical facts more freely, telescope the centuries, "manipulate them like an accordion, at will." While the events of the trilogy remain limited in space (Europe), *Le Soulier de satin* is made up of a whole network of actions that envelop the entire earth. "The stage of this drama is the world," wrote Claudel in one of his first stage directions. The movement of his theatre has been not only to make the flesh of history and the spirit coincide but also to exhaust the meanings of the word "universal"—that is, philosophical and physical, under the aegis of its mystical meaning, Catholic.

The idea was to grasp the moment at which that total experience existed both on a religious and a physical plane. At only one period in history was it possible—that during which Catholicism winning the battle of the Counter-Reformation and the achievement of great discoveries coincide. No doubt nineteenth- and twentieth-century man possesses the world in a more complete way, but in the eyes of the Catholic poet that world is not as satisfying as the world of the baroque age. Protestant sects are established in Germany, England, and America; rationalism has corrupted and split most societies; in fact, ours is a completely divided globe. So was that of the Counter-Reformation, but the struggle was moving in the direction of unification, the great empires were Catholic,

---

1. "The playwright's art, like the painter's, has its freedoms," wrote Claudel in his introductory note to *L'Histoire de Tobie et de Sara*. He explained how he used those "freedoms" when he adapted the deuterocanonical Book of Tobias. He eliminated characters and added others, once he had extracted the deep meaning of the story, with the help of a quotation from Saint Matthew, and had acknowledged Sarah as representative of the human soul. He applied the same method to actual history.

and the Cross was advancing and pushing back the frontiers of Hell (the Protestant world) and Purgatory (the Far East). Claudel chose the period because at that time every human gesture was defined in relation to Roman Catholicism. The whole surface of the globe was either fighting Rome or working for Rome's triumph. It is probable that, except for Dante writing *The Divine Comedy,* no poet has ever had as much the feeling of writing a total work as Claudel during the composition of *Le Soulier de satin.* Every quiver of the characters' flesh is directly and obviously bound to the eternal truths of the Church. And since it concerns the entire world and all the men of that world, of whom we are descendants, Claudel's drama shows, as it were, that all of us, no matter who, all twentieth-century theatregoers, are bound through a common past to that Church. Even if we are its enemies, we are defined in relation to it, and not it in relation to us. Thus *Le Soulier de satin* has the scope of a universal epic.

An epic becomes drama when the accent is put not only on the greatness of the exploits but on the inner and outer conflicts of the heroes as well. Every nuance of the hero's most personal inner life is indissolubly bound to a tremor of the entire universe. Suggested in the somewhat overwhelming allegory of *Tête d'or* and developed in *L'Otage,* such interaction was fully exploited by Claudel in *Le Soulier de satin.* The tormented adventure of Rodrigue and Dona Prouhèze is in itself a great drama of love and faith, but in addition, the fate of our whole universe depends on its every pulsation. Obviously the relation is not a naïve one of cause and effect, as in the historical plays of Scribe or Sardou. It is one of reciprocity in the play of the symbols which make up the skeleton of the visible universe.

That universe itself is dramatic because of the epic simplification which brings out great fundamental conflicts and tensions, such as the distribution of Good and Evil, True and False. In contrast to a profusion of concrete, colorful, and vivid details are clear and distinct divisions among the great principles and great values. Indeed, Claudel's universe is one in which no doubts are allowed.

While his theatre on the whole consists of a simple drama—a conflict between shadow and light, enriched by the Christian dialectic—it is finally that dialectic which introduces all the complexity of human destiny. For Claudel's drama is built not only upon the clarity of a basic universal conflict but also upon the complications of the roads to follow within the conflict. There is no doubt as to values or mysteries, but in the course of what leads to the revelation of those values, there is painful hesitation and a complex struggle. And while there is no doubt as to the duty to please God, there is a problem of choice as to the way to please Him most. Such is the subject of *Partage de midi, L'Otage,* and *Le Soulier de satin.* Suffering springs from the fact that in order to do one's best, one has often to do the worst, and doing the worst, along with the heroism of acceptance and the victory that consists in *wanting* to do what one does reluctantly, constitutes sacrifice. In fact, Claudel's drama often appears as a long sacrificial rite.

After the fiftieth performance of *Le Soulier de satin* Claudel wrote, "Sacrifice . . . somehow provokes the Divine part. By willingly withdrawing, we make room for an incited action of Grace, as it were; we are playing on the side of the All Powerful for an enormous profit."[2] This is actually a kind of Pascalian wager, but the wager is terribly complex. Violaine's way, like that of Ysé and Mesa, Sygne, and Dona Prouhèze and Rodrigue, is made up of detours. Of course, the face of evil is always recognizable: it is Mara, Amalric, Turelure, or Don Camille. That evil is necessary, however. There is no purity without impurity, no Paradise without Hell, no salvation without sin or apparent sin, which would mean that Claudel's works are authentically Christian in emphasizing the corruption of Creation after Adam's fall. But the detours imposed by sacrifice are often what would seem like a passage through Hell—a passage that has little to do with traditional

2. *Le Soulier de satin* (Paris, Club du Meilleur Livre, 1953), Appendix, p. 20.

ethics. For example, Sygne de Coûfontaine's way of salvation lay through betrayal, and Mesa's and Ysé's through betrayal *and* their indirect murder of De Ciz. Claudel's Christian dialectic requires that strong souls be humiliated by means of the most profound abasement.

Sacrifice is more especially complicated since it involves one individual who sacrifices not only himself but others, and it requires a choice, which is complicated by the fact that the terms are masked:

> This notion of sacrifice is tightly bound to the great Christian idea of the *Communion of Saints,* in which it would be naïve to imagine the inoffensive workings of a benevolent society. Religion's commandment: "Love one another!" has more of a relation to nature's commandment: "Eat one another" than one would think.[3]

The conditions for the salvation of a soul are cruel when looked upon from this world, and many critics have not failed to become indignant.[4] But there is no doubt that such cruelty saves Claudel's Christian theatre from sentimentality and the easy good conscience of certain optimistic sects.[5]

In *Strait Is the Gate* André Gide drew a moving and ironic portrait of a Calvinist sacrifice. Claudel demands much the same sort of sacrifice from his heroes, but in Claudel not only is the gate strait but several pass through at the same time—and without irony:

> There is deep mystery and an infinite source of tragedy in the fact that we are the condition of eternal salvation one for the other, that we alone carry within ourselves the key

3. Ibid.

4. Joseph Chiari *(The Poetic Drama of Paul Claudel)* protests against the cruelty that Claudel attributes to God and refuses to believe that His designs were that distorted or that merciless. In fact, Claudel's God is hardly more unrelenting than the Greek Nemesis.

5. See Henri Peyre, "The Drama of Paul Claudel."

to the soul of some one of our brothers, who can be saved only by us, and at our own expense.[6]

Claudel's dramas are built upon the idea that souls are destined one for the other or elect one another. To that extent, not only is the sacrifice of oneself necessary, but that of certain others. Ysé has the key to Mesa's soul, and Mesa the key to Ysé's, and the union of those two souls is well worth the sacrifice of others. The union cannot be immediate, for if it were, it would be only a trap. It is, on the contrary, in the refusal of that union on earth, in the trial of separation and through that trial, that the souls destined one for the other will be led to exemplary acts which will save worlds (*L'Otage, Le Père humilié, Le Soulier de satin*) and save themselves at the same time. Providence, using now outer obstacles, now the action of the characters themselves, provokes and reinforces the separation. Ysé is already married; she goes with Mesa but leaves him for Amalric so that they may be more powerfully reunited at the moment of death. Dona Prouhèze is already married, but when she is finally free to marry Rodrigue, the letter she sends him goes astray between the continents. In *Le Soulier de satin* the problem is further complicated by the fact that two men need Dona Prouhèze—Don Rodrigue and Don Camille:

> Whence the importance of Don Camille's role. He needs Prouhèze more than Rodrigue does. He needs something in Prouhèze that is beyond Rodrigue's desire. A Prouhèze detached from any human attachment, preferring nothing to the eye of God, whatever it may be—a pure star in the ray of her Creator! It is that Prouhèze, that Prouhèze alone who is the condition of his salvation.[7]

In these more or less complicated adventures, based on reversals of attitude or often surprising situations, but all connected to a rather simple basic model, there is quite obviously a lesson. Claudel

6. *Le Soulier de satin,* Appendix, p. 20.
7. Ibid., pp. 20–21.

wanted to bring out the ambiguity of certain vocations, the nature of perfect love, which lies in God and not in the flesh, and God's hidden benevolence, masked by a cruel and unjust destiny, which makes it possible for souls to unite in perfection or quite simply be saved. It would be a mistake to see any Jansenism in such severity and absurdity, for Claudel vigorously repudiates the Jansenist notion of predestination as well as the affirmation that only very few will be saved. Yet not only does he reject all complacency and would, "like Mauriac, rather assert that Christianity enters into souls in order to divide them,"[8] but he emphasizes the absolute individuality of destinies and vocations. While it is true that Grace is possible for all men, there is no question that certain men—and they alone—are marked out for the highest and most agonizing adventures. And it is they who become dramatic heroes.

The adventures of Dona Prouhèze, Rodrigue, and Don Camille can be lived only by them. Every anecdote is individual—that is, unique and possible only with a particular protagonist and no other. There is no anecdote that is universal in itself; souls are not interchangeable. When Claudel writes that "we alone carry within ourselves the key to the soul of some one of our brothers," he implies "and no other." In Claudel's theatre each one answers "with a particular name, his own! *Adsum!*" thus making Claudel's religion a source of drama—first, because it uses Christianity's notions of agony, renunciation, inner conflict, and "Providence's circuitous ways," but also because it emphasizes the singleness of destinies and considers the characters as irreplaceable. In a universe where the poles of Good and Evil are already defined in all orthodoxy, each man, torn between the attractions of one and the other, lives his inimitable destiny, dated historically but representative of an eternal truth. An epic theatre in its choice of extraordinary characters—extraordinary in their political positions or richness of adventures and in the dimensions of the space they occupy and the transformations they bring to the world—Claudel's

8. Henri Peyre, "The Drama of Paul Claudel."

works are also, and perhaps especially, a theatre of the individual.

Since the individual is never alone, his vocation being to open the soul of another and to sacrifice himself for one or several others, the drama is always the double one of love and action. The adventure is lived by strong, passionate beings who act and are acted upon at the same moment, in the same gesture. Christianity's paradox, a source of heresies and schisms, is the conflict between freedom and predestination. In Claudel freedom is manifest and arrogant, even sometimes very Corneillian in tone. The characters are always free to damn themselves. By giving her satin slipper to the Virgin, Dona Prouhèze partially gives up her freedom: "But when I try to rush toward evil, may it be with a lame foot!" Man is free to miss his vocation. Sygne de Coûfontaine was perhaps meant to save Pope Pius VII by marrying Turelure, but as the priest Badilon told her, "You alone must do it of your own free will."

However, the conflict in Claudel is less that between what in man is free and what predestined than the struggle between all in man "which miserably clings to things, one by one and successively" and "what is most essential, God's image." It is the continually reaffirmed difficulty of that choice, which, beyond any dogmatism or controversial judgment and in its creation of a lyrical pathos close to that of Greek tragedy, has provided Claudel with a lay public. A theatre neither of doubt nor of anguish but of a rather Corneillian agony and effort, Claudel's works, by rejecting the complacency of easy devotion and with the help of Catholicism's enormous and magnificent storehouse of images, present an image of individual man whose paradox is to be implacably himself and at the same time always something other than what he is.

A public that might be put off by a systematic asceticism finds that Claudel, in his passage from the world to the supernatural, does not exclude the world but rather embraces it. The carnal universe is the place of action, the theatre of the struggle for salvation. Although Claudel's judgment on anything that is not Catholic would sometimes seem injurious, he does not dismiss those "enemies" or "successive things." They are always present, transfigured but preserved in a kind of baroque integration, and somehow "saved" by the symbol they carry within themselves. There is nothing monastic about Claudel's renunciation. Amalric's sensuality is necessary to Ysé's and Mesa's adventure, just as noise and confusion, colored plumes, the Chinese, and the great farcical masks of the Spanish Empire are to Rodrigue's. Don Rodrigue is perhaps humiliated, mutilated, and stripped bare at the end of *Le Soulier de satin,* but the play itself is not. The poet takes an obvious pleasure—and often a pagan one—in playing with such material. That vigorous part of his temperament may have drawn him toward Hell, but it put rich blood and gluttonous life into the carnal world of his theatre.

While the conflict between Christian renunciation and richness of spectacle would seem to provide excellent theatrical material, Claudel's plays were slow to conquer the general public or even be performed. Indeed, to the reader they often seem devoid of any consideration as to the conditions and possibilities of performance. Claudel refused to bow to the usual restrictions of the stage, or at least he never facilitated the director's task. Moreover, in writing a work of the length and spectacular complexity of *Le Soulier de satin,* he was little concerned with the physical resistance of actors and spectators alike. Claudel wrote for the stage, but for a stage that had not yet been constructed.

Today most of Claudel's dramas have been performed. If the texts are no longer considered "unperformable," it is because the notion of what theatre is has been considerably enlarged since 1890 as a result of the antinaturalist reaction, on the one hand, and also the discovery and partial assimilation of conceptions far from those of Western theatre since the seventeenth century: Greek staging, medieval staging, Balinese, Chinese, and Japanese plays and staging. Claudel, whose plays were performed very early in his career in avant-garde theatres, has gradually conquered an increasingly large public and has finally been played at the Comédie Française and commercial theatres. While there is no doubt that his success since the 1940s has been due in part to a wartime and postwar religious revival, it is due chiefly to the theatre's progressive acceptance of texts that had long been considered unperformable.

The great test was the Comédie Française's production of *Le Soulier de satin* in 1943. Here the meeting of Claudel and Barrault was decisive: Claudel's most scenically difficult play was performed after a few changes and with enormous success. Then the Comédie Française and Louis Jouvet did new stagings of *L'Annonce faite à Marie;* Barrault brought back *L'Echange* and introduced *Partage de midi, Le Livre de Christophe Colomb,* and, most recently, *Tête d'or;* the Paris Opera staged *Jeanne au bûcher;* and the T.N.P. produced *La Ville,* while one of the little theatres staged *Protée.* Claudel, at first considered avant-garde or reserved for a chosen few, has become an eminently successful playwright.

Barrault was enthusiastic about Claudel's works largely because the idea of "total theatre," found in Antonin Artaud and in the theories of Barrault himself, is illustrated or embodied in plays like *Le Soulier de satin* and *Christophe Colomb.* Claudel is "unperformable" according to nineteenth-century standards because his works absorb, with little discrimination or practical sense, all the possible enlargements of our conception of theatre. His experiments with ballet and pantomime (in *L'Homme et son désir* and *La Femme et son ombre*), his partial although real knowledge of the arts of the Far East, and his translation of Aeschylus' *Oresteia* enabled him to escape from a limited conception of theatre. His use of music, puppets, and cinema completes the list of his devices. Through disrespect for the theatre, Claudel appears today as one of its most authentic liberators.

To take only one example, Claudel's use of the film screen is particularly effective. It serves not only to juxtapose two actions that are distant in space—something which has often been done in social-problem or detective-story plays—but to actualize the symbol. Since, in *Christophe Colomb,* as in *L'Histoire de Tobie et de Sara,* the symbol appears as both real and endowed with the two-dimensional nature of a motion picture image, the spectator is provided with the multiple sight of God. While the stage is the world, the screen reveals the deep meanings through close-ups. Thus in *Christophe Colomb* the sailor's death in Columbus' arms is, *at the same moment,* seen in its entirety—with the movement of bodies and the surrounding space—and in its intimacy, in the enlarged detail of the protagonists' expressions. In other words, both dimensions of the event are portrayed: every death, every act, is private and can be revealed only at close range (a view never before provided by the theatre) and in an intimacy that contains the true adventure of souls; at the same time, in the context of the action, the act involves a universe of gestures and a world of adventures and of boats plowing through space. Previously, the cinema had been used in the theatre in the opposite way: real actors act out the private drama, while the screen enlarges the spatial world and presents the mob scenes, without ever portraying the same character in the same action at the same time. It was Claudel and Jean-Louis Barrault who understood that the space suggested by the stage itself is the universe and that the feeling of intimacy or divine indiscretion is provoked by the motion picture close-up.

This is but one example of the "totality" of Claudel's drama, a totality as much on the scenic as on an ideological level. Music, ballet, and pantomime are used in the same spirit of theatrical imperialism, with theatre absorbing all the arts and uniting them in the actualization of a unique and exhaustive work, in the same way that the Catholic vision accounts for the entire universe.

The Claudel-Barrault collaboration, even more than the Giraudoux-Jouvet collaboration, is one of the major events of the modern French stage. To read or hear Barrault, one might think that Claudel played the part of the Father, whose Word was embodied by the Son, Barrault. Here the mystique of theatre is merged with true mysticism. "Our souls became homothetic," wrote Barrault concerning his collaboration with Claudel. Bar-

rault was not satisfied with merely staging the enormous first
version of *Le Soulier de satin*. He himself cut a certain amount
and suggested many changes to Claudel. The agreement between
poet and director arose from a common vision of life and theatre:
they shared not only a taste for the universe in its totality—that is,
in the simultaneity and figurative relation of the visible and invisible—but the belief that a sacred character should be conferred
on two means of expression par excellence, the Word and the
Gesture, and the conviction that one and the other, while representing transcendency, spring from the body itself, from its
rhythms and organic pulsations, so that a link is established between the creature (all flesh) and the Creator (pure Logos or pure
Meaning). Claudel threw himself body and soul into Catholicism
with an impetuousness and almost pagan vigor that corresponds
to the passion and cult of Life which has carried Barrault along
during his entire career. Claudel's "baroque" was exactly what
was needed to charm the complex mixture of intense sensuality
and spirituality characteristic of Barrault's art, and vice versa.

In such theatre as both Claudel and Barrault wanted, language
—the Word—is lyrically expressed according to a calculation of
rhythms, intensities, and even pitch which is close to the operatic
recitative.[9] It is a kind of sacred recitation (occasionally interrupted by coquetries, platitudes, or vulgarities) which keeps the
drama—even when apparently earthy, like *Le Pain dur*—constantly in the perspective of its ultimate meaning, the Divine.
One of the constant tensions of such theatre is therefore the
unchanging relation between the body (whose pulsations are
perceptible in gestures and language) and the supernatural—between the breath of man's lungs and the breath of the Creator.
The Gesture, which in dramatic liturgy of this kind is of major
importance, is indissolubly both itself and the meaning it symbolizes, like the gestures of a priest during Mass. Claudel never

9. The Comédie Française printed an edition of *Le Soulier de satin* which
indicates, in the actual typography, the values of every syllable in the text.

hesitates to devise tableaux more allegorical than dramatic if they are apt to strike the imagination by communicating a meaning suggested by the body's position: Cœuvre putting his foot on Lala, who is stretched out at his feet *(La Ville)*; Violaine kissing a leper *(L'Annonce faite à Marie)*; crucifixions or crawling about onstage *(Tête d'or, Le Soulier de satin)*; and, above all, a symbolic use of the hands (Ysé's and Mesa's hands at the end of *Partage de midi*, the double shadow in *Le Soulier de satin*, the hand of God in *Christophe Colomb*).

Although Claudel was sometimes little concerned with the possibility of staging his suggested tableaux, he still demanded them throughout his works. During the staging of *Le Soulier de satin* he wanted Barrault to keep him informed as to the slightest detail of the spectacles, he wanted to participate in their preparation, and he actually set up the staging of the *Oresteia* on paper. Indeed, the whole visual aspect is essential in Claudel's works: color and moving bodies represent the visible world, which cannot be ignored since it is a vehicle for the invisible, the perceptible support of higher meanings. His is a theatre not only of language and gesture but also of spectacle—and, in the case of *Le Soulier de satin*, what the French call "the great spectacle" (sumptuous costumes and decor, crowds, machines), which until then would seem to have been reserved for the cinema and children's operettas at the Châtelet.

Finally, Claudel's theatre maintains a state of theatrical "double consciousness." Deliberately poetic and antinaturalistic, it presents an imaginary universe which the poet asks us to accept both as a real universe and as a fabricated object, a man-made creation. While the fantastic and even absurdly comical aspect of proper names in the most serious plays is already a signal, it is in *Christophe Colomb* and especially in *Le Soulier de satin* that Claudel most obviously exploits the notion of dramatic *play:* what happens onstage is the product of human devices and should not be taken too seriously. No doubt "the poet," as Jacques Madaule points out, "takes God's point of view, and that is why he sometimes feels like laughing at the most pathetic moment."[10] But it is also because, in a Christian perspective, theatre is indeed presumptuous in trying to compete with Creation, and to avoid sacrilege, it must be given an aspect of farce and be made to mock itself. It would seem here as if the Church's traditional distrust of theatre led Claudel to avoid any Promethean pretensions in his art. Given his ambition for totality, the contrast produced is one of the strongest in French theatre, especially in *Le Soulier de satin*. In this gigantic drama, with "the stage as the world," the Announcer, in his rather heavy jesting and his nonchalance regarding the characters and the actors themselves, evokes a mixture of Pirandellian devices and fairground theatre. It consequently lowers the whole to the level of an improvised masquerade and so keeps alive the consciousness of its human fabrication, inseparable, in true theatre, from any deep participation in the unfolding drama. Everything happens as if Claudel's personal conflict of temperament, tremendous pride, and Christian humility had been the source of that somehow supplementary but always necessary tension.

The combination of a drama and a scenic display that is both self-conscious and inseparable from the drama's symbolism is helped by the Christian doctrine of the immanence of Meaning in the Sign—the paradox of the presence-absence of God. It is difficult today to attend the performance of any attempt at a modernized Mystery without thinking that such an attempt had already been far more successfully carried out by Claudel, for his theatre is an aggregate of devices, audacities, and truly functional discoveries—one of the rare moments in French theatre when innovation does not seem experimental.

Claudel borrowed the key of the world from Christianity, carved it, decorated it as would a good craftsman, and presented it to his public with the imperturbable certainty that it was the only key

10. In Claudel, *Théâtre, 1,* xix.

possible. The universe appears as a comedy that God puts on for Himself, with men for actors, who are endowed with just enough freedom to give the impression that they may ruin the spectacle.

But there is more. Claudel's epic drama and the actual history of humanity have, fundamentally, one point in common: they are both parables of the Drama of divine love, told to God and man, and repeated indefinitely. For the comedy is essentially a drama of love. God suffered and was crucified out of love for man, who betrayed Him. The betrayal poisoned the reciprocal love of God and the first man, and only by the sacrifice of one and the other can that love, that union in love, be restored to its perfection. Thus earthly adventures are adventures of love, which always contain the moments, progressions, and reversals in the history of the relations between God and man. Each man is a unique person, just as Christ was a unique person; each individual sacrifices himself for another, just as Christ sacrificed himself for every man in particular—and in every hero's sacrifice, Christ's sacrifice is repeated.

In what, then, does this drama of love consist outside the Christian doctrine? It is, first of all, a metaphor for the dual feeling attached to the flesh—a source of ecstasy and dissatisfaction at the same time. It is also a metaphor for the feeling of transcendency: the world is transcended by its own meaning. It is the embodiment of a paradox—that of the feeling of immanence—for transcendency is within man. And finally, it is the idea that through the detours of love, through the very suffering to which it inevitably leads, and through the dialectic of renunciation, the true essence of love and of self will be attained "at the same time and indissolubly."

PART II


BACK TO MAN

# CHAPTER 4

# MAN IN TIME AND SPACE:
# ARMAND SALACROU

During the thirties, while Cocteau was laying his traps and while Giraudoux was trying to put the gods back in their places, Armand Salacrou was gradually formulating a theatre of man, stripped of ghosts and demons, angels and magicians. In contrast to the enchantment of metaphors of the supernatural, the spectacle he created shows man at grips with himself, aware of transcendency, but a transcendency represented by others, by the mystery of passing time, and by the physical cosmos, infinite and incomprehensible.

Early in his career Salacrou wrote works similar to the surrealist experiments, modernist compositions, and the theatre of dream. Imaginary countries, circus fantasies, and dream projections are woven into very freely constructed and garrulous scenes, in which the poetry is often interrupted by discussions on the meaning of life and love, in a style sometimes more parodic than ironic. Then his form and tone gradually changed, adopting some of the rigor and naturalism of conventional plays, with the result that his theatre became less obviously poetic. While the poetic disorder and "the play within the play" of *Le Pont de l'Europe* (1925) led critics to evoke Shakespeare, the later *Histoire de rire* (1939) derives from Boulevard *vaudeville,* and *Comme les Chardons* (1964) from the kind of bourgeois drama that penetrates into family secrets.

Indeed, in many of the plays written by the mature Salacrou poetic imagination seems to be dominated by realistic observations. They would appear to be a return to a study of customs and manners, essentially bourgeois or lower-class—financial transactions, class prejudices, the fear of scandal, shameful adultery—set mostly in provincial milieus, and even precisely situated in Le Havre, Salacrou's birthplace. The dialogue itself is of course artfully written, but it is made up of "realistic" details taken from life (in *Les Fiancés du Havre* Salacrou went so far as to distinguish between the different accents of a tiny section of Normandy)—the dream of yesterday's naturalists. As for the characters, they are often endowed with all the dimensions required by naturalist theatre: a complete psychological structure, details that are somewhat caricatural or typical, and manners in tune with their environment or social origins. In fact, they are what in the past was called "true-to-life." Moreover, they apparently forced themselves upon their author, not as theatrical metaphors, but as real beings: Salacrou himself tells how one of them, Madame Berthe—a nasty old woman madly in love—of *Un Homme comme les autres,* became an obsession he was unable to throw off. Thus in many respects his theatre is a presentation of perceived reality, a clinical study of certain customs, a gallery of living portraits. Daily life, as in conventional theatre, is the very substance of the plot—not transformed but photographed.

Haunted by the real, Salacrou has even attempted historical reconstruction. *Les Fiancés du Havre* (1944) had already been built around a local anecdote from Le Havre when in *Boulevard Durand* (written in 1959, performed in 1961) he devised a "non-fictionalized chronicle"[1] in which, except for a few changes in name, he tried to reconstruct, as precisely as history allows, the story of a strike and the trial of an agitator, his conviction, his release, and his final madness. Thus his theatre became documentary—a historical theatre, a theatre of "truth"—making public all the evidence involved in a trial. "I tried to proceed with the subject without doing any kind of so-called literary or theatrical research," wrote Salacrou in an appendix to the play which consists of the historical documents used in his dialogue—and, for the most part, reproduced word for word. *Boulevard Durand* represents an extreme point in Salacrou's works, of course, but by carrying naturalism to an extreme, he paradoxically became a pioneer—the forerunner of Adamov's *Le Printemps 71* and the recent epic frescoes of Armand Gatti.[2]

While one of Salacrou's chief concerns has been to reconstruct scenically a living and actual reality, especially one that he has personally experienced, from afar or from close to—life in Le Havre (which has come to be like Balzac's or Zola's Paris or Simenon's provinces)—and while he is perhaps the naturalist playwright that the French stage was unable to produce at the turn of the century, the realistic elements in his works are actually a pretext. Customs and everyday life are used for an end that transcends them. This is sometimes made apparent by a very simple device: for example, although most of *Les Fiancés du Havre* would seem to be the study of financial difficulties and a *mésalliance* in a bourgeois family, Salacrou meant the anecdote to unfold in a decor created by Raoul Dufy, which immediately gives it a nonrealistic and indeed very theatrical dimension. Moreover, while the plot of the same play is based on a real story, it gradually moves in the direction of the improbable: the whole business of an exchange of children, whose real identities are not revealed until twenty-eight years later and with consequences carried to an absurd extreme, ultimately gives a truly poetic dimension to

1. *Théâtre, 8,* 259.
2. See below, pp. 196–208.

what might well have been a play in the manner of Dumas fils
or Emile Augier.

Using a basic substance anchored in tradition, such as naturalism
or Boulevard comedy, Salacrou diverts it, as it were, giving it an
unusual significance. *L'Archipel Lenoir* starts out like a cruel
naturalist play, supposedly tending toward a collective murder,
and ends up as a farce; *Histoire de rire,* on the other hand, has all
the characteristics of a Boulevard *vaudeville* but shifts to melancholy, makes the traditional cuckold into a dignified, pathetic, and
wise human being, and ends with an attempted suicide and the
now celebrated words, "A funny story? How very sad." Salacrou's
theatre is thus not all that comfortable: it involves the spectator
in familiar situations and characters only to change the value of
the situations and unmask the characters. A drama leads to
comedy, or a comedy turns out to be merely the surface of tragedy
or pathos. The spectators' habits are altogether unsettled both on
the level of reality and on the level of theatre—and on those two
levels Salacrou's works are an attempt to expose illusions.

Such techniques would lead to no more than simple satire if
Salacrou did not give expression to an anguish which, beyond
sarcasm or some personal obsession, allows him to make a statement of universal value about man's place in the cosmos. Aside
from realism, historic chronicles, studies of customs and manners,
and character portraits, Salacrou's theatre is based on the drama of
time—more precisely, past time. Behind the sordid little stories of
common individuals (one of his plays is entitled *Un Homme
comme les autres*) is the notion of the point of no return, the
Racinian leitmotiv "It is done," or the existential idea of the past
as an object. In *L'Inconnue d'Arras* all the words that the dying
hero Ulysse had pronounced during his lifetime are presented as a
cloud, a swarm of flies. The past is irremediable, unchangeable,
but it is precarious; it exists once and for all, but only in the
memory of man. The monstrous injustice that led Jules Durand to
madness, as well as the good will of his defenders, is immobilized

in the past. There is no middle course: all is nothingness if the memory of man forgets it. In *L'Inconnue d'Arras* Ulysse clings to one moment in his life—a kind gesture he once made for a woman who may have been a skillful prostitute or may have been just a poor girl; he never knew—but as he is dying, the relived moment is nothing more nor less than a kind gesture and uncertainty. There is no question in Salacrou's works of a Romantic or Proustian nostalgia: they are concerned with the fixed nature of events, which are annihilated if no memory records them and which are nothing more than what they were if memory preserves them.

With *Boulevard Durand* the playwright-historian re-creates for his audience an event that had concerned the past of a whole nation. In other plays, to oblige his characters to face their own pasts, Salacrou uses all the devices of theatre, even the most facile —such as the unexpected glimpse of a face out of the past, which has been intentionally or unconsciously obliterated, in the form of a relative who bears a likeness to the original (*Les Fiancés du Havre, Comme les Chardons*). The past is an object, but it is only the object of consciousness. And that is the tragedy implied by Salacrou's works: the past either is ignored—thus reduced to nothingness, with individuals or communities living in the good conscience of an inauthentic present—or is recalled, with its incomplete and irremediable nature making the present unlivable. In many respects such plays anticipate the subject matter of Sartre's dramatic meditations on the past and on the sum total of the acts of a lifetime. But whereas Sartre, in his optimism, grants free consciousness the possibility of choosing the meaning of the past, Salacrou, haunted by determinism, arrives at conclusions that are a dead end.

Of course a charming decor by Dufy may poeticize such stories of the past, but the play then becomes a dream. Or the playwright may invent a world that moves backward, as in *Sens interdit*, where time is reversed, death comes before birth, and elderly or peevish couples make their way, over the years, toward the dazzling wonder of first love, adolescence, childhood, and the stupid bliss of babies; that is his poetic right, but it is also a kind of reductio ad absurdum. When what we call the "future" is given as the past, and what we call the "past"—that is, lost happiness—is given as the future, the play becomes a burlesque evocation of a paradisaic world, where good comes *after* evil, where salvation is time reversed; but such an impossible wager is the desperate caprice of a playwright temporarily under the illusion that he is taking the place of God.

The most dramatically original and the richest of Salacrou's plays concerned with this problem of man and time is *L'Inconnue d'Arras*. It is filled with all his naturalism: a man like the others, faithful or unfaithful women, a satire on the bourgeoisie, middle-aged decay, and the desire for escape, success, or heroism. Its first title, "La Mort est le rendez-vous des vivants," catchy enough at first glance, is actually more explained by the play than it explains the play. That is to say, the play is demonstrative—not as crudely as *Sens interdit* but certainly with as much intellectual audacity. Indeed, what it presents is an intellectual metaphor. Working from the old idea that a dying man relives his whole life in his last few seconds, Salacrou constructs the action within the time it takes for the bullet that Ulysse shoots into his head to reach his brain: the play begins and ends with the same pistol shot. But what might have been a pretext for a kaleidoscope of more or less dreamlike images is structured in such an artificial and intellectualized way that the improbability of it all becomes a virtue. Actually, *L'Inconnue d'Arras* is a tour de force: using all the freedom allowed by the unverifiable basic assumption, Salacrou found the means to make the action of a hundredth of a second into a kind of well-made play which lasts more than two hours.

In a setting that rises in tiers, all the dead and the living who had played some part in Ulysse's life meet with him, demand their rightful places in his last memories, argue among themselves, try to justify themselves, proclaim their sincerity or their bad faith, clear themselves or assume their responsibility, and so on. In fact, all the characters have but one reality—that which Salacrou grants them onstage for the duration of the performance, since they are required for his demonstration. Only one ghost hovers around without being mentioned—Pirandello's, of course, for these characters are only half in the mind of the dying man: most of the time they act as they would act if they had met in flesh and blood at the bedside of a Ulysse who was taking weeks to die in a hospital. And yet no character manages to be more precise than Ulysse's image of him. Since Ulysse doesn't know the name of the unknown woman from Arras, she doesn't know her own name. A character may be a combination of the various images that Ulysse has of him: his old friend Maxime, for example, exists simultaneously as what he is at thirty-seven and what he was at twenty, and the two images fight one another. These are not allegories, for the characters are not personified abstractions but rather three-dimensional, naturalistic, and even picturesque embodiments of the maximum that anyone can know or imagine about the people who are close to him, whether out of love, indifference, or hate. Intellectual constructions they are, however, for they crowd the stage as a group of witnesses, each of whom wants to assert—before the hero's final descent into nothingness—the validity of his own starring role in an individual life. Once Ulysse is dead, a line will be drawn and the sum or reckoning be calculated—not only of Ulysse's life but also of the others', in relation to him.

The real question the play raises is, For whom and why does Ulysse kill himself? In the name of some happiness irremediably past or of some present and momentary unhappiness? Because his wife Yolande is unfaithful to him or because he betrayed the glorious image he had of himself at twenty? The whole confusing avalanche of witnesses, none of whom is impartial, is unable to supply the answer. All that is left of Ulysse's life is a series of banal events, adolescent ambitions, and bourgeois compromises, along with a few daring and happy moments that have faded in time, some people who once meant something but have turned out to be disappointing, deceitful, or cowardly, and the one shining but terribly ambiguous little spark of a brief encounter in Arras.

It would not be true to say that Salacrou is showing the futility of a life, but it would be no more accurate to say that Ulysse's life has value because of his encounter in Arras. The whole play is made up of the tension between the value of a moment at the time it is experienced in joy or in despair and the incomprehensibility of the sum total of a lifetime. One is reminded of Malraux's words, "A life is worth nothing, but nothing is worth a life." As early as the 1930s, well before Sartre, Camus, and today's playwrights, Salacrou was struck by that paradox, as well as by the play of time, its irreversibility, and the impossibility of understanding the past as existing and not existing at the same time—that is, by the absurdity of a life hemmed in between birth and death.

"Time is a dream," said Lenormand in 1919. It is even the title of one of his first plays, whose hero has an extratemporal experience in the manner of J. B. Priestley. For Salacrou time is a frightful reality, and reversing it is merely a playwright's trick: presented as a trick, it is intended to stress the fact that all man's unhappiness comes from time's irreversibility. Actually, this endeavor of his is as illusory as that of Jacques, who, at the beginning of *Une Femme libre,* tries to master space by installing a reduced model of the entire solar system in the house. To the distress of the irremediable, Salacrou adds a sharp awareness of man's solitude in the cosmos.

Living in a lost world, comparing the earth to an anthill or saying that it is only one earth among others, likening men to poor birds or flies, evoking the stars and outer space, seeing things from on high, situating the action of a play in relation to the Milky Way—such allusions abound in Salacrou's plays. There are of course variations in tone—the anguish may be full of pathos, as in *L'Inconnue d'Arras,* or transformed into a burlesque justification of immoral acts, as in *Une Femme trop honnête*—but anguish is one of the signatures of Salacrou's works, whatever the genre. It sometimes evokes Pascal ("the eternal silence of infinite space") and sometimes Voltaire ("the viewpoint of Sirius"). And as in Pascal and Voltaire, it has nothing to do with some vague Romantic ecstasy but, rather, is created by an intellectual awareness of the space of modern science and from philosophical reflection on what that conception of space means to man. The infinite mechanism obviously works to perfection, but, just as obviously, its infinity and its perfection are precisely a sign of the fact that man has no cosmic privilege.

One fact remains: men suffer. "The advantage that the universe has [over man] is that the universe knows nothing of it," said Pascal. Salacrou often brings to mind Pascal, and he anticipates themes of existential literature. The naturalism of his plays not only represents man as an object of the positive sciences; it points up how unjustified and unjust that state is. No longer an answer to questions about man's nature, naturalism is a matter of astonishment, anguish, and metaphysical revolt. There is no doubt that a man like the others, belonging to a particular milieu, will in some ways necessarily be cowardly or commit adultery or lie: it is a socio-biological law. But that such a law exists is absurd, if there is no God, or if there is, what a fearful God! In *Dieu le savait,* a very talky and undramatic play, the characters discuss the subject, throwing determinist or theological arguments at each other. The play may be too direct an intellectual debate rather than a drama, yet it throws significant light on the atmosphere of cosmic anguish that colors the rest of his works.

A title like *La Terre est ronde* is just as enlightening, and the play that bears it is worth any formal debate. Along with *L'Inconnue d'Arras, La Terre est ronde* is one of Salacrou's most complete works. Time plays its part—not in the form of memories, but from minute to minute, in the very surprising changes in behavior from scene to scene and in the almost Shakespearean changes in attitude of the Florentine mob before, during, and after the dictatorship of Savonarola. But the relativity of all things in space also expands the play to cosmic proportions. The action takes place in 1492 ("We are in 1492, and in Florence," says a character in the very first scene), and though the events surrounding and attendant on Savonarola's dictatorship are shattering and tremendous—to the inhabitants of Florence—what a petty and ridiculous adventure when seen from the perspective of the discovery and the whole cosmic notion of a new world. If one were to telescope, poetically, the dates, one could summarize this play by putting the destruction of a Botticelli painting side by side with Galileo's "Eppur, si muove!" In the play Savonarola has all the works of the Renaissance burned, but he himself is then burned—and the earth turns round in infinite space. *La Terre est ronde* reveals the corruption and true suffering of man from day to day, but it equally reveals the cosmic truth of their insignificance. For if there is no God, what has just unfolded is merely a brief comedy in an infinite and indifferent space. And if God exists in the terms of Savonarola, "Understand that you are nothing, and that what was before was nothing, and that what will be afterward will be nothing. Everything is as nothing. And nothing exists if not thee, Light of God."

In *Mes Certitudes et incertitudes,* an explanatory and autobiographical text written in 1953 and published in Volume 6 of his *Théâtre,* Salacrou, after energetically affirming his belief in a mechanistic determinism, added, "It is not impossible that 'my theories' are merely a shelter, and that I take cover in that total mechanism, having no other choice open to me for enduring my birth, my life, and my death." This inner calm is completely relative, however, for such faith leads only to an awareness of the absurd. "In my anguish, it is the transition from the ineluctable future to an ineradicable past that grips me." Unable to accept the Christian idea of God and rejecting, on the other hand, Sartrean freedom, Salacrou has set himself up as a witness to the discovery of determinism, the transformation in the individual consciousness of chance into necessity—and the fall into darkness. Now it appears that man feels a desire for eternity and a desire for freedom and responsibility, but such "feelings," like the feeling "that the sun turns around the earth," lead to the tragedy (and it permeates all of Salacrou's works) that "determinism crops up in our daily habits with as much incongruity as universal gravitation —determinism, stupefying as the roundness of this earth, which is hung from no thread in the apparent emptiness of the sky."

Salacrou the man has not, for all that, renounced action. His relative wisdom consists in living *"as if* [his] flesh were not a collection of small molecular structures, *as if* [he] were master of [his] decisions." His participation in left-wing political activities seems meant to give his "life, which has no meaning, a temporary usefulness." Nor has Salacrou the playwright renounced that temporary usefulness, for his theatre is often "committed": *La Terre est ronde, Les Nuits de la colère,* and *Boulevard Durand* are denunciations of injustice, indifference to the suffering of others, and cowardice. But his plays are, above all, answerless questions, the theatrical manifestation of an anguished surprise in the face of existential contradiction. A testimony and a protest, they show man's capacity to overcome anguish by way of theatrical games and are thus the symbol of an ambiguous victory.

# CHAPTER 5

# THE AGONY OF SOLITARY SOULS:
# HENRY DE MONTHERLANT

Henry de Montherlant is the first to use a psychological vocabulary with regard to his plays and his characters. Pride, esteem, hate, scorn, sadism, love, and purity of heart are terms he uses constantly in explaining his characters' adventures and problems in prefaces, postscripts, analyses, and answers to critics. Indeed, he describes the Infanta of *La Reine morte* as "a neuropath like the King." In 1954, in the postscript to *La Ville dont le Prince est un enfant,* he wrote, "People speak to us of 'psychological theatre' as a certain form of theatre. For me there is only one form of theatre worthy of the name: psychological theatre."[1] What interests Montherlant in *Le Maître de Santiago* is not the hero's struggle or relationship with God but the inner mechanism of the psychological phenomenon of faith, that phenomenon combined with intransigence, and the ambiguity of abnegation and pride. Whereas Claudel's

1. Montherlant, *Théâtre*, p. 947.

*Le Soulier de satin,* performed at the time Montherlant was writing *Le Maître,* is a Catholic play, Montherlant's work is a play
*about* Catholics. Claudel's play is similar to the Spanish *autos
sacramentales:* the hero's supernatural destiny is objectively affirmed. Montherlant, who writes about the same period and the
same atmosphere, at no time treats the supernatural as such but
describes an emotional and intellectual attitude toward it.

Another of Montherlant's concerns, and one that he has reaffirmed several times—often to defend himself against the critics
—is that of "the imitation of life." By that he means that no rule
of composition, no pre-established principle of what a dramatic
character must be, should turn the playwright away from the
faithful reproduction of psychological flux, its surprises, even its
incoherence. "Unity of style? Never heard of it. There is no
unity of style in life," he wrote concerning *Celles qu'on prend
dans ses bras,*[2] a play in modern dress, in which a Spanish tone is
combined with very Parisian vulgarities and occasional farce. As
to the sudden turn-about-face of Georges in *Fils de personne:*
"That instability *is* life," he said in 1943.[3] For Montherlant man
is essentially a psychological mechanism whose workings do not
follow a logical development. He can be described in terms of
classical psychological categories (not in those of what Montherlant calls "dime-store psychoanalysis"); he is made up of contradictions; he surprises others and surprises himself. And the objective of theatre is to bring out the workings of the mechanism
by means of exemplary anecdotes.

Such psychologism and fidelity to life might have led to a more
or less naturalistic anecdotal theatre, similar to Boulevard productions of the twenties and thirties. Moreover, Montherlant's refusal
to integrate the discoveries of modern psychology, obstinately
holding to a general "intuition," might have turned what was
meant to be a uniquely psychological theatre into a simple repetition of supposedly eternal themes that have in fact been long since

2. Ibid., p. 831.
3. Ibid., p. 273.

reinterpreted and transcended. Even the French classical writers of
the seventeenth century, who were convinced that "everything has
been said," treated man from a point of view quite new for their
time and used categories that were developed by Descartes, the
Jesuits, or the Jansenists. Indeed, in a play like *Celles qu'on prend
dans ses bras,* Montherlant, through fear of dime-store psychology,
fell into a type of psychology midway between *vaudeville* and
Porto-Riche. Yet the greater part of his dramatic works transcends
the application of his two principles, and the return to man that
he represents does not mean a pure and simple return to a form
of theatre which has had its day.

There is no doubt that Montherlant clearly refuses certain techniques of traditional realism, devices that go back to the eighteenth-century bourgeois reaction to classical language. He believes in the necessity of a theatre of language and, like Giraudoux,
of well-written language, without the "spaced periods" so dear to
Diderot and the naturalists. "People call a play that is well written
'cold.' What they want are a great many spaced periods," wrote
Montherlant in his "Notes de théâtre."[4] In the same text he
complains about actresses who feel the need to add "ah!"s and
"oh!"s, "but"s and "well"s, to their scripts. He rejects the pauses
and interjections used to make the script seem true to life, for the
truth and life he seeks cannot be situated at the level of a photographic or documentary copy of human behavior. Montherlant's
notes and prefaces also show his concern with finding a good
balance between conventional or impersonal acting and methodi-
cal "characterization." Certain actors "do too much," others not
enough. In acting as in language, one well placed "ah" is effective,
one detail of behavior is suggestive. A repetition of "real details"
falls into verism and turns the attention away from the drama
toward scenic realism.

In spite of such comments, Montherlant's interest in actual stag-

4. Ibid., p. 1070.

ing is small and could hardly be compared to Cocteau's material
love for the stage and its tricks, Claudel's theatrical imagination, or
Giraudoux's true knowledge of actors and directors. He is far more
interested in the literary quality of his plays than in the actual
problems of theatre. In fact, he sometimes even prefers to ignore
theatre:

> My taste [for theatre] has diminished even more since the
> war, as it were. I have not been to the theatre *once* by choice
> since 1919, although the duties of society (friends' openings)
> or someone's insistence have led me there four or five times.
> It is not disdain for the art, but seeing a play performed al-
> ways gives me a weaker impression than the one I had
> reading it.[5]

Such was his feeling in 1929 as expressed in the preface to *L'Exil*.
In 1954, in the postscript to *La Ville dont le Prince est un enfant,*
he concluded: "Whoever says theatre (performance) also says loss
of time. I had already lost much time with *La Ville*—from the
minute it stopped being only a *volume*."[6] In his explanatory texts
Montherlant alternates from one state of mind to another—an
alternation similar to that by which he explains certain of his
characters—now devoting long pages to the work of an actor or
the story of how one of his plays was produced, now claiming to
disregard anything that is not the text itself.

His plays are ambiguous in much the same way. There is no
doubt that Montherlant writes for the stage, but there is also no
doubt that the characters speak—well and a great deal—far more
than they act. They stand opposite one another and pass the time
describing and analyzing themselves or describing and analyzing
each other. The *tirade,* frequent in Montherlant, is sometimes a
logical discourse as in Corneille, sometimes a narrative as in
Racine. But where the tirade in Racine and Corneille is the source
of action or transformation of character, in Montherlant it is es-

5. Ibid., p. 9.
6. Ibid., p. 950.

sentially the analysis of an emotional state of indecision. The first
two acts of *La Reine morte* constitute a prolonged state of expectation, during which King Ferrante probes within himself. The
end of the third is marked by a decisive act: Ferrante has Inès
killed. Similarly, all of *Le Maître de Santiago* is the analysis of a
state of refusal. Alvaro spends his time describing and justifying his
attitude by giving a portrait of himself and of others. The final
conversion of his daughter is the only "act" in the play. The same
is true for *Fils de personne,* an analysis of a particular situation that
lasts until the final sacrifice.

Yet a Montherlant play does move. It is fundamentally the
portrait of a soul, but a portrait relative to, and at the moment of,
a crisis, a choice to be made. The most active of his plays in that
respect is doubtless *La Ville dont le Prince est un enfant.* The
Abbé de Pradts' decision to authorize Sevrais' and Sandrier's
friendship is a serious act and provokes a whole train of action.
The resulting scandal due to a misunderstanding, its shaking effects, the head of the school's decision, and his explanations at the
end of the play represent a dialectic of situations which, without
taking anything away from the psychological portrait, adds an
outer dynamism that is missing from certain of his other plays.
Those others, however, are just as dramatic. Their treatment of
one apparently static situation is frequently found in French
literature, mostly in the novel (*Adolphe, Dominique,* certain of
Gide's novels) but also in theatre (Racine's *Bérénice* and Sartre's
*Huis Clos,* to take extreme examples).

In *La Reine morte* (the portrait of an old king whose political
plans are undone by his son's secret marriage) and in *Fils de
personne* (the portrait of a father disappointed by his son's mediocrity) the heroes, because of the misbehavior or shortcomings
of others, are forced to examine their own consciences. Nothing is
resolved during most of the play despite a certain amount of
secondary action, but as a result a permanent state of tension is
maintained. For static and repetitive as the analysis often is, it is
always *against* others. It leads to analyses and counteranalyses

until finally all the characters have been covered, the analyses being always in relation to the basic conflict. The very repetition of the hero's fundamental attitude produces a cumulative effect that makes the decision or final action seem like the necessary explosion at the end of a continually mounting tension. In *Port Royal,* a play in which everything has been decided in advance, so to speak, the entire subject matter consists in the nuns' and the archbishop's growing knowledge of themselves and of each other. Each one hopes for a compromise from the other, but each one is just as certain that he himself will never come to terms. The play consists of that increasingly clear confirmation of two opposed intransigencies.

A clear distinction must be made in Montherlant between the action itself, often within, in the classical manner, and the action onstage. *Malatesta,* considered by Montherlant as the counterpart of *Le Maître de Santiago* and in which he presents a hero as eager for life as the hero of *Le Maître* is for nothingness, is an agitated and lively play. But this "pagano-Christian salmagundi," as Montherlant calls it,[7] does no more than show the hero's character in all its facets by means of a few adventures. Malatesta's expedition to Rome to assassinate the Pope and his residence there under guard are only meant to keep him in a state of having perpetually to ask for recognition. The necessity of Malatesta's death does not come from within his own character, as do the final actions of Ferrante, Alvaro, or Georges. A lively portrait of an Italian Renaissance adventurer, with his pride, his appetites, his cultural and ideological confusion, *Malatesta* is a series of intensely dramatic scenes that mark out a mad adventure, yet the resolution of the drama is created not by an unbearable increase in tension or by a cumulative effect leading to an explosion but by a murder that comes from the outside: Malatesta is poisoned by his biographer. Montherlant's more satisfying plays—his linear and least agitated ones, such as *Port Royal* and *Le Maître de Santiago*—resolve the

7. Ibid., p. 431.

drama by means of the elements of the conflict itself and leave the spectator with the impression of having taken part in the flow of an intense and implacable action.

Therefore, and contrary to Claudel, Montherlant is most convincing in his austerely constructed works. It is in such plays that he is most successful in creating a portrait of the man who is somehow at the end of his rope and who liberates himself by a definitive act: murder or sacrifice. For Montherlant's theatre is chiefly concerned with the man who can bear it no longer, the man who is already aging, who has lived out his life, whose first loves are long past, whose children are born and grown, whose tasks in politics, war, or a profession have been accomplished. In fact, some of his heroes are getting older and older: his Don Juan is sixty-six; his Cardinal in *Le Cardinal d'Espagne,* eighty-two. Montherlant gives the leading role, and sometimes the only important one, to the "old King" of tragedy.

Some particular circumstance leads the aging man to watch himself live; he thus becomes dual and dramatic, for he struggles between what he is and what he wants to be, what he seems like in his own eyes and what he says he is, and, of course, what he seems like to others. Each of Montherlant's characters has a strong tendency to talk about himself, to describe his own figure. Malatesta, Ferrante, Georges, and Alvaro quite naturally spend their time probing into themselves, explaining themselves to themselves, justifying themselves. But an incident always intensifies the tendency. For example, the more Malatesta feels frustrated in not receiving the recompense or recognition that is his due, the more vigorously he draws his own portrait. "I" is one of the more important words in Montherlant's plays. All of his heroes would seem to be built around the remark, "How can they do that to me? Me, who . . . ," and they're off! They draw their own portraits or make their own analyses by way of explaining that they do not deserve their misfortunes—as the Infanta does when she is humiliated by Don Pedro's avowal, and King Ferrante when he is hurt by his son's disobedience, and Alvaro when he is asked to go and seek his fortune in the new world, and Georges when his son shows his vulgarity or is about to be taken from him, and the Abbé de Pradts faced with young Sandrier's "betrayal." Their indignation when faced with injustice is an impassioned reaction, almost immediately justified by moral considerations. Montherlant's portrait of man is that of a creature in which there is little distinction between passion and ethics. The hero who is hurt not only suffers but considers himself the embodiment of a moral value.

The element of ethics in Montherlant's plays has led to great confusion among critics as to the meaning of the plays—a confusion kept alive by certain of Montherlant's own comments. He sometimes seems to want his theatre to preach the greatness of souls, yet he often denies that he has any intention of moralizing. In his preface to *Pasiphaé* Montherlant declares that in his "imaginative works" he wants "to be both a moralist, that is, one who makes a study of passions, and a moralizer, that is, one who proposes a certain ethics." The fact that since 1938 Montherlant would seem to have changed his mind, claiming in articles and letters that he emphasizes character study at the expense of the moral lesson, does not keep his public and critics from seeing moral propositions in his works, for his characters express themselves in moral terms. They claim to be on the side of Good (greatness, purity, intransigency) and use maxims in the analyses they make of themselves and others. But do the maxims express the characters' ethics only or Montherlant's as well? Are they meant to complete a character's portrait or make a model of him?

While almost every dramatic work implies an ethics and calls for a judgment on the part of the spectator as to the value of the characters' behavior, other values generally transcend the judgment. To the extent that the spectator, for example, identifies with Phèdre in her personal tragedy, in which a whole web of complicated emotions envelops the character, he accepts the idea of the crime against which she struggles, so as to give his entire attention to the beauty and pathos of the struggle. Although Montherlant clearly aims at a modern equivalent of the classical struggles, in his characters' inner conflicts he puts particular emphasis on the ethical values they affirm—with the result that the audience often has the impression of being asked to approve of certain values rather than be moved by the pathos of the conflict itself.

The ethics proposed by his heroes is not the currently accepted "vulgar ethics," considered by Montherlant as a "codified opinion of the moment"—not a social ethics but an ethics of the individual. Although as a good student of Barrès he implies that France and man will be saved by a cult of the ego, he is fundamentally less interested in the results than in the code of morals itself. His heroes are conscious of being supermen. They are convinced that they are of "superior quality" or among the "elect," like the Jansenist nuns of *Port Royal*. The world is thus divided into two ethical groups: men of good quality and men of bad quality. Montherlant's heroes belong to Gobineau's category "the sons of Kings." For some they represent a continuation of a Corneillian heroism, for others a resurgence of Stendhalian egotism in degraded form.

*Fils de personne* and its sequel *Demain il fera jour* are striking examples of the ambiguity of Montherlant's attitude with regard to the moral significance of his works. In the first play Georges Carrion is entirely involved in the cult of human quality, and just as Ferrante in *La Reine morte* sends his son to prison "for mediocrity," so Georges ends by letting his son go off to danger and possible death because he is disappointed in him. Since the son Gilou is presented as a little fool, sometimes sentimental, sometimes indifferent, and interested only in movie magazines, Georges' disappointment might well seem legitimate, and he attracts the spectator's moral sympathy. In *Demain il fera jour* the same Georges Carrion really sends his son to his death, but this time out of fear. He needs a guarantee that will save him in case the victorious Resistance movement decides to pick a quarrel with him. Montherlant explains the character's transformation as follows:

> Georges has collapsed. He has seen the Occupation and he predicts the consequences: his incentive is shattered. In another respect, nothing remains of his love for his son: the spring has run dry. The champion of *quality* will go so far as to commit a frightful act. In 1941 he sacrificed his son to an ideal. In 1944 he sacrifices him to his own fear. And it is the same man.[8]

The hero, compared to a "samurai" in the first play and also called a "Jansenist freethinker," now shows himself as "vile under the influence of fear." Montherlant explains at length the psychology of his degradation and rightly defends himself against accusations of incoherence or improbability. Actually, the two plays and their justifications throw light on many important aspects of Montherlant's drama. There is no doubt that it consists of an ethics of "quality" and "greatness" and that such an ethics is an ideal proposed by the writer. But something else leads Montherlant to explode those values, as if he himself believed that they were no more than abstractions, a kind of moral dream that he imposed on his characters and which he is the first to deflate:

> The double faces of Malatesta and Georges, so different from what they think they are; of Ferrante, so different from what he wants to be. Georges no more defends a certain idea of man, no matter what he says, than Ferrante defends the reasons of state, no matter what he says.[9]

Thus the idea of man with which Georges would have liked his son to coincide and which seemed to be the motive for his behavior is merely an illusion or, in any case, a false motive; it is on the contrary, his fear in *Demain il fera jour* that is real.

---

8. Ibid., p. 743.
9. Ibid., p. 371.

Certain of Montherlant's comments seem to suggest that his theatre represents the drama of the individual who is mistaken about the motives for his acts, more than the conflict between those who live according to an ethics of human quality and the mediocre world that surrounds them. In fact, the drama is one of pride or, to use the vocabulary of classical psychology, of an attempt, out of self-love, to justify oneself in one's own eyes and in the eyes of others. Montherlant's heroes are not really great men; they are men who want to see themselves as great.

Montherlant's comedy *Brocéliande* clarifies the meaning of his works even more than his own explanations. The protagonist Persilès, a rather timid bourgeois, begins to speak like a hero as soon as he believes himself a descendant of Saint Louis. His illusion of aristocracy transforms his attitude: he becomes haughty, convinced of his superior quality, avid for purity and grandeur. His supposed superiority consists essentially in its affirmation, for in fact it is based on an illusion. In this very amusing comedy Montherlant mocks his own serious heroes. They, too, affirm their superiority in language, using a vocabulary of grandeur, but the motives for their actions are quite different. Alvaro's Christian intransigence in *Le Maître de Santiago?* Rather, a desire for nothingness, a surrender to "nada." Philippe de Presle's and Geneviève's patriotic heroism in *L'Exil?* Rather, passionate friendship and maternal love. Ferrante's grandeur and regal intransigence in *La Reine morte?* Rather, the lassitude of a tired old king.

There comes a time in many of the plays when the character breaks down. In a moment of weariness he relaxes and confides in a third person. Such moments are interesting both dramatically and psychologically: they disclose the character's hidden motives, and they are excellent theatrically in that they represent an unmasking. The mask of greatness and moral exigency is removed, revealing a face that is marked solely by emotion or passion. Here Montherlant is in the classical tradition of the search for truth, the unveiling of souls, the psychological undressing that is fundamental to action in the works of Racine or Molière. Montherlant's first play, *L'Exil,* written in 1914 and never performed, presents his method in a most obvious and elementary way. The young protagonist Philippe de Presle, at first cynical and hostile to wartime obligations, then impatient to enlist, reveals—both indirectly throughout the play and directly in a long scene with his mother at the end of Act II—that his attitudes and comments are motivated not by any solid principle but solely by a passionate friendship for Senac. In a parallel way, his mother's patriotism collapses when Philippe talks of enlisting. The hearts of Montherlant's heroes are like blank pages on which passions are expressed in moral terms.

When Ferrante confides in Inès and the young page Dino del Moro in *La Reine morte,* when the head of the school confides in the Abbé de Pradts at the end of *La Ville,* when Christine gives in to Ravier at the end of *Celles qu'on prend dans ses bras,* each one exposes himself and shows that his haughty tone is no more than a cover for a whole obscure mechanism. In a note written in 1954, "En relisant *la Reine morte,*"[10] Montherlant explains Inès' murder in terms of Ferrante's masculinity, his sadism, and his disgust with life and children. During most of the action the heroes are of bad faith, by the playwright's own admission. The moral values they claim to embody are an objective more than an attainment. Their ethics is not an absolute but an ambiguous state of consciousness.

In this respect, Montherlant has much the same attitude as La Rochefoucauld in the seventeenth century, who did not deny the courage of certain acts but investigated the motives behind the attitudes of courage and charity. He discovered that ethics is not a motive but a result, that there are essentially no moral intentions, only bursts of passion justified a posteriori by the characters' rationalizations or the outer sanction of appearance.

Everything happens as if Montherlant, in choosing the subject matter for his dramas, went out in search of the great spectacular

10. Ibid., pp. 253–59.

acts which history, custom, or the heroes themselves explain in moral terms, and then devoted his play to unraveling the reasons for them. Every act has two meanings, and the play discovers the real meaning, the original meaning, contained in the characters' psychological makeup. His method is the reverse of Sartre's in *Huis Clos* or *Les Mains sales*. While Sartre presents an action in terms of its significance, which comes *after* the action, for Montherlant man is a dramatic being, swinging between his values and the determinism of his psychology. He occasionally succeeds in living in the rarefied atmosphere of his principles, but his agony comes from the fact that he refuses to acknowledge the very source of those values.

Montherlant does not belong to the race of unobtrusive writers who let their works speak for themselves. Even more than Cocteau, he surrounds each of his plays with analyses, prefaces, postscripts, and answers to critics, sometimes written many years after publication or performance. He comments upon his own works better than any critic has been able to do. He analyzes them from the inside out and supports his arguments with his own maxims or those of his characters. He is not a writer who cuts the umbilical cord once the work is submitted to the public.

In spite of the fact that he denies putting himself into his works, it is clear that he remains very close to them. His insistence in choosing solitary heroes who claim to be discouraged by the current way of the world, who vehemently cling to the idea of superiority, and who then show how their motives are not always as noble as their attitudes or at least more passionate than moral— such insistence reveals the temperament of Montherlant himself. His theatre might be considered as the masquerade, perhaps not of his actual ideas and passions, but of his inner struggle. In the conception and construction of his plays he often gives the impression of hesitating as much as his characters. He uses them as spokesmen by identifying with certain of their outbursts and goes on to dissect them, judge them, and turn against them. At a performance of a Montherlant play the spectator takes part not only in the sudden changes and metamorphosis of an entirely objectified work but in two tangled dramas: the character's and that of the writer who struggles with him, identifies with him, tries to reject him, and more or less succeeds in all respects.

Montherlant sometimes gets rid of his actual subjects in the same way as he does his characters—with cruelty. He completed *Fils de personne,* an ambiguous play, with a short Boulevard comedy, *Un Incompris,* "a counterpart that borders on caricature," "a little work that also brings out uncertainty, which is what we should feel concerning the very nature of heroism,"[11] and with *Demain il fera jour,* in which Georges changes from being heroic to being despicable. Similarly, *Brocéliande* might be considered a kind of sacrifice through mockery—this time a sacrifice of all the works preceding it. The movement seems to be a double one: the hero, who sacrifices everyone mediocre, is finally sacrificed in turn by the writer, who makes him grotesque or despicable.

The double sacrifice reveals an exigency which is never satisfied—an exigency and a fear: the exigency of always being aware of oneself and the fear of being taken in, caught, hurt. One must be able to answer for oneself at every moment—hence the extravagant rationalizations as well as the destruction of the very content of those rationalizations. If the attitude seems contradictory, there is always a ready answer: so is life.

Although such an attitude makes the audience uncomfortable when it is applied to the relationship between the writer and his characters, it gives the characters themselves, seen objectively, an unquestionable richness, a true dramatic ambiguity, and, because of their dilemma, a tragic dimension. The hero is a sacrificer like his creator, and his act itself, which should prove the integrity and authenticity of his chosen values, in fact shows the nonmoral motive for his attitude.

Certain critics, and Thierry-Maulnier in particular,[12] have

---

11. Ibid., p. 397.
12. Quoted by Montherlant in Note IV to *Fils de personne,* ibid., p. 363.

noticed that Montherlant's heroes' sacrifices of others are somewhat similar to exorcisms. By killing or exiling the person they
consider as weak or mediocre, they think they have killed or driven
out their own weakness or their own mediocrity, as in the case of
Ferrante imprisoning his son or having Inès de Castro killed, or
of Georges letting his son go off to possible death. Montherlant
seems to subscribe to the interpretation and adds to it elsewhere
with a theme he is partial to in his novels: the bullfight. Thus his
heroes' sacrifices have ritual value, and the ultimate meaning of
the whole should be sought beyond the often oversimple moral
maxims, in their cynicism, beyond the analysis of a classical psychological device, in an attitude of magic. Just as the matador
immolates his own animality or fear by killing the bull, so heroes
like Ferrante and Georges sacrifice, through others, that part of
themselves open to tenderness, abandon, indulgence, and even
happiness.

Such characters are reflected in the others. They see in others
their own temptation, the face of what they do not want to be but
what in a kind of way they are. The tragic irony comes from the
fact that in sacrificing what they do not want to be, that very
dimension of themselves becomes perceptible or acknowledged.
*La Ville dont le Prince est un enfant* is once again the richest and
most subtle example of the process. The play's setting itself, a
Catholic school, is favorable to the casting of spells. The teachers
who work not only on their pupils' minds but on their souls, the
religious coloring given to all feeling, all emotion, all affection,
the ritual of friendship among students or students and teachers—
all make it possible for the writer to transcend the conflict between
a moral attitude and its psychological motivation and move toward
a rather strange poetry made up of both the most murky elements
and the greatest purity. The Abbé de Pradts, expelling Sevrais so
that his favorite pupil, Sandrier, may be removed from what he
believes to be Sevrais' bad influence, learns, through a kind of
backfire, that Sandrier is also to be expelled so that he will no
longer be under his own bad influence. Sevrais' expulsion reveals

that the Abbé was unknowingly in the same position as the child he had accused. Thus, without realizing it, he was making Sevrais pay for his own weakness. The play's setting is favorable to self-analyses and reciprocal confessions and allows the writer to play with all the subtleties of his characters' bad faith, up to the final elucidation.

The dialectic of sacrifice is not present in all of Montherlant's plays, but it is frequent enough to throw light on his works as a whole. Montherlant's characters become rigid within an image of themselves—an image to which they can attribute qualities of greatness, magnanimity, purity, lucidity, or brilliance. The motive for their rigidity is the Pascalian "self-love," which, "unable to destroy truth in its essence, destroys it as far as possible in his own knowledge and in that of others."[13] Thus the greatness of Montherlant's characters lies not so much in their ideal or in the rules of action they propose—sometimes tempting, sometimes tiresome or naïve—but in the intensity of the very drama that tears them apart. Their greatness is theatrical not human. They succeed in being admirable by so persistently trying to coincide with a proposed image and, more especially, since they occasionally, in the course of the play, succeed in convincing their creator himself. Moreover, the images they hold up for themselves may be detestable, but they are rarely dull. The grotesque arrogance of the hero in *Brocéliande,* like the mystic renunciation in *Le Maître de Santiago* and Ferrante's regal haughtiness or the Abbé de Pradts' cult of beautiful souls, is suggestive of highly colored theatrical attitudes. About the only exception is Ravier in *Celles qu'on prend dans ses bras,* whose contemptuous sneers are as distressing as his psychology in love.

Beyond the real value or truth of the image man holds up for himself—which varies from Don Juanism to mystic asceticism, from a totally humanistic life to complete renunciation—Montherlant offers us a definition of man independent of the con-

13. Pascal, *Pensées,* trans. W. F. Trotter.

crete content furnished by ethics, politics, or even individual passions. It lies in the notion of effort toward a certain self-realization.
In the course of his works the effort is sometimes taken seriously,
sometimes shown as illusory, sometimes considered for itself
beyond all judgment. Man is not fundamentally political or charitable or religious or capable of love. All those characteristics are
secondary. He is, first and above all, a being who strives toward a
chosen image. The hero is he who strives the most vigorously, the
most steadfastly, and often with the most cruelty.

There is nothing metaphysical in the idea. In fact, it belongs to
the order of psychology, for what is under consideration is not the
objective itself but man's movement toward it. And Montherlant's
description is of man in that pose.

French critics are clearly divided over Montherlant. It is never
easy to find an impartial judgment concerning him. Either the
critical essays devoted to him are the works of admirers blinded
by their enthusiasm, such as Jacques de Laprade, or of ferocious
disparagers. It is interesting to note that foreign critics, who are
more apt to consider the works in themselves and not in their
immediate relation to the French scene, and who seem especially
sensitive to their grand style, are high in their praise. For Eric
Bentley, Montherlant's works represent "a grown-up theatrical
art."[14] For John Gassner, Montherlant is "the most authentic
genius for dramatic writing discoverable in France after 1940."[15]
And indeed his theatre is both ambitious and serious. Montherlant
expects a lot from his public: he writes plays that require a taste
for great style and a capacity for constant attention. His characters
express themselves in classical French, clear and elevated (except-
ing the vulgarities of *Celles qu'on prend dans ses bras* and *Don
Juan*), a language of unquestionable dignity and precision. However, the beauty of form is often a mask, and some particularly fine
speech, which seems to give the key to the play's subject, in fact

14. *In Search of Theatre*, p. 48.
15. *Masters of the Drama*, p. 722.

gives the key to a false subject, the true becoming apparent further on. The ideal spectator for a Montherlant play is therefore one who does not accept the characters' explanations outright but who is capable of admiring their quality without immediately jumping to conclusions.

Montherlant has often complained about the incomprehension of both critics and audiences. Yet because of his oversubtlety in analyzing the characters and his attempt to show that the true meaning of the action does not lie in the characters' own comments about it, his intentions go unnoticed. Quite recently, apropos of *Don Juan,* Paul Guimard[16] laughed at those who, in describing the play, use words such as "catch a glimpse of," "secretly," "perhaps," "without seeming to." Montherlant, however, intended the audience to "catch a glimpse of" the tragedy hidden within the farce. But by completely reducing a mythical character to his most elementary motives, he submerged the play's hidden intentions in a vulgar farce. The legendary rebel and seeker of the absolute or Molière's arrogant freethinker becomes quite simply a sixty-six-year-old lecher. Montherlant's meaning comes through in a change in the play's tone when Don Juan and Ana meet, and also at the end, when the death mask worn by the hero sticks to his face and becomes one with it. A tragic dimension is restored to the character, who is the prisoner of a vulgar and grotesque sensuality, but a lucid prisoner. Yet it would seem that the attempt here of pushing man's incoherence to the extreme only makes the play itself incoherent. The French critics of 1958 found it no more than a painful farce that does not hold up.

Montherlant has always inserted a hidden element in each play, which is in fact the key to the play's meaning. Robert Kemp, at the time of *Port Royal,* spoke of "well-covered poison" with respect to the analysis of the one nun's disbelief that subtly but definitively orients the play's meaning. While there Montherlant did not break the work's aesthetic harmony, that is doubtless one

16. *L'Avant-scène,* No. 188 (January 1, 1959).

of the dangers of his art. The misunderstandings that constantly attend his works come not from the difficulty or obscurity of the actual subject matter but from the veil he throws over his subjects in order to "imitate life."

Once the spectator has understood, he has only to play the writer's game. He will then recognize one of man's faces, that of his solitude—not a whining solitude, waiting to be repudiated, but a solitude so vigorously accepted that ultimately it seems to be chosen. It is reinforced by a contempt for others, the price attached exclusively to the ego, and the construction of a whole system of values (which vary according to the play) to justify it. Great gestures, acts, values, and language are all meant to glorify it, exalt it. Montherlant has an authentically ironical vision of man, since it is inseparable from a doubt as to the basis for the solitary hero's grand attitudes and a doubt as to the meaning of the final revelations. For in wanting to remove that very doubt, men perform the definitive acts that reveal the deep ambiguities of self-love.

# CHAPTER 6

# FROM DISAPPOINTMENT TO PLAY:
## JEAN ANOUILH

While Anouilh is of course a writer, he is chiefly an all-round *homme de théâtre,* and probably more so than any other great playwright of his generation. Not only do his works, like Sala-crou's, essentially consist of plays (along with a few scenarios, some unsigned—certainly no novels or philosophical essays), but he has gradually become his own director, and for the past few years would seem to have stopped writing his own plays in order to adapt or direct the plays of others—plays in which he finds, or on which he imposes, elements of his own spirit and leanings: Molière's *Tartuffe,* for example, and Roger Vitrac's *Victor ou Les Enfants au pouvoir.*

No doubt Anouilh's works are essentially characterized by his conception of theatre as an absolute value and by the pleasure he takes in the stage. Inspired by his discovery of the theatrical magic of Giraudoux, Molière, and Shakespeare, and by his acquaintance with Louis Jouvet, Anouilh owes much of his success with the most

varied audiences to the fact that any spectator with some knowledge of the stage, whether or not he is in sympathy with Anouilh's
general "philosophy," is forced to bow to the evidence: seated in
the theatre, and whether delighted or annoyed by the point of view,
he undergoes an authentic theatrical experience.

The naturalism of Anouilh's early plays is of course striking. The
protagonists of *Jézabel* (never performed), *L'Hermine, Le
Voyageur sans bagage,* and *La Sauvage* stand out, in all their
bitterness, violence, or despair, against a background of brutality
or sordidness. The substance of their world is money, adultery,
promiscuity, cruelty, the degradation of poverty, the division of
classes, and the fundamental vulgarity of the common people. As
in cheap popular novels, the hero or heroine may dream of rising
above his lowly condition by way of murder, as in *L'Hermine,* or a
"good marriage," as in *La Sauvage*—both simple dramas based on
the conventional tension between a desire for happiness and the
obstacles created by society (the family or a difference in class)
or by reality in general. At first glance, this kind of tension, which
is found in all of Anouilh's works, seems banal. Yet it is complicated by the fact that a further desire—for purity or, in any
case, for some beautiful ideal—necessarily conflicts with both the
sordidness of reality and the desire for happiness. From play to
play, Anouilh has enriched that triangular dilemma, adding ambiguities to the notion of purity and even, in some of his latest
works, holding it up to ridicule or showing the dangers involved
in it, while at the same time substituting practical realism for the
sordid.

These moral variations would take little away from the basic
naturalism if Anouilh, from the very start, had not been alive to
the need for theatricalism. While the subject matter of *Le Bal des
voleurs* (written in 1932, although not performed until 1938) is
itself centered around a young girl's escape from the boredom of a
world of idlers, the play overflows with scenic invention, masquerade, and unreality—that is, pure theatre. Most of *Le Voyageur
sans bagage* (1937), with its amnesiac protagonist in search of his

past and his family, consists of revelations of egotism, family hatred, attempted murders, and adultery, under the eyes of low-minded servants, yet various devices create a distance from the horror of the real, the most important being the final twist, which changes the tone of the play: an ironic note is introduced when, at the cost of a lie, the hero goes away with a little boy straight out of an English engraving. Anouilh's main subject has always been the conflict between the weight of an ugly and difficult reality and certain men's desire for the absolute, but he has gradually found the solution to that conflict in what he had sensed from the very beginning—theatre itself.

The weight of reality in Anouilh is that of the world of men, their natures, and their appetites—as they exist today. While a theatrical dimension is often added by the whimsical picturesque quality of certain periods (frequently the beginning of the century), it is the world of today that is in question. A universal myth like that of *Antigone* is closely linked to the problem of the Resistance and collaboration in the 1940s, in the same way that *La Foire d'empoigne* (concerning Napoleon and Louis XVIII) is a portrait of the possible attitudes of today's politicians. Even in the details, contemporary allusions are obvious: the guards in *Antigone* are twentieth-century policemen; the little monk in *Becket* is a modern young terrorist. And in all of the plays, even the historical ones, the familiar bourgeois world of the twentieth century is satirized in period costume (Henry II's royal family in *Becket,* for example).

Such anachronisms or distortions are of course similar to certain of Giraudoux's or Cocteau's devices. The times of Romantic local color or historically accurate reconstructions are over: the past now has meaning only in relation to the present. But in Anouilh the link established between the historical past and the contemporary world has a very special purpose: not to show that the "gods" are still around, or that our world is visited by the "chosen," or that a young glazier is in fact an angel in modern dress, but to denounce history in the name of the present, and the present in the name of history. Anouilh relates the sordidness of today's world to the crimes or exemplary adventures of antiquity or of the past in general and sees the crimes or exemplary adventures of antiquity as no more than manifestations of a reality as ridiculous as that of today. Such parallels make the present grandiose, but only by showing a past that is degraded in terms of present baseness. While with comparable devices Giraudoux or Cocteau transformed our times into a temporary embodiment of mythology or eternal magic, Anouilh levels off the historic past and present, situating them on an intermediate plane, where the spectacular wonders of the one serve as an aesthetic ornament to the other, and where the other imposes the image of a condition eternally blocked in its mediocrity, despite individual aspirations.

There is a restful side to Anouilh—just one of many, to be sure, but it does explain part of his success—a quality similar to that of certain historical plays by Scribe and Sardou and the kind of melodrama that "makes Margot weep" (Musset): we are all just as good as the great characters of myth or history, and, by the same token, those characters were no more than poor human beings, all tangled up in their own little natures, like the rest of us. For this is a theatre of demystification—of twofold demystification, in fact. Certain dubious heads of state are dragged in the mud—but not so fast! They happen to belong to the race of Creon. And, vice versa, Napoleon is set up, out of admiration or hatred, as a tremendous mythical figure—but beware! He actually was no more than a poor actor, whose chief concern was to make a spectacular exit. A little upstart in the Resistance, who is getting his mean personal revenge, is likened to Robespierre, while Robespierre himself, one of the rare "pure" heroes in French history, was, according to Anouilh, merely jealous of the sexual prowess of other men. Masked suppers (*Pauvre Bitos*), ancient tragedy performed in modern dress (*Antigone*), the use of the same actor to play two antithetical parts (Napoleon and Louis XVIII in *La Foire d'empoigne*)—by such purely theatrical tricks Anouilh demystifies.

Anouilh's awareness of all the theatrical possibilities enables him to use still other devices of demystification, in this case quite similar to Salacrou's. He borrows from established genres (*vaudeville,* bourgeois comedy or drama, eighteenth-century comedy), switching over in midstream from one genre to its opposite, or shows, through forms meant to maintain the public's good conscience, all sorts of reasons for having a bad conscience. *Ardèle ou La Marguerite,* for example, has the form of a *vaudeville* but leads to a double suicide and very sad discoveries indeed, and *Le Voyageur sans bagage* starts out as a comedy, goes on to the horrible discoveries of an almost detective-story and naturalist investigation, and ends with a poetic escape. By using devices of this kind, Anouilh confronts the public with an established and satisfying modern mechanism, only to more successfully destroy the motives for satisfaction. An ordinary spectator is at first pleased to find himself in the presence of a traditional kind of plot and characters or precise allusions to contemporary problems, but he is soon shaken in most of his opinions and in his tendency to be satisfied with himself and his world. The traditional genres are shown to be false, the allusions are found to be accusations, reality is finally denied by poetry, and the mythical imagination ends by collapsing under the blows of common sense. The shimmering changes in style, tone, and mood come, not from a super-logic à la Giraudoux, but from a deep bitterness that demolishes all established illusions out of fear of being the dupe of false values and superimposes the higher value of theatrical entertainment.

Note, however, that the attitude of not wanting to be deceived does not exclude a certain basic ideology, which derives from what the French, until 1958, called "the right." Inherited wealth confers a kind of grace, elegance, and ironic lucidity—even on those who live in boredom and vice; the exercise of political power as a craft is a modus vivendi whose necessarily sordid aspects are rehabilitated by the notion of "a job well done"; and so on. But what one might call Anouilh's "bourgeois aristocratism" could be considered merely a surface element of his works, for his thinking has

evolved. Pol Vandromme, in his recent book on Jean Anouilh, has
pointed out the "reactionary" turning point in his life: directly
after World War II the still hesitant playwright, who seemed to
believe in the generosity of the pure and the oppressed, found
himself involved in an attempt to save the collaborator Brasillach
from being condemned to death and discovered that some of those
who allowed Brasillach to be shot may have done so not only out
of patriotism but also out of cowardice or personal revenge.[1] In
fact, Anouilh has always been a reactionary, but in the manner
of Molière's Alceste. His attitude is less a political stand than a
fundamental disappointment in the reality of the world. He grants
that human beings have great value, but that value, by the very
nature of things, is never realized. It may sometimes sparkle, however—in the rich, in those who simply say No to life, and, finally,
in the illusions of theatre, if one accepts once and for all the idea
that theatre *is not* life.

The dramatic expression of Anouilh's disappointment reaches out
to many areas of everyday existence. The grandeur of man is never
found where one often thinks it will be. It is customary, for example, in the Christian world to glorify unhappiness as the source
of virtue and redemption, but on this point Anouilh has taken a
conspicuously anti-Romantic position. Never in French literature
has there been a more repetitious and vigorous denial of Alfred
de Musset's formula, "Nothing makes us so great as a great sorrow." In *La Répétition* most of the characters suffer or end by
suffering, but the misery, caused by jealousy, wounded pride, or
unsatisfied passion, is either held up to ridicule (as with Villebosse)
or presented as a source of moral decay and ignoble acts (Hero, and
the Countess herself in her schemes to destroy Lucile). Generally,
in Anouilh, suffering leads to shame and acts of moral and physical
self-destruction. Similarly, in regard to poverty, the myth deflated
is not that of the emotional suffering which ennobles the victim

1. Pol Vandromme, *Jean Anouilh, un auteur et ses personnages* (Paris,
1965), pp. 116 ff.

but the myth of the virtuous heroism of the poor. As early as *L'Hermine* the hero Franz admits that "poverty made [his] youth into a long period of pettiness and disgust." Poverty leads Anouilh's characters to petty calculating, rancor, bitter dreams. And when the poor take refuge in dignity and intransigence, they become spoilsports: they upset the game, become hateful in their excessive purity, and are the ruin of the others, like Julien in *Colombe*.

Destroyed also, although sometimes only partially in that the plays leave it unresolved, is the theme of the one and only love. When Anouilh puts two young people together for the first time, they may fall in love at first sight and make highly impassioned speeches about the eternity of their love *(Eurydice, Roméo et Jeannette)*. But then they have to commit suicide before their love can degenerate, before the impurity of others and their own natures can show them the vanity of their love. Or else love is part of an unreal divertissement *(Le Bal des voleurs, Léocadia,* and *L'Invitation au château)* in which the playwright's technique itself emphasizes the fantasy of the final happy marriage. There are no united and happy couples in Anouilh's theatre. All the mature couples who appear onstage are always involved in a farcical situation and treated rather lightly or with an accent on the situation's sordid or bitter aspect. The only ones who escape, until a new passion comes along, are the couples who have established a "good friends" relationship *(La Répétition, Ardèle)*.

In this respect, one device that provokes even more pathos than the poetic presentation of the lovers' death in *Eurydice* is the unexpected flashback at the end of *Colombe*. After having shifted the action from the idea of purity to the idea of happiness, after having shown Colombe's delight in her corruption and the vanity of Julien's illusions about the eternity of their love, Anouilh takes the spectator back to the past and ends his play with the first romantic meeting of the two young people. Similar to certain of Salacrou's techniques, this reversal of time in extremis has a very powerful dramatic effect: the joy of the moment, the sudden harmony of the boy and girl, is shown in the absolute of the present—*its* present—but not until the end of a long spectacle whose purpose was to give the lie to the permanent value of that past moment.

Anouilh uses a comparable device at the end of his play about Joan of Arc, *L'Alouette*. The work as a whole is altogether theatrical, in that the characters are neither actors reproducing Joan's adventure nor infernal ghosts meditating on it anew. By a decree of the playwright, they are all, including Joan herself, both alive and reliving their adventure onstage and hence are indefinable outside of what Anouilh has made of them. But in that purely scenic and poetic universe, where real human beings are able to live and at the same time to put their lives in order, time can be manipulated both as the author wishes and, in the present case, as a national legend wishes: the play follows the historical chronology of Joan's vocation, her trial, and her burning, but before the curtain falls, the characters decide that the last tableau will show Joan not at the stake but in the cathedral at Reims, standing beside the King of France at his coronation.

Just as in *L'Alouette* the popular image of the legend prevails scenically over the reality of a sad political adventure, so in *Colombe* the image of a magazine for young girls prevails scenically over the unbearable reality of the necessary corruption of people who devote themselves to happiness. In both cases there is the implication that real life is precisely the opposite of the final denouement: it is only by way of poetic artifice that joy comes *after* sorrow. These two examples are characteristic of Anouilh's double game—theatrical poetry and bitter realism.

Anouilh continually focuses upon the fact that, considering life in its chronological flow, there is an inevitable curve from an inner ideal to all the possible challenges to that ideal. Every one of his protagonists begins with the hope of some beautiful achievement—any kind of beautiful achievement, but always one situated outside evil. Money makes for happiness, poverty makes for virtue, devotion to an ideal is either satisfying or effective, love at first sight means love that will last forever. But then time modifies such notions and shows them to be false: How can a rich girl be happy when "somewhere there will always be a poor lost dog" *(La Sauvage)?* How is one to believe in the virtue of the poor when that virtue turns into lowly revenge *(Pauvre Bitos),* or when one discovers that social and financial inferiority causes gangrene of the soul *(Le Voyageur sans bagage, La Grotte,* and many others)? How is one to think that devotion to an ideal has any value when it leads to a complete negation of the world and of oneself or to a useless catastrophe *(Antigone, L'Alouette, Becket)?* How is one to believe in love at first sight when one discovers either the sordidness of the past *(Eurydice)* or watches love melt away in the face of the reality of the world or the real demands of happiness *(Colombe)?*

To emphasize clearly the fatal degeneration of any ideal, Anouilh peoples his theatre with little boys and little girls, children who in fact are well past twenty. Over the years he has perhaps increasingly decided in favor of characters—from the old duchesses of his early plays to the politicians belonging to the race of Creon—who have viewed their childhoods from a necessary distance, repudiated them, and become true, realistic adults, not at all worried about dirtying their hands. But apart from this extratheatrical stand, he has constantly, from his very first plays to his most recent, created the ambiguous character in whom there is a mixture of an ideal that derived from ignorance and a corruption due to experience, the adult who never manages to repudiate completely his original purity. It was no accident that he recently directed Vitrac's *Victor ou Les Enfants au pouvoir,* a surrealist farce whose hero is a child genius, nine years old and six feet tall, who dies after having discovered and denounced the ludicrous behavior (adultery, madness, stupidity) of adults.

Indeed, Anouilh's own characters often recall "the little boy that I was." And when childhood is thus recalled, it generally seems open to all the great ideals and all the great passions. It also carries within itself the seeds of the corruption to come as soon as there is a relationship between two people. Then begins the jealousy, the longing. Two children are the beginning of a society and therefore the beginning of corruption. Moreover, the observation and imitation of the adults' corrupt society leads to the degeneration of the children (Toto and Marie-Christine imitating the adults in *Ardèle*).

When the characters actually remain children, the situation is not livable. One cannot be both a child and an adult, for the persistence of the child in the adult leads to catastrophe. The catastrophe may be admirable, as in the case of "little Antigone," or it may consist in incoherence, passion, and murder, as in the case of the "little boy" Henry II in *Becket*. In other words, the corrupting world is definitely not for them.

But the play of purity and sordidness is ambiguous. Taking *Colombe* as an example, the purity Julien wants to impose on Colombe is withering and deadly, whereas the corruption she undergoes in the company of actors makes her live and brings her happiness. Moreover, the accuser whom Anouilh introduces into such worlds of shame is controversial, and from play to play he has become subject to increasingly contradictory judgments and is shown to be far from a paragon of virtue and justice.

Such ambiguities remain in the category of the realist portrait, and Anouilh could well have stopped there—as he in fact did in his first plays. But during the course of his career he overcame the naturalist conflict, with its moral implications, by rejecting the conflict itself. The heroes of his great plays finally transcend good and evil through a clearer and clearer refusal to play the game of life. That refusal leads to two extreme solutions, often combined in the same play: the tragic catastrophe brought about by his abstract No and the substitution of the game of theatre for the game of life.

Since Antigone, at the beginning of Anouilh's play, has buried her brother for very precise reasons, similar to those of Sophocles' heroine, at first glance the subject of *Antigone* seems to be the conflict between two "laws" and the painful choice it imposes on exacting or responsible people.[2] But in the course of the play the conflict between political realism and a refusal to compromise is not resolved by the choice of one as against the other. Instead, it takes the direction of an affirmation of two different loves of life and the real world. Opposing Creon, for whom reality is praxis, stands Antigone, for whom the world is a kind of Garden of Eden. It is thus easy for Creon to break down what one might call her "Greek" reasoning, and her attitude then becomes a denial of life out of love for life. Her final No is less a refusal to collaborate with Creon's politics than a rejection of any collaboration with the problem as a whole—that is, with the double face of life itself.

Antigone's extreme attitude is typical of the higher refusals of Anouilh's other great heroes, who are presented in more specific contexts. The world is a mechanism for corrupting man, lowering him, keeping him from being a man. The dramatic hero is aware of the situation, caught between the obligatory degradation of life and a will to escape from it, despite his love for life in all its concrete richness. Sometimes he succeeds in a grotesque way, like General Saint Pé in the "Pièces grinçantes"; sometimes he discovers that his dignity lies in absolute negation. Even the Inquisitor in *L'Alouette*—one of the possible symbols of the universal conspiracy against man and against the concrete beauty that life could have—when confronted by Joan of Arc is forced to acknowledge that

> There will always be a man to hunt down somewhere . . . who will finally be caught and killed, and who will once again debase the Idea at the height of its power, simply be-

2. It was this aspect of *Antigone* that was picked up by the critics and audience at its first performance in Paris in 1923: a choice between the resistance to an order considered unjust and collaboration with it.

cause he will say No without lowering his eyes. *(Full of hatred, he hisses between his teeth, looking at Joan.)* The insolent breed!

Antigone's or Joan's insolent attitude is also that of Thomas à Becket in *Becket ou L'Honneur de Dieu*, a play that might be considered the height of Anouilh's production to this day. On one level the historical drama is a pretext for very contemporary allusions, sordid family scenes, and denunciations of political corruption and disenchantment (a disillusioned King of France, a clownish Pope). On another level it is a tragedy of passion. The mechanism of unrequited passion in Henry II's friendship for Becket is shown in all the complicity of the game of love and hate, despair and jealousy. It is a little boy's intense misery upon discovering that his best friend has forsaken him; nevertheless, since the character is adult, there are times when Henry II behaves like one of Racine's heroines. Very symbolically, the barons who go off to murder Becket walk to the rhythm of his heartbeats. The King's passion has a most Anouilhian function, however: it destroys the illusions which are the very structure of the characters' world. On the other hand, it appears to be based on illusion itself to the extent that it is unrequited, since Becket's friendship for the King is of quite another nature: he is beyond the sordid and beyond love. As the King's friend he plays the part of a fellow libertine and he plays it well. Yet what interests him is not debauchery but perfection in debauchery. When the King appoints him Archbishop, all he does is to be the perfect Archbishop—a far cry from Eliot's Becket in *Murder in the Cathedral*. There is no question of God here—rather, the *honor* of God:

| | |
|---|---|
| *The King:* | So you've begun to love God? *(He shouts.)* And you haven't changed, pig-headed boy, you still don't answer when someone asks you a question? |
| *Becket (gently):* | I have begun to love the honor of God. |

In the conflict between the honor of the King and the honor of God, Becket's choice is not motivated by any logic:

| | |
|---|---|
| *Becket:* | I shan't try to convince you. I shall only say No. |
| *The King:* | But you must be logical, Becket! |
| *Becket:* | No, it's not necessary, my King. One has only to do, absurdly, what one has been entrusted with doing—and to the very end. |

And "absurdly" is the word for it. Becket never for a moment gives a thought to what he considers a duty: it is an imperative which is given without justification and which places him beyond any psychological or political vision. Such an attitude is doubtless one solution to the problem of life which is unlivable—but a desperate one. For since life is necessarily and gradually corroded by the cancer of practical compromises and false, dehumanizing idealism, choosing "absurd" purity is actually choosing against life, killing oneself or having oneself killed in the name of that No which is both the honor of man and his annihilation.

Saying No is the logical conclusion which the more lucid characters come to. But in addition to this moral solution of basic conflicts, Anouilh, in his comedies (the "Pièces roses" and "Pièces brillantes") and in certain of his dramas or tragedies (the "Pièces grinçantes," "Pièces costumées," and "Pièces noires"), emphasizes another kind of solution—theatre itself—presented in the form of fantastic and contrived denouements, such as the conclusion of *Le Voyageur sans bagage* or of *Valse des toréadors*. In the first, the hero escapes from his real past by acting out a lie with the help of an unexpected and heaven-sent little boy; in the second, the plot is nonchalantly resolved by a conventional device from classic comedy—the farcical discovery of hidden filiations. Even more clearly, at the end of *Hurluberlu* the hero, after both his conspiracy to save

France and his marriage have failed, has no other solution but to act in an amateur theatrical, and the curtain falls on the beginning of a play within the play.

Actually, all the works of Anouilh are filled with that kind of theatricalism. The comedies are masquerades; Joan of Arc in *L'Alouette* does not merely live but acts out her life; *Antigone* is presented as the staging of a tragedy. The whole of his last play, *La Grotte,* is presented as an arrangement of characters and fragments from a drama that the author has not yet managed to write, and he himself intervenes in the action to answer his characters' questions, to explain, or merely to stop up the holes. Every one of Anouilh's plays, except for the very first, is dominated by a theatrical vision of life.

In the comedies, the characters—either bored or disgusted—are masked most of the time and play at living a certain conventional or extravagant destiny. In contrast to the young girl, "naked under her little linen dress" (a description repeated in many plays) and in search of a purity that is impossible in this world, there is the rather mad old lady, laden with jewels and lace, masked, and lucidly playing a part that saves her from despair. Many of Anouilh's characters are counterfeits, from Lady Hurf in *Le Bal des voleurs* to Ornifle in *Ornifle ou Le Courant d'air.* Their motives are clearly neither ambition nor shame, but the fear of being bored or of suffering. Madame Alexandre in *Colombe* is a perfect symbol of this "hypocrisy" in that she is an actress, but even characters like Tigre in *La Répétition* or Messerschmann in *L'Invitation au château* live behind masks, each in his own way.

The subject matter of many of Anouilh's plays consists of justifications of the mask, attempts to unmask the characters, and even pure exercises of virtuosity on the theme of the mask. The theme is exploited in a more or less physical way, depending on the play's degree of seriousness. In *Le Bal des voleurs* Peterbono and his two friends disguise themselves by changing costumes and identity three times, and Gustave, four. In other less fantastic "Pièces roses" and in the "Pièces brillantes" a poor young girl is generally disguised as a rich one (Amanda in *Léocadia,* Isabelle in *L'Invitation au château*). The costume party in *Pauvre Bitos,* one of the "Pièces grinçantes," becomes a pretext for Pirandello-like effects and the basis for a scenic simile intended to explain the revolutionaries during the Reign of Terror as well as the psychology of the 1944–45 purge. In *La Répétition* the heroes, disguised in Louis XV costumes for an amateur performance of Marivaux's *La Double Inconstance,* are themselves involved in a cruel adventure of libertinage and passion similar to *Les Liaisons dangereuses.* In *Le Rendez-vous de Senlis* Georges is actually neither masked nor disguised, but he hires professional actors in order to create a family for himself.

Anouilh's use of the mask achieves a double effect. First of all, it brings back one of the essential and original elements of theatre: the assumption of someone else's identity or physical appearance, which begins the very moment an actor pretends to be himself and another. One of the purest and most effective forms of theatricalism consists in producing a kind of chain of false identities, as in Beaumarchais' *Le Mariage de Figaro,* in which a young actress is both herself and Cherubin, a young boy, who during the play passes himself off as a girl. In many respects such theatre would seem to consist in superimposing masks on a face or in taking them off one after another, just as clowns manage endlessly to remove their multicolored vests. Truth plays hide-and-seek onstage, and Anouilh brought the game's more spectacular aspects back to the French theatre of the forties and fifties.

On the other hand, the device is also used to present an ironic vision of life, for Anouilh's characters are closest to certain truths when they consciously assume a mask. At times it is not so much a question of truth as that of a mere feeling of comfort: some characters manage to achieve their purposes only if they dress in the manner that is customary in a particular situation; they are poor actors who need makeup and theatrical costumes to play their parts properly. But on another and deeper level the mask serves to reveal: not until he performs Marivaux does Tigre discover a passion he no longer believed himself capable of; not until they discover themselves as revolutionaries during the Reign of Terror do the characters in *Pauvre Bitos* reveal their deeper selves; not until she wears theatrical costumes and gives in to the artificial life backstage does Colombe discover her true gaiety. In *L'Invitation au château,* when Madame Desmermortes sees Isabelle—a poor girl hired to play the part of a mysterious rich girl—mingle with her guests at a ball, her comment is: "She's the only one who doesn't seem to be acting a part." Anouilh thus introduces an authentic dramatic effect—the revelation of the true by way of the false and because of the false.

Even a serious drama like *Becket* is informed by the vision of the mask. Thomas à Becket, like most of Anouilh's characters, can play his part well only when he wears the costume symbolic of the part. By putting on a monk's habit or an archbishop's sumptuous robes, he succeeds in identifying himself with the honor of God—a serious masquerade, but a masquerade. And it is by playing a part that Becket finds his truth and his own honor. In such a play the close link between the refusal of Anouilh's heroes and the theatrical vision of life becomes clear. In point of fact, they are inseparable. Whereas Salacrou recalls Pascal's anguish, Anouilh states Pascal's theme of divertissement: man tries to save himself from anguish by identifying himself with a role, with a game. Where there is a game, there is a negation of earnestness. But the earnestness is restored in a higher form when there is total identification with the role, as in the case of Antigone or Becket. In the last analysis, Anouilh's theatre is ambiguous: it shows man's defeat in the face of life, but also his victory as a total actor, on whom neither Creons nor inquisitors nor passionate kings have any real hold.

The consequences of such an attitude are twofold. On the one hand, it is the source of a great number of theatrical effects, either original or borrowed from the Commedia del'Arte, Shakespeare, Molière, Marivaux, or Beaumarchais. On the other hand, it gives enormous rights to theatre, since it is not only a metaphor of life but also a solution. Such devices as unexplained flashbacks, a juggling with time and space, and a toned-down avant-garde are not based on magic or the supernatural. As elements of pure theatrical freedom, they represent no more than the playwright's way of telling a story—in other words, the indefeasible power of theatre.

If one decided to judge playwrights according to their mythmaking powers, it would be amusing to consider how—after Cocteau's "enfants terribles" and Giraudoux's "chosen" young ladies—a great many of the young Parisian bourgeois of the forties patterned themselves after the "pure" heroes and heroines made fashionable by Anouilh. And since myths have the habit of being tenacious, many still consider Anouilh the playwright of purity as opposed to the sordid.

In fact, however, Anouilh has gone far beyond a simple conflict that catches a young girl's fancy, on both an ethical and a theatrical level. While his works as a whole, at least to date, certainly present a stylized spectacle of degradation and of young hopefuls who refuse that degradation, they are, above all, a constant meditation on the ambiguity of the conflict. Still more, they bring out the truly dramatic elements of the ethical problem. Among the "pure" creatures, Antigone and Joan of Arc adore life: sand, water, the warmth of a nanny, a strong smell of horsemen—that is, everything that represents the concrete richness of the real, which is both similar to, and more concrete than, the "human values" of a Giraudoux or a Camus. Despite the differences in metaphors, all three playwrights have a keen taste for living things—a fact that many ethereal and intellectual French girls have refused to realize.

Anouilh's heroes and heroines fight as much against abstraction (the Inquisitor's "Idea" in *L'Alouette*) as against the sordid aspects of concrete reality. Some of them take refuge, paradoxically, in idealism, but that idealism is more a nostalgia for happy life than a philosophy and is finally dangerous and negative—hence the source of their tragedy.

What is left for them is an awareness of the situation and a pride in having said No. And what is left for the writer and his spectators is a highly colored portrayal of man's condition, which is re-created but also dominated by all the artifice of theatre: man becomes superior to his fate by affirming, for the duration of a performance, that he is the constant participant in a difficult but entrancing masked ball.

# CHAPTER 7

# MAN AND HIS ACTS:
# JEAN-PAUL SARTRE
# AND ALBERT CAMUS

During the forties, with Anouilh becoming ever more involved in his theatrical game, Salacrou continuing his variations on a Pascalian theme, and Montherlant trying to express deep confusion in clear terms, Sartre and Camus were successfully giving both a modern and an intelligible form to this return to man.[1] Their originality consisted in achieving it without reverting to a scientific viewpoint, a vision limited to psycho-physiological determinism. What might have resulted in a neopositivism—considering the collapse of our supposedly transcendent and absolute values —appears, on the contrary, as an affirmation of man's privileged

1. Germaine Brée and Margaret Guiton, in their book on the contemporary French novel, *An Age of Fiction* (New Brunswick, N.J., Rutgers University Press, 1957), similarly described the *novels* of Sartre and Camus as a "return to man."

metaphysical position. With the added notion that philosophy is more an object of action than of speculation, more a part of life than a play of ideas, the medium for existentialist thought became quite naturally a work of fiction: the novel or theatre.

Starting from the principle that man is alone before man and from the fact that such a situation is understandable or conceivable only in terms of action, Sartre and Camus have tried to create a type of theatre in which the concrete representation of life and their own philosophical concepts are absolutely inseparable. Given their basic philosophical positions, the dialogue is indissolubly bound up with physical *acts*. Whether the plays take the form of historical drama (Sartre's *Le Diable et le Bon Dieu*), allegory (Camus' *L'Etat de siège*), a kind of semi-detective story (Sartre's *Les Mains sales* and even *Nekrassov,* Camus' *Le Malentendu*), or a series of debates (Sartre's *Huis Clos,* Camus' *Les Justes*), the spectator is held by the expectation of rebounds, the promise of extreme and definitive acts, the surprise of certain dramatic effects, and the double question: What is going to happen? How will it turn out? Sometimes both writers do end by creating a rush of physical happenings that border on the unreal (Camus' *Caligula,* for instance, might seem like an arbitrary catalogue of acts of cruelty and madness), causing some critics to describe their plays as "melodramatic."

Physical action, generally violent, takes on a new value as treated by Sartre and Camus, since their basic philosophy consists in destroying the importance traditionally accorded to motives. What really counts are not the reasons for an act but the act itself, its present significance, and the significance it gives to the characters and the world. In other words, the search for the psychological causality of an act is either shown to be vain or replaced by an investigation of the act's significance. This does not mean that motives are altogether eliminated. Although explanations may be reduced to a minimum, they are indeed necessary, for the acts are not gratuitous. Caligula himself, in Camus' play, does not gratuitously experiment with the gratuitous: he is impelled by a "need for the impossible," the "need for something that is not of this world." Yet the motive is presented very briefly and in such terms that it seems more metaphysical than psychological. In certain cases the spectator, accustomed to long verbal explanations, may be baffled. This is especially true in the case of *Le Malentendu,* in which Martha's need for escape, leading to her murdering the wealthy clientele of the Inn in order to get money, is explained rather sketchily and always in the same terms. While a traditional writer of "psychological theatre" would have devoted most of the play to long digressions on the psychology of suffocation, the misery and dismal mediocrity of Martha's life, and so on, Camus merely sums up those digressions in an image of the sun and the sea. For the true subject of his play lies rather in the absurd and fatal conjuncture of Martha's acts and her brother's almost un-explained behavior.

Even in a retrospective work such as Sartre's *Huis Clos,* in which the acts are in the past and the characters try to evaluate them, no emphasis is put on discovering why, through what determinism of the world and men, the characters happened to commit their crimes. Indeed, when they try, as Garcin occasionally does, they fail to reach any conclusion. Since the play is chiefly a study of the different ways in which men "bear" their acts, when any psychological causality is introduced, it is only as an a posteriori rationalization of the characters themselves and is no more than a present state of consciousness. Similarly, in *Les Mains sales* the long flashback that makes up the greater part of the play contributes nothing but plain facts, with no explanation: the meaning of Hoederer's murder is given only in the present and by way of Hugo's decision. As for *Les Séquestrés d'Altona,* the hero is so tortured by the possible historical *significance* of his monstrous war crimes that he takes refuge in madness.

It has often been pointed out that Giraudoux's characters have hardly any pasts and are completely open to their futures. With a very different vision of the world, Sartre and Camus present much the same attitude. What counts for them is the project an act represents or its meaning in the present—a meaning that changes according to the agent's choices and the interpretation of other people. Of course, for the existentialists a concrete situation requires that a certain *nature* be taken into account. No existentialist ever dreamed of denying given elements such as a man's body, sex, age, social class, and temperament. In fact, the weight of those elements, along with a consciousness of it and the effort made to objectify it or reject it, is inseparable from the subject matter of *Les Mains sales, Le Diable et le Bon Dieu,* and *Les Séquestrés d'Altona.* To use the existentialist vocabulary, all freedom is *en situation;* but since Sartre and Camus want to bring out the irreducible element that distinguishes man from the rest of the world, their interest lies more in its manifestations and creations than in the mechanism of "natures" or "essences," which are considered as secondary.

Such emphasis in theatre means a complete reversal of the treatment of action: acts are presented not as products but as inventions. An act is therefore seen as a creation, almost as unique and irreplaceable as a signed work of art, and at the same time as both a source of drama and drama itself, not only at the moment it is committed—when it implies a struggle and a choice—but even afterward, in man's effort to clarify the relationship between it and himself. Sartre's characters' frequent use of the expression "my act" emphasizes the idea of its being both an outer object and a reciprocal bond between man and what he does. His plays are investigations of the different relations of man to his acts, whether he tries to rid himself of them (which is impossible, hence Estelle's painful tragedy of bad faith in *Huis Clos,* Franz' escape into madness in *Les Séquestrés d'Altona,* and Heinrich's devil in *Le Diable et le Bon Dieu*) or completely assumes them. Without denying all the excuses that science gives for his behavior, man is considered in the perspective of the formula: in any case, whatever I do, *I* am the one who does it.

Taking this formula as a central point, the existentialist theatre opens out around it and examines the ethical and political extensions it implies. Men are considered as having no excuses, since from the start it has been accepted that man is thus distinguished from the rest of the world. As a result, the play's intensity depends largely on the seriousness of the acts committed. Everyday acts, taken one after another, can be successfully used in the novel, as in Sartre's *La Nausée*. However, since dramatic economy demands that the weight of dilution be replaced by the shock of concentration, the effect must be produced through a violent or monstrous act—a point of view very similar indeed to the Greek, Shakespearean, or classical concept of exemplary and extreme acts. If it is true that every act brings man's very being into question, what better means is there than murder, where even an illusion of reparation is impossible. Moreover Sartre and Camus, in the belief that great violence is a sign of the times, use murder in all its forms.

The more horrible the act, the more the individual, who always acts *alone,* begins to "question." While the solitude and anguish involved in murder had already been described by Malraux in *La Condition humaine,* Sartre and Camus combine the greatest violence and the deepest solitude in their situations. For them solitude is what separates the would-be murderer from the arguments in favor of the murder. In *Les Mains sales,* for example, Hugo begins to like Hoederer, whom he wants to kill for political reasons, just as Kaliayev, in *Les Justes,* had decided to throw a bomb at the Grand Duke until he saw children in the carriage. Emphasis is put on the isolation of each individual in his action or his suffering, in a vision of the world where, to use Roquentin's terms in *La Nausée,* there is obviously no "communion of souls"; for, as he says, "I have not fallen so low." My suffering is *my* suffering just as my murder, even in the case of collective action, is *my* murder.

The isolation of man in action is often symbolized by the choice of heroes whose basic situations are exceptional. Orestes' background has made him a stranger to all the cities in Greece *(Les Mouches),* Hugo is a young bourgeois in the Communist party *(Les Mains sales),* Goetz is a military leader and a bastard born of

a nobleman and a peasant *(Le Diable et le Bon Dieu)*, Lizzie is a
prostitute on the fringe of American society *(La Putain respectueuse)*, Nekrassov is an adventurer *(Nekrassov)*, Kean is a great
actor *(Kean)*, Caligula is an emperor *(Caligula)*, and Kaliayev is a
poet *(Les Justes)*. Sometimes, of course, there are more specific
reasons for the choice of certain characters: in *Les Mains sales*,
for example, Sartre was speaking directly to the young bourgeois
Frenchmen attracted by communism at the time. In general, however, the characters' exceptional situations are meant not to imply
that humanity is naturally divided into heroes and the superfluous
rest of mankind but to express, in the form of a hyperbolic metaphor, the similar agony of any man faced with himself.

The agony here is metaphysical. Although the hero may be
acting out of passion or in the name of some value, what suddenly
strikes him is the bare fact of his own existence and the dizzying
vacuum of the nothingness it implies. Whether the hero be Camus'
Caligula or Sartre's Garcin, Goetz, or Hugo, his hopeless discovery
is that the world is absurd and his acts the unjustified creations of
his freedom.

"You are no more than the sum of your acts," says Inez to
Garcin in *Huis Clos*. The traditional idea that man commits some
particular act because he is thus-and-so is replaced with its opposite: by committing some particular act, man makes himself
thus and so. Nothingness to start with, man spends his life giving
himself an essence made up of all his acts, and it is through acting
that he becomes conscious of original nothingness. The anguish
that grips him is provoked by that nothingness, the absence of
justification, and the metaphysical responsibility which makes him
the creator of his own essence.

The idea is alien to many minds. First of all, it is uncomfortable.
More importantly, however, it eliminates the notion of human nature, a fundamental concept in Western thought, and treats human
destiny in itself as meaningless and useless agitation—in other
words, as absurd. Since the dramatic hero also finds the idea diffi-

cult to accept, the conflict between his awareness of the absurd and his need for justification constitutes the strongest dramatic tension in Sartre's and Camus' works.

Once the hero accepts the idea—if he does—a second dramatic conflict is created: What is he to do now? The choice is simple. Either he can fall back into blindness and bad faith—that is, into a belief in reasons, eternal essences, and the value of established orders, human or divine, with a meaning given in advance—or he can assume his acts and his life, fully aware of the world's absurdity, and accept the crushing responsibility of giving the world a meaning that comes from himself alone.

In his first play, *Les Mouches,* Sartre showed the transition from frivolous freedom to the discovery of terrifying metaphysical freedom. He also showed that the discovery is unbearable (Electra's collapse) and at the same time how, unbearable as it may be, man can save himself and others when he assumes his act, as Orestes did.

Orestes is an apprentice, as Caligula is to a certain extent in Camus' play and Goetz in *Le Diable et le Bon Dieu,* except that Orestes is in the privileged position of not being from anywhere and participating in nothing. When Jupiter tells him about the crimes of Clytemnestra and Aegisthus, he answers: "I couldn't care less. I'm not from here." A bit later, when he begins to dream about the lives of men who are anchored in one place, with their possessions and their worries, he feels a touch of regret but continues all the same to congratulate himself on what he calls his "freedom": "Thank God I am free. Oh! How free I am. And what a superb absence is my soul." There Sartre, with the help of the Greek myth, skipped a certain number of stages. His hero is already outside the blind conformity of collective behavior. Having begun life with the illusion of disengagement taught him by his cosmopolitan pedagogue, Orestes, at the cost of a great struggle and a double murder, succeeds in creating the "royal way" that leads him to assume his own acts. In addition to his pedagogue's impossible frivolity, he has to avoid two temptations: the attitude of those who belong to the oppressed social group, convinced that their oppression is in the order of things, and its correlative, the alliance with a divine order, symbolized by the terrifying and grotesque figure of Jupiter. In other words, Orestes must avoid the freedom of the "spider's web that floats ten feet above the earth at the mercy of the wind," as well as the human and divine traps that transform man into something determined, into "stone." By murdering his mother and her lover, he discovers that an act is nothing more than an enormous and obscene presence, a parasite of man, both exterior and possessive, and he understands that the act is his and only his. He also understands that it has objective consequences: a tyrant's death frees the oppressed people, whose bondage stemmed only from the tyrant. But as far as the act itself is concerned, only the agent can determine its weight, only the agent bears the burden. *Les Mouches* is thus a sumptuous metaphor intended to show men that responsibility is not synonymous with guilt and that the world of men is made up of the impact of actions, whose meaning comes only from the men who committed or suffered them. The play also indicates that the plague (and here we partially rejoin Camus) exists only to the degree that men accept it. Since the plague is in fact no more than the imposition of responsibility on others from the outside, man has the power to counter that act with a contrary act.

This point of view has brought true overtones of tragedy to the theatre of Sartre and Camus. Their heroes love life. They have no particular desire to die, nor do they seek any glorification in death. But they prefer death to a degradation of the man within them. They fall from a high state in that, whether emperors or proud terrorists, they are reduced to suicide, prison, and physical or moral torture. Furthermore, the catastrophe is always accompanied by an awareness which makes them superior to that which crushes them. Their awareness, however, implies not the recognition of a superior order but rather a recognition of man as the one and only value.

On this level Sartre's and Camus' plays can be divided into

two categories: those in which emphasis is put on the agony itself (*Le Malentendu, Huis Clos*) and those in which both writers, succumbing to a kind of proselytism, seem to want to prove that the only way of really being a man among men is to assert one's freedom by rebelling against established orders, mere masks of the absurd (*L'Etat de siège, Les Mouches*). In the second category the theme of the efficacy of action prevails over that of its absurdity. In *L'Etat de siège* the hero dies, but his revolt continues and sea air purifies the pest-ridden city, whereas in *Le Malentendu* Martha's suicide leaves the spectator with a bitter impression. Not that her death is useless, for it has the ultimate value of a protest, but at the end of the play the world closes in on Martha's testimony, just as the heavy, blind earth will cover her body. Yet in both categories, whether the action is effective or only a desperate protest, the basic tragedy and heroism are the same, and the writers' intentions were the same: to bring out, from behind the false face of humanity, man's true condition.

Here the return to man excludes a tableau of daily life and mediocrity. Men are truly men not in their petty and niggardly daily acts but rather at the moment when the idea of man is heroically brought into question through themselves. Consequently, when everyday banalities are suggested, it is only to emphasize their *inauthenticité*—that is, their power to dehumanize the individual by blinding him to his own freedom. In the belief that the portrayal of beings and situations at their most ordinary and average constitutes a misunderstanding of humanism, Sartre and Camus make a distinction between a false humanity—which doubtless merits being portrayed, but not as the true definition of man—and a true humanity, which in the world today can be found in any individual at moments of great crisis or in extreme situations. At such times man really wonders what he is. What counts is the portrayal of man stripped of his pettiness and "the most man possible"—that is, not positively defined but rather suspended between possible definitions—for man can be defined as being outside any definition and at the same time bewilderingly in search of one. The best means of concretely expressing this point of view is the portrayal of characters caught in a paroxysm of situations and acts.

While both the existentialists' and Camus' way of considering the relation between man and his acts is profoundly dramatic in itself, the addition of a supplementary element, bearing also on the basic philosophy, makes the plays of Sartre and Camus not only dramatic but theatrical as well.

In the three chapters devoted to Albert Camus' theatre in her book *Camus,* Germaine Brée comes back time and again to the theme of the play within the play and the characters' own staging of it. The "play" that Caligula deliberately puts on as an answer to the blind performance of the Roman patricians and humanity in general is the most striking example. In *Le Malentendu* the action is made up of two opposed scenarios: Ian's return to his homeland —both written and played by him—and the scenario of melodramatic murders enacted by Martha and his mother. The Plague in *L'Etat de siège* stages his own arrival by sending a comet into the skies of Cadiz as a Prologue; he then transforms the decor and forces the people to play parts, stipulated in advance, in a vast allegory of oppression and dehumanization. Even the heroes of *Les Justes* are cast as actors who are conscious of the roles assigned to them, wear disguises, and devise the staging for a political assassination. Thus Camus' characters are made up of those who write their own dramas and play the parts of their own choosing and those who are subjected to a scenario written by others.

Sartre also seems to have had a similar theatrical vision in most of his plays: the characters in *Huis Clos* act out precisely the drama expected of them by the powers of hell; Goetz is the stage director of Good and Evil in *Le Diable et le Bon Dieu;* Jupiter and Aegisthus organize the collective spectacle of men and the universe in *Les Mouches;* the leading characters in *Nekrassov* and *La Putain respectueuse* are made to play parts written in advance by the powers of this world; and the problems of the actor himself are portrayed in *Kean*, an adaptation of Alexandre Dumas' play.

On the whole, such references to a theatre of life give an especially theatrical savor to the works of Sartre and Camus. Their devices are somewhat comparable to those of Cocteau and Anouilh, but the implications and significance are different. The use of an imposed scenario or a play within the play is meant to furnish a means for action rather than provide a solution to life. The job of the stage director consists in assigning a place and a function to everyone and everything in relation to a given end and a plan of the whole. Defined as part of a whole, things and individual beings must sacrifice their spontaneity and freedom. The tension thus created generally results in an explosion of the elements outside the game or of anyone who freely refuses to enter in. Sometimes the stage director's order wins *(La Putain respectueuse);* most often the unpredictability of the absurd *(Le Malentendu)* or of freedom *(Les Mouches, Les Mains sales, Le Diable et le Bon Dieu, L'Etat de siège)* reduces man's scenarios and the metaphoric scenarios of the gods to nothing; and on occasion the individual or private self, the person who answers for his own fears, loves, and so on, stands out at the height of the action as isolated and separated from the overall plan *(Les Justes, Morts sans sépulture).*

The great directors are the oppressors, the liberators, and the experimenters. Jupiter and Aegisthus, the Plague, the American senator, and in certain respects the Communist party belong to the first category; the revolutionaries and Martha, in relation to herself, to the second; Caligula and Goetz to the third. In other words, this particular form of second degree theatre, as compared to that found in other works, is presented not as an aesthetic solution of the absurd but as a metaphor of the oppressive order as well as the necessary means to explode its lies and injustices. Whether mask or antimask, it takes the form of a scenario written in advance and, through a necessary antithesis, evokes the themes of freedom and contingency. Anouilh also used the device in

*Antigone, L'Alouette,* and other plays in which the heroes refuse to play the game of a scenario written in advance, but his solution lies in the play itself, in the very theatricalism of the conflict, whereas in Sartre and Camus theatrical creation is always a means, never a reconciliatory end.

In *Le Diable et le Bon Dieu* Goetz is an extraordinary actor who identifies with the roles of his choice. Several times during the play he is called "buffoon." He acts for an audience—God— but finally discovers that his "play" has been no more than a bloody farce and that the spectator he counted on was missing: from the balcony of the sky only a gaping emptiness looks down upon him. Just as in Camus' play Caligula tried to be pure Evil, Goetz tried to be one hundred per cent Good. While both are inventors and challenge the order of the world, their social experiments leave them with emptiness and negation, since a desire for the absolute in the name of man leads to the destruction of man and the loss of humanity. As Germaine Brée points out, such imposition of the absolute is much the same as the Plague's absolute and abstract order in *L'Etat de siège.*

Having brought their heroes to the experience of nothingness and the consciousness of a universe without hope and without illusion, both writers found it necessary to reintegrate life. In *Caligula* Cheréa, who "lives within the truth, without hope and without delusion . . . recognizes the relative human order in which reign 'those truths of the flesh' that are lived and not demonstrated."[2] Others return to life through the concrete tasks imposed by urgent poblems: Goetz finally agrees to use his talents as a military leader by helping the peasant rebellion; Diego, in *L'Etat de siège,* succeeds in convincing his fellow citizens to open the doors of the city and let in the sea air.

The basic conflict, then, is threefold: the comedy of a world of illusions (false justifications) as opposed to the theatre or antitheatre of those who seek the absolute, and both opposed to the

2. Germaine Brée, *Camus,* p. 167.

plain fact of existence as it is lived or to be lived, individually and collectively. In Camus existence as such is expressed more or less allegorically in the character Cheréa in *Caligula* and the Mediterranean richness of certain images in *L'Etat de siège* and *Le Malentendu*. Sartre expresses it less poetically in Hoederer's vitality and relation to objects in *Les Mains sales,* Hilda's love in *Le Diable et le Bon Dieu,* and *Nekrassov's* gaiety. But since it is most often outside the play, it can only be alluded to. Man's unchanging tragedy lies both in the search for it and in the tension between the first two elements of the conflict.

Despite great similarities in basic philosophy and theatrical vision, Sartre and Camus differ profoundly on the aesthetic level, just as in a comparable way *La Nausée* differs from *L'Etranger,* or *La Peste* from *Les Chemins de la liberté.*

Sartre's dramatic universe is nearer to realism or traditional naturalism. Eric Bentley[3] points out the fact that *Huis Clos* is essentially Strindbergian in tone and a drawing-room comedy in form. Indeed, three Boulevard melodramas can easily be made out of each of the three characters' lives: a frivolous young lady who killed her child, a rather nasty lesbian who led her friend to suicide, a pacifistic journalist who deserted in time of war—all psychological dramas with social implications and perfect material for a "well-made" play. Even the setting for each drama is suggested: the lesbian's room with its gas stove, the newspaper office with the editors in shirt sleeves, and the elegant room in Switzerland with its windows giving onto the lake. Sartre deliberately chose three rather typical news items and kept certain "true" details—that is, their naturalist color.

When Camus chooses a news item *(Le Malentendu),* he chooses an exceptional one and then strips it of anything that might evoke everyday life. Moreover, he eliminates any familiarity or banality from language. Actually, Camus' characters all speak the same

3. *The Playwright as a Thinker.*

language—a kind of stylized and intense common denominator which wipes out any naturalist implications behind their purified intentions and feelings—whereas Sartre, although he brands his characters with his own images and syntax, fills their dialogue with expressions and devices that closely copy naturalist "reality." One has only to compare the hangman's lines in the fourth act of *Les Justes* with those of Hoederer's bodyguards in *Les Mains sales* or the guards of Apollo's temple in *Les Mouches*. In the case of characters who would normally use slang, Camus keeps it to a minimum, while Sartre deliberately uses it as much as possible, along with syntactical ellipses.

Much the same may be said in regard to form. In Sartre there are frequent references to traditional or familiar genres: *vaudeville*, drama, historical drama. The decors themselves are conventional: real rooms, real garrets, and real German countryside. Even a fantastic setting like the Second Empire drawing room in *Huis Clos* is fantastic because of its realism: the Barbedienne bronze statue, the Louis Philippe couch, and the bricks that obstruct the window are scenically effective only if they look real and are not artistically suggested. In that respect, Sartre has contributed considerably less to the development of theatre than Camus, who avoided most references to familiar genres, aimed at a very special economy in his settings as well as language, and launched out into experiments of highly stylized total theatre.

Yet Sartre had reasons for what he did. He wanted first to get the spectator on familiar ground and then gradually bring him into existentialist drama, far from that familiar ground. In *Huis Clos*, for example, the naturalism of each character's "case" and the realism of language and decor create an image of the beyond that is acceptable to audiences accustomed by films and theatre to seeing death represented in very earthly forms. The true subject of the play, however, is revealed on a third level. Beyond the anecdotal interest of a few adventures or perversions and the modernist pathos of the allegory of hell, it concerns the relation of one consciousness to another, the search for a definition of the self with

the help of others, and the realization that the presence and judgment of others is necessary and yet leads to an impasse.[4] On that
level the whole takes on all its meaning, and we discover that the
play is not a metaphor of hell but that the image of hell is a metaphor of the hopeless suffering of individuals in search of their
definitions in the eyes of others, yet constantly brought back to
themselves.

Garcin's reticence in telling how he deserted and especially how
he physically fell apart at the time of his execution is an excellent
subject for a naturalistic psychological drama (the pacifist has a
shameful secret: he acted out of cowardice), and part of the dialogue is directed toward that drama but at one point turns away
from it and moves toward an existentialist perspective. Once it has
been established that an inquiry into the motives for an act does
not reveal the act's meaning, Garcin's hopeless tragedy lies in the
fact that he is unable to determine the meaning of his life by himself and is condemned to live between two women—one totally indifferent to the question and the other who, needing "the suffering
of others in order to exist," decides that he has been cowardly and
is thus satisfied with the spectacle of his shame.

Sartre's plays lead the spectator from the universe of perception,
common sense, and psychological or aesthetic habits to an existentialist conclusion, often difficult in its newness. What he shows
essentially is that his vision of the world is inherent in the normal
universe. His method consists in bringing it out progressively, and
often the progression itself makes up the greater part of the play.

*Les Mains sales* is presented as a politico-detective drama in the
form of an investigation and a trial, based on a simple question
comparable to the suspense-provoking questions in melodrama:
Why did Hugo kill Hoederer? The suspense is all the more acute
in that the spectator knows that Hugo's life depends on the answer.
The investigation itself, which takes up six of the seven tableaux,
is in the form of a flashback concerned only with the simple fact

4. *Huis Clos* was first published in *L'Arbalète,* No. 8 (Lyon, 1943), as *Les
Autres* or *The Others.*

of Hoederer's death, leaving the murder committed by Hugo in all its ambiguity. Sartre played the game of detective-story melodrama according to the rules, but he stopped short of melodramatic satisfaction. The "secret" one is supposed to uncover is not uncovered and it becomes increasingly clear that it is impossible to uncover it. In a sense the naturalistic melodrama destroys itself under one's very eyes, leaving hero and spectator open to whatever lies ahead. Having finished his long demonstration and created the necessary vacuum, Sartre can then go on to lead both hero and spectator into the true subject of his play: in the last fifteen minutes one discovers that the meaning of Hoederer's murder does not lie in Hugo's reasons for it, which in any case remain ambiguous; his true motive is the one he chooses *afterward,* when, fully aware of the situation, he determines—through his own death—the meaning of the situation and the value of Hoederer's life and his own. Somewhat the same gradual transition takes place within Goetz and the spectator in *Le Diable et le Bon Dieu,* although its dialectic is not as clear because of the play's vast proportions.

In Camus' plays also, spectator and hero are led to make a common discovery, and the element of detective-story suspense—the interest in what will happen next—is one dimension of his theatre. But the level of the play's true subject is given straight away. There is almost no transition from one vision of the universe to another. *Caligula* begins with the Emperor having just discovered the world of freedom and the absurd. Had Sartre written *Caligula,* he would doubtless have shown the hero making his decisive discovery in the first act, beginning with Drusilla's death, and would go on to show how Caligula was shocked by it and how it led up to his final experiment. In Camus' play the curtain goes up on an imaginary world whose dimensions are given from the very beginning and once and for all—hence the dual impression of classical economy and intransigence.

Camus' uncompromising aesthetics is based on a symbolic vision, far indeed from Sartre's. The Germany of *Le Diable et le Bon Dieu,* deformed and stylized as it may be, *is* Germany during the period of the peasant revolts, whereas the Rome of *Caligula* has as little reality as the Naples of certain of Molière's comedies or the Poland of *Ubu Roi.*[5] Sartre takes a historic event and brings out its significance. Camus starts with a general dramatic conflict and then embodies it fictionally. In other words, symbol prevails over locality. Thus, despite a few clear allusions to the present state of Spain, the Cadiz of *L'Etat de siège* represents as imaginary a locality as the North African city in his novel *La Peste.* It is quite simply a city in a dry, sun-scorched country near the sea, which enables Camus to make use of his familiar myths.

While Sartre generally first tells a story, rich enough in realistic elements to be self-contained, Camus constructs a poetic allegory based on a conflict. In her book on Camus, Germaine Brée points out that Camus' most obviously anecdotal play, *Le Malentendu,* "is entirely symbolical." In *Caligula, Les Justes,* and *L'Etat de siège* the traditional creation of characters is replaced by the symbolic embodiment of possible attitudes to a dramatic conflict. Consequently, Camus lays himself open to the traditional criticism of allegorical literature—the contrived embodiment of ideas or entities. But in all aesthetic sincerity and by means of an immediate stylization of dialogue and characters, Camus does present his plays as intellectual creations from the moment the curtain goes up.

Less popular than his other plays but more ambitious and per-haps closer to the "modern tragedy" he sought, *L'Etat de siège* represents a synthesis of Camus' aesthetics and general ideas, com-bining the philosophy of acts and extreme situations with a certain form of symbolism. In his preface Camus explains how Jean-Louis Barrault, inspired by Artaud, was haunted by the meaning and symbol of the plague and wanted to create a play around it. Camus, having just published his novel *La Peste,* was the obvious

5. Despite Camus' research. See Brée, *Camus,* p. 146.

man to write the script. In this case the symbol was given first. Since he had already worked with it on several levels in his novel, Camus' job consisted in making the maledictions that crush man coincide with the physical ravages of the plague. Moreover, the metaphor is not spontaneous; it is the result of the collective effort of Artaud, Barrault, and Camus. *L'Etat de siège* is thus characteristic of Camus' art in that it is the development and extension of a simile he had already worked out; it is a theatrical exercise on a given subject: organized totalitarianism as the plague of the modern world.

The plague itself is embodied in a rather portly man in uniform, who takes over the government in Cadiz with the help of his secretary, Death. The symbol is obvious and becomes increasingly so at the beginning of the second act, when the Kafkaesque satire on bureaucracy starts to sound like Courteline-become-metaphysical. In addition, every character in the play, when confronted with the Plague, embodies a simple attitude, a commonplace opinion or way of behaving—the most important, next to the rebellious hero's, being that of Nada, who by his very name represents man at the level of nihilistic despair. Allegorical as it may be, however, the play is no less "existentialist" in its general philosophy: the hero successfully counters the established order with the refusal of a free being—a refusal which, ironically enough, almost seduces Death but for which the hero finally does pay with his life. Moreover, the play contains symbols of all the necessary existentialist stages: *inauthenticité,* rebellion, confidence in life despite everything.

A "total" play in its themes, Camus and Barrault wanted also to make it a total play on a scenic level: abstract dialogue, lyrical tirades, individual and collective pantomime, spectacular effects. Both totalities are meant to correspond in the alternation between the comments of the real people (lovers, fishermen, and so on) and the speeches of personified abstractions (the Plague and Death). While the play fails in part because of the fact that the whole is more an intellectual allegory than a living synthesis, it is one of the rare attempts at uniting modern philosophy and modern theatre.

Camus' and Sartre's aesthetics are as different as their general ideologies are similar. Where in Sartre innovations in form are secondary to content, in Camus aesthetic consciousness is inseparable from the substance. Yet their intentions are much alike in that both have tried to give French audiences theatre that is neither an agreeable repetition of past masterpieces, even recent ones, nor a purely modernist aesthetic thrill. They have also agreed on the idea of an art that is completely concerned with and conceived in terms of our times. Their common purpose has been both to describe the man of today and to write for the man of today. Such is doubtless the intention of all writers, but in Sartre and Camus it takes the form of a conscious rule, affirmed and reaffirmed as a writer's first duty. An acute consciousness of the modern world and a true identification with its problems and demands have determined the themes and aesthetics of both. And although Camus had time and again refused to be labeled "existentialist," he *can* be considered committed or *engagé,* if literary *engagement* is taken in its broadest sense, as writing for one's time, directly or indirectly about one's time, with man's freedom as an ultimate goal.

In the light of such an attitude many literary positions must be rejected as survivals of a dead past. Psychological analyses in classical terms, reducing man to a determinism which is now thought to be precisely not man; historical and picturesque reconstruction for itself; freezing man in the ice of dead essences; the exclusive cult of beauty; placing the meaning of the world outside man—all are eliminated, not absolutely but relatively: the present and man's tragedy at this moment of history are considered more important and rich enough to take precedence over any other concern.

Thus the central problem of Malraux's novels has been brought to the theatre by Sartre and Camus. They chose their subjects among the most burning issues of our times: wars, oppression, rebellions, revolutions, and through them reached the so-called universal themes—but stated them in new terms. Instead of traditional psychologism, the entire human being is called into question.[6]

Camus' allegorization and his refusal to emphasize, as does Sartre, the topical aspect of his dramas show that he aimed at a nonhistoric universality. He does, however, keep today's problems always in the foreground. His choice of the plague as a symbol was determined less by its timeless universality than by its particularly violent activity at the present time. "Today the technique is perfected," says the Plague in *L'Etat de siège,* after having gone over the plagues of the past "when the idea was there. But not the whole idea."[7] In other words, although the plague is doubtless continuous and permanent, it is at its height in the modern world. "Codified" to perfection, it is close to an absolute victory over subjugated man. Yet today is also a time of hope among men who have understood that they are free.

In trying to make this clear in their plays and to reach the largest possible public, Sartre in his works as a whole and Camus in *L'Etat de siège* were often forced, given the difficulty of their philosophies, into simplifications and sometimes even concessions. Sartre compromised by using Boulevard details and facile naturalist techniques, especially flagrant in *Les Séquestrés d'Altona.* He also spelled out certain of his arguments in easily assimilated formulas and, by seeming intellectually clearer, sacrificed many nuances necessary to a complete understanding of his philosophy, while losing in dramatic reality as well. As for Camus, his often abstract maxims, used as articulations, are sometimes more intellectual than dramatic.

6. As if by chance, a whole group of "committed" plays appeared on Paris stages during the forties and fifties, presenting the point of view of the right as well as the left. Aside from the Anouilh plays that skirt existentialism, the most interesting works, in reaction or in imitation, were, at the time, Thierry-Maulnier's *La Maison de la nuit* (1953) and Colette Audry's *Soledad* (1956).

7. The term Idea, as an expression of the abstract system that crushes man, can also be found in the Inquisitor's speeches in Anouilh's *L'Alouette.*

For theirs is a theatre of ideas—exactly the kind Gide had hoped to see created by Giraudoux. Neither Sartre nor Camus are primarily playwrights. Sartre is, above all, a pofessional philosopher. Camus is obviously more of an artist and was always active in the world of theatre,[8] but all of his works are dominated by intellectual searching and the examination of ideas. What distinguishes their plays from other "philosophical" theatre, however, is the absolutely dramatic and concrete nature of their philosophy itself. The fundamental problem of the definition of man and the world is truly embodied in living acts.

8. For example, his collaboration with the "Théâtre du Travail," founded in Algiers in 1935, and his many adaptations.

PART III


DIALECTIC CONTINUED

# CHAPTER 8

# POETIC WORDS AND DEEDS:
## AUDIBERTI, GHELDERODE, VAUTHIER, SCHEHADE

Historical perspective has made it relatively easy to distinguish the major playwrights of the prewar period—Giraudoux, Claudel, Cocteau—and there is no great problem in isolating those of more recent date, such as Salacrou, Anouilh, Montherlant, Sartre, and Camus. During the late forties, the fifties, and the early sixties, however, many new and disparate works—always revolutionary, often promising, sometimes enchanting—have kept French theatre in a constant state of alert from one year to the next. Among the new crop of writers Eugène Ionesco, Samuel Beckett, and Jean Genet are the unquestionable masters, and even though their works have recently been bypassed by certain types of neorealism—in the form of chamber pieces or epic drama—they remain central to the new theatre in France.

It is possible that the next years will bring revelations of the magnitude of Beckett's *En Attendant Godot,* Ionesco's early plays, or Genet's *Les Paravents*. And such works may well be created by certain of the playwrights catalogued in the following chapters. Of course some of those mentioned are already dead—Ghelderode, Audiberti, Boris Vian—but they died so recently that no one can say whether or not their innovations and very individual perspectives will form the basis for some future theatre. In any case, living or dead, the playwrights considered in the following catalogue represent, in a somewhat unsifted mass, the life of French theatre during the last few years—that is, theatre as we indirectly have tried to define it throughout this book: ambitious, significant, historically original, and (at the risk of sounding redundant) eminently theatrical. Some may turn out to be peripheral, others may end up as mere curiosities in a literary museum, still others may be remembered as no more than momentarily dazzling reflections; yet at the moment they would all seem to exploit the new possibilities of the stage, and they all speak to audiences of today in the terms of today.

Within this arbitrary arrangement of necessarily disordered material, many of the playwrights mentioned would perhaps be surprised to find themselves placed side by side. Yet they may be grouped together by reason of their common interest in extending the possibilities of theatre that had already been discovered and exploited by their elders, in the realms of language and scenic freedom. Furthermore, they are not trying to make theatre comfortable; indeed, all of them more or less specialize in discomfort, whether it be provoked by an image of violence, existential anxiety, or a strange inner universe. To achieve their effects, many use the devices of farce, a genre that has been very actively revived in France during the past twenty years. The farces of Molière and the *vaudevilles* of Labiche and Feydeau have been restaged not only in state but in avant-garde theatres. Imitations, almost pastiches, of traditional farce, such as Claude Santelli's *La Famille Arlequin,* have been produced. And, most importantly, there has been a glorious revival of Alfred Jarry's scandalous *Ubu,* first on stage, then on television. In fact, Jarry's monster sets the tone for modern farce: while its form varies from the acts of the Frères Jacques to the plays of Ionesco, its humor is always sacrilegious—and consciously, in fact deliberately so. Its humor is also "dark," since life itself is brought into question. Carried to an extreme, this tendency results in certain of Beckett's short plays: farces that don't make one laugh at all.

Nevertheless, while farce is one of the dominant notes of this new theatre, it would be as much a mistake to lump all the plays into that category as it would be to systematically label them "absurd." In some, lyricism stifles the farce; in others, an earthy well-being triumphs over apparent absurdity. That certain characters are comical or pitiable does not necessarily mean that they are clowns or miserable buffoons; that the style of certain playwrights is enigmatic and distorted does not necessarily imply that it denies the existence of an order, however obscure. Moreover, some of the writers have had their taste for the absurd tempered by the influence of Brecht and a new sense of the epic form; others have found their taste for farce subdued by the notion of human grandeur—often of a very gloomy sort but, relatively speaking, no gloomier than that of many characters in ancient tragedy.

Perhaps these playwrights of a new theatre, all of them caught up in a general movement that is constantly varied by diverse or even contradictory influences and by their individual temperaments, can best be described as "rocks lost in the middle of the sea."[1] In any case, they may be divided chronologically and by the dominant tone of their works. On the whole, a distinction may be made between the poets, the playwrights of the absurd, and, deriving from the absurd or countering it, those who aim at a new kind of epic drama. This chapter will deal with the first group.

In 1946, when he staged Jacques Audiberti's *Quoat-Quoat,* André Reybaz opened the door to a new invasion of the theatre by those

1. The comparison was made by Guy Dumur in "Les Poètes au théâtre," *Théâtre de France,* No. 4 (1954), p. 46.

who might be called poets—that is, by playwrights whose most striking originality lies in their verbal imagination. Audiberti himself once declared that a play is a literary genre like any other and does not depend on being performed. While he gradually discovered the exigencies of performance and tried to comply with them, he remained primarily a manipulator of language. In fact his joy in writing words was so narcissistic that when one of his last plays, *La Fourmi dans le corps,* was performed in 1962 at the Comédie Française, some of the Parisian critics were still accusing him of verbalism and of writing gibberish.

Yet Audiberti's technique is more than logorrhea. In most of his adventure-comedies the poet's imagination is given free rein. Indeed, it draws on all the sources (farce, the Boulevard, melodrama) and goes off in all directions. Audiberti does not disdain apparently facile effects: the intrusion of type characters, such as the volcanic and revolutionary Mexican woman in *Quoat-Quoat,* or quick-change artists like those in *Les Naturels du Bordelais* and *L'Effet Glapion;* behavior that is contrary to the situation or state of the characters, such as the Prime Minister's arrogance toward his king in *Le Mal court,* the Princess' striptease in front of the Cardinal in the same play, or the puny son's unexpected success with thirty women in *Les Femmes du Bœuf;* and the distortion of historial characters like Joan of Arc in *Pucelle* or Turenne in *La Fourmi dans le corps.* Even if such devices are not very original in themselves, they do have shock value, whether comical or disturbing, and their boldness creates anxiety, horror, or mystery. The scene in *Quoat-Quoat* in which the hero tells his secret to the captain's daughter, the moment in *Le Mal court* in which the Princess describes her own body, the transformation of the characters into crickets in *Les Naturels,* the final horrors of *La Hobereaute,* Turenne's clownery with the cannonball in *La Fourmi* are so many quasi-surrealist or terrifying extensions of situations otherwise parodic and simple.

The effect of Audiberti's imagination—uncontrolled in regard to the quality or quantity of its products and at its most inventive in the matter of events or deliriously colorful language—is to disclose a monstrous reality behind all the jesting or beneath the absurdity of a preposterous adventure. For his drama is built on the relations between a surface life and deeply hidden primitive forces. The surface, whether contemporary or historical, consists of a chaos of events that is made to appear funny by a use of comical images, puns, and distortions of syntax. But that tumultuous and sparkling verbal flow both contains and reveals hidden forces: the god Quoat-Quoat, the Evil that spreads, the earthly and mythical forces of *Ampélour,* the natural forces of *Les Femmes du Bœuf* or *Pucelle,* the beast of *La Fête noire.* One of these forces recurs regularly—the power of the flesh, sometimes included in the general idea of Evil *(Le Mal court)* and sometimes concretely represented *(La Logeuse, La Fourmi).*

No doubt the dramatic tension of Audiberti's works is created by an awareness of the fact that such forces exist, and in this respect his universe is close to Antonin Artaud's. In general, the buried forces are monstrous, and when they break out, they do so epidemically, violently, and degradingly. True, Audiberti would seem to waver: the concrete richness of his vocabulary and the "healthy" way he sometimes evokes flesh and sensual appetites combine real terror with an often joyous force of attraction. If the Princess in *Le Mal court,* having willingly lost her virginity, becomes a savage queen, the canoness Pic-Saint-Pop, who forced her friend Du Marquet to rape her in *La Fourmi dans le corps,* gives in to the joys of the senses. The canoness having discovered love thanks to a little foundling, ultimately transforms that love into charity: when the baby is taken away from her and she is given, in its place, a drooling dwarf who barks like a dog, she adopts him, saying: "Poor dogs that we are! Poor race of bears and wolves!" Of course, Du Marquet and Pic-Saint-Pop will marry—but Evil continues to spread.

Despite the ambiguity that colors the moral consequences of succumbing to the hidden forces, it is their haunting presence— both dreaded and desired—that characterizes Audiberti's drama. Although they come to the surface in such obvious ways as sex or murder, Audiberti generally invests them with semireality, thus allowing the spectator to believe in their existence but also in their supernatural nature. The language, descriptions, and allusions create a state of belief in their possible incarnation, but if the incarnation has to be too precise, it is hidden: both the baby and the dwarf in *La Fourmi dans le corps* are heard but never seen, just as at the end of *La Fête noire,* at exactly the right moment in the spectacle, there is a mixture of concrete phenomena, all characteristic of the monster, but not the monster. Actually, *La Fête noire* is resolved by a murderous act that is strictly human. Thus Audiberti's imagination, like that of certain of his poet-heroes, moves to the very edge of the incarnation that leads to man's ruin or that devours him, but never goes so far as allegory or personified abstraction. When in *L'Effet Glapion* he popularizes the theme of the creative or evocative imagination, he divests it of its disturbing magic. But in his best works, on the contrary, Audiberti uses language and plot in such a way as to suggest the mystery of life in all its horror.

Doubtless a good example of poetry *of* the theatre, Audiberti's works are also and unfortunately too often an example of poetry *in* the theatre. While the verbal delirium evokes the richness of a threatening or threatened reality, it sometimes ends by turning in on itself, evoking, in its complacency, neither the absurd nor the mysterious: all that is left are words—and obscurity. Although the onslaught of curious images, mixing the familiar with the fantastic, and the variations of the variations on a central theme communicate the writer's joy of freedom and give the plays their poetic atmosphere and their savor, often the verbal techniques attract more attention than they should, become wearisome in their useless abundance, and somehow make the mask opaque instead of contributing to its transparency.

In 1949 another poet was introduced on the French stage: Michel de Ghelderode, a Belgian who had been writing for the theatre since 1919 and had been performed in his own country since 1925.

French directors have been drawing upon his plays for their repertoires since 1949; his complete works have been published by
Gallimard; and in the United States, after David Grossvogel had
given him primary importance in his book *The Self-Conscious
Stage in Modern French Drama,* university dramatic groups and
off-Broadway companies have taken the lead and produced certain
of his works.

The surface characteristics of Ghelderode's universe are dazzling. In many of his plays masqueraders, grotesque figures, living
corpses, gluttonous and lustful men and women frantically move
about in a decor of purple shadows, full of strong smells, and throw
violent, foul, or mysterious phrases at each other in highly colored
language filled with Belgian idioms, archaisms, and shrieks. Even
in the plays where the language is closest to modern French, the
dialogue and long speeches are profuse and frenetic. There is no
rest in Ghelderode's theatre; the shock is permanent. Everything
is pushed toward a paroxysm of language and spectacle—a flam-
boyant theatre, based on Flemish culture, its legends, its humor, its
puppets, and its painters, from Brueghel the elder to James Ensor.
But in overstressing Ghelderode's Flemish background, so obvious
in itself, one is in danger of losing sight of his works' deeper
value and of seeing them only as an overwhelming display of
folklore. A joyful or macabre kermis, his theatre uses the village
fair, the mountebank's stage, overcrowded cabarets, and the swarm-
ing streets of the red-light districts as an image of man's condition.
Thus the picturesque quality of this tumultuous world becomes
more than just a curiosity: rather than set up a barrier of exoticism,
it heightens the colors of man's everyday world.

Ghelderode was aware of the reciprocal relations between life
and the masquerade of carnival. The plays that most clearly present theatricalism as a theory are those devoted to the world of
theatre itself—*Sortie de l'acteur* and *Trois Acteurs, un drame.*
Often a character and his theatrical image are opposed or juxtaposed. In *La Mort du Docteur Faust,* Faust meets the actor who is
playing Faust; the devil in the play within the play is ridiculed by a

real devil; and of course there are two Marguerites. In *Barabbas,* while the Crucifixion takes place behind the scenes, a clown mimes the Passion on the fairground stage. Again in *La Mort du Docteur Faust,* once the actor Faust is killed in the street by a crowd who has taken him for the real Faust, the latter—also wanting to kill the actor, who had escaped from him—shoots *himself* in the chest. In *Barabbas* the clown who was miming Jesus knifes Barabbas in the back. Although these effects, midway between Pirandello's and Genet's, may sometimes be somewhat oversimple or, on the contrary, rather obscure, they do help to make Ghelderode's works a kind of theatre of theatre. Using clowns, mimes, jesters, and masqueraders, Ghelderode opposes more charitable images of Creation with his vision of life as a parody of Creation, as a painful Farce. In the end the Farce is reality, the grotesque mask is the truth of all beings, and the madness of the macabre kermis is the underlying drive of souls.

One substance of this enormous Farce is felt in all its frankness and weight—the flesh. It may sometimes have its charms, as in *Hop Signor!,* with the executioner Larose, the "handsome blond athlete" who chews roses. But usually it is deformed, obscene, stinking, and always demanding. Brought into play by every possible means, it nails the characters to earth. Even in suffering it is the object of baroque acceptance, not of negative distress, as in Beckett's theatre.

More generally, Ghelderode's theatre is made up of matter, a stuff that is forced on all the senses. Flesh, crimson velvet, gold, and excrement are an essential part of both the spectacle and the language. Ghelderode's poetry consists in constantly harking back to that bath of matter. Lavishly handled, it leads to nothing other than itself and to the appetites of which it is the object: avarice, gluttony, or sexual desire. Constantly present to all the senses, matter is the stuff of the characters' actions and excitement.

Ghelderode used the device of baroque amplification to create a burlesque of man's condition. Most of his characters are kept in a state of indignity by the weight of their bodies, their physical deformations, their sensual relations with other matter. Any objects that would ordinarily be accepted as signs of grandeur are shown in decay or given monstrous forms, so that the usual symbols are replaced by the recognition of matter as such: in *Hop Signor!* the garden resembles "some old forgotten cemetery," and in *Fastes d'enfer* the hangings in the episcopal palace are falling in shreds.

All this would be no more than a savage masquerade and pure farce, colored by a theatrical awareness of life, if every play did not have a more or less explicit higher appeal. Some of what Ghelderode is saying is fairly simple. For example, in *Christophe Colomb* Columbus does not set out to discover America, that material object which satisfies such puppets as the character l'Homme-Foule; he sails away out of boredom, seeking "the ideal sphere" and, in fact, his own true essence. In *L'Ecole des bouffons,* while rebellion seems to be the solution that would bring Folial's disciples out of their misery, a reversal of the situation reveals a higher truth: the condition of all great art is cruelty. But the pole of dramatic tension opposed to the massive and weighty presence of matter is chiefly represented by death and its mysteries. The allegory of *La Ballade du Grand Macabre,* Lazarus with roots growing out of him in *Mademoiselle Jaïre,* all the hangmen, all the corpses are concrete manifestations of death, which haunts Ghelderode's works. Death is within matter itself, eating it away, deforming it, tearing it apart.

The actual evidence of the flesh is what gives rise to the mystery of death. And the very fact of inevitable death, sometimes at the end of the farce, brutal and ironical as in *Magie rouge,* sometimes the very subject of the play, as in *Mademoiselle Jaïre,* gives Ghelderode's theatre its tragic aspect. On the whole, the plays are constructed according to two different patterns: either they are similar to certain types of baroque and classical comedies of intrigue, although the artificial happy endings of traditional comedy are replaced by a necessary death—a negation of the life of the flesh and the senses, of indeed the very motivation of the plot *(Hop Signor!,*

*Magie rouge)*—or both levels are constantly juxtaposed, so that an awareness of their permanent relationship creates the play's tension *(La Ballade du Grand Macabre, Mademoiselle Jaïre, Fastes d'enfer)*. Fundamentally an annihilator of the characters' universe of intrigue and sensual pleasure, death is also the bearer of meanings that give tragedy its transcendency and always more or less transform the play into a mystery: in *Sire Halewyn* the union in death of Purmelende and Sire Halewyn, a frenzied and gothic transposition of the theme of Judith; in *Hop Signor!* the union of the executioner Larose and Marguerite; in *Mademoiselle Jaïre* the union of Jaïre and Lazarus, both risen from the dead, modified by the expectation of a second death and a fusion with God.

Since the conflict is, above all, one between death and the flesh, it is only natural that Ghelderode often allude to the mystery that best expresses it: the raising of Lazarus. It is also natural that within that mystery he choose and develop the theme of *jam putet* in all its horror. Like the customers' wives who frequent the cabaret in *Pantagleize,* living humanity "has the embalming stench of a mortuary."[2] The smells of the kermis are comparable to the odors of corpses, which are themselves held up to ridicule in the enormous olfactory confusion at the end of *Fastes d'enfer*. Ghelderode's force lies precisely in the skillful mixture of the greatest horror and the most knockabout farce, which may be compared to a terrifying ceremony of the Spanish Inquisition mimed by the merry players of a Flemish fair.[3] Neither element can exist without the other; each issues from the other. When the farce is not vigorous enough, as in *Sire Halewyn,* the play is reduced to a pompous Romantic-symbolist melodrama; for the mystery of death is so grandiose that it must be enveloped in rites, in ceremonies, which of themselves turn to buffoonery.

Ghelderode's theatre indicates a way toward the realization of a primordial drama in which tragic horror and the frankest guffaws are indissolubly mixed. His use of local tradition carried to its

2. *Pantagleize*, Act I, scene 2.
3. See Pol Vandromme, *Ghelderode*, pp. 72–87.

extreme possibilities is not far removed from the method of the Elizabethans and the Spanish dramatists. He touches on the primitive joys of the body, its appetites and their satisfaction, which are inseparable from the ambiguous fear of individual or collective death. Antiphilosophical and even anti-intellectual, his works are the long and instinctive cry of a soul in misery, imprisoned in matter that is both sumptuous and rotting. A thousand forms of death and the devil pervade Ghelderode's universe, as in the Middle Ages. Even Christ has his place in it *(Barabbas),* but he keeps stubbornly silent.

In contrast to the spectacular luxuriance of Audiberti and Ghelderode is the scenic concentration of Jean Vauthier, whose characters number two or three at the most, and whose plays are set in in a single enclosed room, recalling Strindberg or Sartre's *Huis Clos.* Yet Vauthier has this in common with the poet-playwrights: his characters' verbal delirium and a suggestion of transcendent mystery.

With their endless monologues and dialogues written in a frantic style, mixing bold metaphors and philosophical formulas with the vulgarities of modern speech, Vauthier's plays are characterized by a permanent and ever-increasing tension, resolved at the end by a single and violent act that is meant to bring redemption or revelation—at least to the characters. Each play is presented as a kind of verbal and physical ballet or corrida. When two characters are onstage at once, they never stop looking for each other, pushing each other away, touching each other, or trying to avoid each other's hands or eyes; when they talk, they interrupt each other or ignore each other or seize on an apparently innocuous word of the other's and blow it up into a sign of sin or of lying or of hatred. In fact, the action takes place completely within the characters and is extremely savage.

Such theatre would seem to aim at creating, on a small stage, a kind of pure drama which at the same time would be a total theatre. Indeed, the growing exasperation of language and physical movements within a closed space dazes not only the characters but the audience and the actors themselves, leading everyone toward a both exhausting and liberating climax. Even the playwright is deeply involved: Vauthier's desire to go through the whole theatrical experience himself is indicated in the published texts, where he usually makes only typographical distinctions between the dialogue, his actual invention of the dialogue, the staging, his personal comments, and the general impression he is trying to communicate, thus becoming not merely an author but his own director and his own audience.

On the surface Vauthier's situations could not be simpler: the relationship between a man and a woman *(Capitaine Bada)*, the relationship between a man, a woman, and an old nurse *(Les Prodiges)*, and a man in search of his past *(Le Personnage combattant)*. But these simple situations are pretexts for plunging deep into the souls of his characters, endlessly questioning their sincerity, cruelly dissecting human relationships in general, and pointing up a kind of metaphysical egotism. Vauthier's male characters vainly seek salvation, and in the process they experience the most frightful inner destruction, which they communicate to the audience through the spectacle of their desperately strained bodies and their shrieks torn from the depths of anguish.

*Le Personnage combattant, fortissimo* is at the most extreme point of this extreme theatre. When he performed it in 1955, Jean-Louis Barrault accomplished as great a feat as he did in 1935 with Faulkner's *As I Lay Dying*. The play presents a character struggling with himself in a universe of objects and noises. He is a "character between two texts"—an elegant writer in a hotel room, trying to rewrite a novel he had begun in the same room many years before, when he was still young. At present he is opposed to the writer and young man that he was. With no allegorical personification of the past to destroy the living synthesis of the present, the world of objects through which the young man had sought to make contact with the real is both described as he had formerly experienced it and newly experienced in the present. The Character tries desperately to reconstruct the conditions of his past experience, for he believes that his salvation lies in being able to grasp the objects as such.

But the objects have somehow betrayed him, for they are no longer the same. The room has been strangely decorated and has been contaminated by others. Even what happens outside does not correspond to his expectations: the noise from neighboring rooms interrupts his work and his experience; the trains that pass just outside his window do not come by at the appointed hours. Besides, he himself has changed. He has become rich; more importantly, he has matured. From time to time, as if to mirror that growth and aging, the hotel employee appears, shady and brutal—an adult form of the little homosexual boy the Character had known in the past.

The Character struggles in a prison made up of time that has passed, the resistance of objects, absurd and uncontrollable circumstances, and his own nature. Constantly thrown back on himself, powerless to break the walls of his prison, he experiences a night of agony, in every sense of the word, at the junction of every possible exasperation. He is between two definitions of himself—an exemplary situation—and his cries and agitation are thus valid for any anguished struggle.

The conclusion of a Vauthier play is always ambiguous: though allusions are made to liberation or even to the salvation of the male character, irony (*Capitaine Bada*) or obscurity (*Les Prodiges*) leave the spectator in a state of doubt as to the effectiveness of the brutal act—murder or accident—which immediately precedes the end. The final impression is more one of theatrical release than of a real metamorphosis or metaphysical salvation. Therefore the struggle is more interesting and more shattering than the denouement, and the end of the struggle is welcome less for its actual significance than because the spectator's nervous and mental fatigue has reached its limits. Indeed, the originality of Vauthier's theatre consists in the unrelieved spectacle of characters *entangled* in things. Theirs may be struggles of the soul, but their agonies are not suspended in a vacuum. A character's being is always a being-in-the-world.

In *Capitaine Bada* and *Les Prodiges* the "thing" the characters are entangled in is woman. In the first of these plays the variations on the theme of chastity show that Vauthier's heroes are haunted by the traditional notion of carnal sin, giving their destinies virtually Christian extensions. Less traditional is the stress laid on the inevitable presence of the other person as an object. Alice *(Bada)* and Gilly *(Les Prodiges)* are, above all, living and suffering *things,* against and apropos of which Bada and Marc try to define their solitary souls. Vauthier's plays are not so much tragedies of the couple as portraits of the individual suffering of man, struggling against the traps and betrayals of what *is,* and to which he is fatally linked: others (woman), the past, the modern world, furniture, his own nature.

With the spectacle of an awesome struggle against a universe of things, Vauthier has managed to bring to the stage a very modern tragic vision. He has translated the well-known mystery of sin and the dangers of the flesh into what might be called existentialist terms. He has also found a new function for poetic language: instead of being a mere instrument, he has made it into the very substance of the characters' psychology. Vauthier's is one of the most poetic attempts to create a genuinely contemporary theatre, and its final success depends on the good will of the spectator, who must agree to be shattered by an intense verbal bombardment.

Among the poets of violence and paroxysm Georges Schehadé appears to be something of a lost sheep. Behind him loom the shadows of Musset, Maeterlinck, Vildrac, and Supervielle. Indeed, he would at first seem to be an heir to Romanticism and a delicate symbolism. Discreet and magical, his works began to be performed on the French stage in 1951, a few years after Ghelderode and Audiberti were introduced, and just before Vauthier. Farcical, parodic, and tragic elements are mixed in his works, as they are in those of the other poet-playwrights, but in contrast to their explosions are his aerated poetry, his refinements and nuances, and his subtle play of metaphors, which evoke not the flames of hell, the tortures of the flesh, or the horror of existence bound up with things, but the diamond of youth and purity and a kind of very Romantic escapism.

All very banal, one is tempted to think. And in fact the reviewers were quick to discover that certain of Schehadé's plays, with their prudent suggestion of a spiritual ideal, recalled the charming naïveté of many old-fashioned and limited works. "Over there . . . over there . . . the marvelous clouds!" said Baudelaire in *Le Spleen de Paris,* and critics have been known to reduce Baudelaire to that platitude. Some did the same to Schehadé and have even compared his play *Le Voyage* to the escapism of the thirties, represented by Marcel Pagnol's *Marius.* Such criticism limits Schehadé to a commonplace, however, to an elementary pattern that his play uses but transcends. True, the very title *Le Voyage* and the dream of the play's hero, Christopher, are related to that literature of escape which now seems to belong to another age: the story of a young shop clerk who dreams of adventures at sea and of exotic islands. In fact, the central character of Schehadé's plays is often the old-fashioned poet, filled with purity and faithful —sometimes unto death—to an inner universe that rejects a reality in which "action is not the sister of dream," as Baudelaire phrased it. But the discretion of Schehadé's works is misleading in that it sometimes obscures—and this is perhaps their flaw—his use of the traditional figure of the hero-poet for a very original purpose, created by very original means.

Actually, Schehadé's theatre as a whole is misleading, for each play goes out to meet the spectator on his own ground instead of beginning with a dazzling avant-garde attack. A valet informs the spectator that his master is about to leave *(Monsieur Bob'le);* in a rather ordinary inn a gowned magistrate flirts with the innkeeper *(La Soirée des proverbes);* a young officer is lost in a sinister forest *(Histoire de Vasco);* a young English shop clerk of 1850 dreams of sea voyages and pays no attention to the girl who loves him *(Le Voyage)*; in a pretty boarding house a young girl seems unable to choose between her three fiancés *(Les Violettes)*. Even when the opening scene is intriguing, its strangeness is somewhat familiar. Then the language becomes increasingly metaphorical, the images increasingly obscure, the situations increasingly unreal or threatening. One gradually realizes that some danger is hanging over the charming and engaging characters, that a difficult and perhaps deadly adventure is awaiting them. Everything happens as if the poet were taking the spectator by the hand and leading him slowly into his universe of enchantment or terror, in the company of characters who, from tableau to tableau, have been imperceptibly drawn into a mysterious adventure. Just as Argengeorge *(La Soirée des proverbes)* abandons Hélène to go and discover the secret of the rendezvous at Les Quatre Diamants, so Christopher *(Le Voyage)*, who has gone so far as to put on a real sailor's uniform, becomes the defendant in a strange trial in which he is accused of a cowardly murder, and so Mme. Borromée's boarders *(Les Violettes)* are gradually led into the wake of evil by the devil of modern times, the atomic scientist Kufman, who wants to use the nuclear energy of violets to destroy the world.

Characters and spectators wander about in a world of strange and comic antics and wonders, a maze of wrong tracks and enticements, in search of Truth or signs of Truth. The play of this theatre of enigmas seem like detective or adventure stories: mysterious rendezvous and secret missions suggest questions, but the answers are always delayed. As the hat-maker Max says in *La Soirée*, "Truth has many faces, falsehood but one." A glimpse of Truth is caught amid the lies, but it appears only to slip even further away. Somewhere behind the words of Monsieur Bob'le, in the snows of Hunter Alexis' "fifth season," in the meeting of Marguerite's dream and Vasco's innocent fear, it is so fleeting, so manifold, that all the poet's imagery is needed to suggest it. Simple and clear symbols are enough for the lie (Judge Domino's gown or the soldier's unsubtle disguises in *Vasco*), but Truth is the discovery or the product of the will and imagination of pure creatures—hence its ambiguity, its elusive nature, and the doubt that hangs over it. For actually, at what level should it be sought?

In *Le Voyage* Schehadé has gone as far as possible in his use of this ephemeral paradox. Situated at the center of the play is the testimony of two "witnesses" to a murder committed at the other end of the world. There is first a concrete presentation of an ignoble and treacherous killing that took place over a prostitute and her pimp father, among lecherous, cantankerous sailors; this flashback is based on a description of the crime given by a witness (an intelligent parrot!) to self-appointed judges. Then Christopher, who has agreed to pass himself off as the killer-sailor whose uniform he is wearing, gives his version of the murder, about which he in fact knows nothing. His beautiful and sentimental story about rivals in love, in a world of generosity, friendship, and gracious despair, is also presented as a flashback, with just enough lack of realism for the spectator to feel that the actual adventure is the *lie,* and that the *truth* is the product of a young poet's imagination. Now this truth of a poetic lie is effective, since through Christopher the sailor-murderer is acquitted. But the happy ending is colored with melancholy and irony: Between a parrot's testimony and a poet's reconstruction, who, in good faith, would have chosen the parrot's testimony? And Christopher finally gives up the voyage of his dreams, not only because he has contributed all the money he has saved to build a monument to the murdered sailor, but because, what would he find "over there" if not the treachery and crime witnessed by the parrot?

Clearly, at the end of each adventure Schehadé does not lead the spectator back to his own ground. On the contrary, he launches him out into an even vaster mystery, that of death: the death of a dream sometimes, as in *Le Voyage;* the death of the pure hero, as in *La Soirée* or *Vasco;* the death of a whole collectivity who had betrayed the simple poetry of life, as in the atomic and burlesque finale of *Les Violettes.*

Between the two poles of the adventure a constant tension is maintained by the distance between things, people, familiar words, and all that they permanently symbolize, which is itself impossible to grasp. Schehadé's theatre is a fireworks of equivalences. In his universe everything is a sign: words, objects, crows, costumes, names. In *La Soirée des proverbes* even the fish Marcellus in his jar is one: the symbol of silence—"or even worse!" adds Frightful Philippe. The characters live in that kind of dangerous zone. Sometimes they refuse the mystery; other times they clumsily search for the key to it—as do the guests in *La Soirée,* who struggle with proverbs that are unsatisfying or visions that terrify them and bring out their bad faith. But each play has at least one hero, endowed with an innocence called Poetry. In *Les Violettes* the Baron Fernagut finally betrays his own ideal, but young Pierrette remains faithful to her universe of love, and ironically converts the devil to it. In the other plays the hero holds out to the end, unto death. Bob'le, Vasco, Argengeorge are all poets of purity and truth, but a purity and a truth that have many faces: wisdom, curiosity, courage, a rejection of time, and even what is generally considered cowardice, which in time of war is innocence.

Psychology, of course, has little place in such theatre. The characters are less motivated personalities than points in space, which attract swarms of images, grouped by affinities. Psychological coherence is replaced by poetic coherence, equally capable of representing passions and bringing out modulations of intensity.

Critics have emphasized Schehadé's Eastern origins. His poetry is very close to the enigmas and charms of Persian tales. But, more generally, in a world of lies, violence, and, with *Les Violettes,* a race for total destruction, Schehadé stands up as an opponent, as a comical and melancholy guardian of the subtle truths of the soul and its real destiny. Using all the charms of a subdued style and whimsical characters, Schehadé—free of the anger of his contemporaries—finally and skillfully asserts the value of man, and the rights of poetry as well.

Immediately after World War II, along with Audiberti and Ghelderode, another poet came to the French stage—Henri

Pichette, whose verbal frenzy and theatrical imagination gave great hopes. *Les Epiphanies* is essentially no more than poetry recited onstage, however, and *Nucléa,* whose first part is a great spectacle of war, a theatrical and very effective synthesis of shrieks, violent verbal images, and deafening stereophonic noise, ends with interminable recitations of alexandrines aimed at the devil and in honor of love and poetry. Despite his noble intention of setting up a splendid image of man rising above the calamities of the modern world, Pichette never really achieves great drama, and except in the first part of *Nucléa,* he would seem to use the stage for presenting genres other than theatre itself. Besides, since 1952 Pichette the dramatist has been silent.

What Geneviève Serreau calls "the feast of words,"[4] and which has been carried on by Vauthier and Schehade, continues to produce new poets. Since 1960 René de Obaldia, for example, has amused and shocked audiences of the Théâtre National Populaire and the Boulevard by his nonchalant way of stringing together verbal antics and outlandish situations. *Genousie, Le Général inconnu, Le Satyre de la Villette,* and *Du Vent dans les branches de sassafras* are perhaps minor works, but in a burlesque way they evoke a whole current mythology (theatre in life, Lolita, science fiction, television, Westerns), manage to neutralize its horror or vulgarity, and by means of the false naïveté of very loquacious dialogue, give it young freshness. More recently, Romain Weingarten sent "new chills" down the spine of French poetic theatre with *L'Eté,* a play based entirely on the mysterious relationships between two talking cats, a brother-sister couple, and two lovers who are never seen onstage.

Obviously, rebellion, the absurd, and Brechtism have left room in the theatre for a drama that is more conventionally poetic yet still very modern. But up to now Jean Genet is the playwright who most powerfully and originally combines the "feast of words" with a feast of dramatic and scenic imagination.

4. See her *Histoire du nouveau théâtre,* pp. 24–36.

# CHAPTER 9

# THE ABSURD HAS MANY FACES: VIAN, ARRABAL, DURAS, DUBILLARD

The awareness of an eminently dramatic situation—man confronted by the incomprehensible or unjustified aspect of his own condition—can be expressed in hundreds of ways. Whatever the solution (nihilistic acceptance, poetic transformation, or final confidence in a free will capable of overcoming that state of mind), the so-called absurd has in fact haunted playwrights of all times. Greek tragedy is based on it, as are Elizabethan theatre, Corneillian tragedy (with its values that result in a glorious nothingness), Racinian tragedy (where everything happens mechanically, in relation to a God—but a *hidden* God), and Romantic drama (in which the cry "fatalitas!" is no more than a rhetorical device). Without the absurd, taken in the broadest sense, there would be no drama. When theatre becomes reasonable (as, for example, French eighteenth-century bourgeois theatre), it becomes drama repudiating drama, and one wonders why some writers have spent so much time writing plays only to say, in effect, that the drama of life can be resolved by reading three pages of rationalistic philosophy. André Malraux once commented that "reason cannot account for man." He may be wrong, but if one believes he is wrong, one denies the validity of theatre.

Much great literature is the expression of an impatience with the absurd. Playwrights of the past sometimes showed that impatience through a rational ordering, a presentation of perceived disorder in conflict with a style, a form, or even the structure of an anecdote that expressed either the poet's desire for harmony or what he believed to be a hidden intention of God. Today's theatre of the absurd is characterized by an emphasis on the inhuman or irrational pole of the conflict. And this is perhaps one of the real differences—taking into account, of course, the stylistic modes of the various periods—between the theatre of the past and the new theatre that has been proliferating since around 1952.

For the poet-playwrights discussed in Chapter 8 the horror or incoherency—both real and perceptible—of man's condition are essentially reflections which are unbearable but which can be justified by the existence of a reality or a transcendent order, whether diabolical, divine, or simply and vaguely poetic (in the symbolist sense of the word). The link is established through frenetic or imaged language, with no concessions made to rationalistic optimism. To these poets, who stress the absurdity of life in itself, man's condition is a farce (tragic, grotesque, or graceful as a ballet), but a farce that has a purpose: to amuse God, who one senses is the Devil, as Cocteau has said. Such metaphors to explain metaphors are not valid for any other playwrights, however, and those we shall discuss here stand in somewhat the same relation to the poets as Sartre did to Giraudoux or Cocteau. Their vision of the world derives from a return to man; that is to say, they express a dramatic transcendency that has to do with consciousness, not with poetry or the supernatural.

These playwrights paint a direct portrait of agonized consciousness as an individual experiences it through the gestures and language of everyday life or in ordinary situations related to the customs of today (divorce, a *Reader's Digest* variety of psycho-analysis, modern war). Any metaphors involved are those of man at grips with his condition—not of a mystical or poetic beyond. Arrabal's virgins crowned with thorns are fantasies of an eternal child who was never able to dissociate his first Communion from his erotic discoveries—not images of the real presence of the Virgin and Christ in the world. Dubillard's Master who dies in his complex house is the individual surprised by the Cartesian mystery of the union of soul and body within himself—not a symbol of God worried about the fact that His Creation is about to go down the drain. In the same way, Ionesco's rhinoceroses are metaphors of an individual consciousness' horror of others—not the symbol of some "black beast" in the manner of Audiberti or the embodiment of a diabolical evil that existed *elsewhere* before subjugating the world.

Indeed, it is in relation to Ionesco and also to Beckett that this new group of writers must be considered. For their means are somewhat similar: verbal incantation, expressionistic tricks, what appear to be the most old-fashioned naturalistic details (reminiscent of Zola, Courteline, and Jean-Jacques Bernard), cabaret or vaudeville acts. By concentrating on the individual confronted by his absurd condition, even in the most personal or intimate situations, and with great freedom in their use of theatrical devices, these few playwrights have managed to create a kind of "chamber theatre."[1] Even when they deal with collective adventures like the Spanish revolution or war in general, their theatre brings the spectator—whether through laughter or horror—back to that awkward and pathetic "self" whose sphere of action never exceeds

1. This expression is borrowed from the first volume of Jean Tardieu's *Théâtre* (Paris, Gallimard, 1955). Although primarily a poet, Tardieu as a playwright combines elements of Adamov, Ionesco, Vian, and even Beckett. But his theatre is essentially a linguistic meditation and an occasionally theatrical illustration of the rest of his writings.

the space of a small stage. Pascal described that self as "hateful," but Boris Vian, Fernando Arrabal, Marguerite Duras, and Roland Dubillard tell us it is all we have, absurd as it may be.

It took some time for the dramatic works of Boris Vian, who died in 1959, to finally be performed. A poet, novelist, trumpet player, and dramatist, Vian was a kind of new Jarry—but a melancholy and tender Jarry. His works convey a taste for life in all its forms and also—like those of Ionesco or Raymond Queneau—an obsession with death. Death is not the sumptuous horror of decaying flesh or the supernatural phenomenon that it was for Ghelderode, but extinction in itself, a nothingness in the face of which man's agitation has little value.

This attitude led Vian, in two of his plays (*L'Equarrissage pour tous* and *Le Goûter des généraux*), to poke fun at the ambitions and incoherencies displayed by mankind in performing the act it would seem to take most seriously: war. Greedy, opportunistic, or simply childish, Vian's characters—generals, politicians, soldiers, and civilians of all nationalities and all leanings—take part, with an almost Ubuesque lack of awareness, in what seem like cabaret acts. According to a tradition dear to French children, the generals, properly dressed in the uniforms of today's army, have a tea party, during which they take a few alcoholic drinks on the sly (out of fear of an overpowering mother) and organize a war in all its detail—until they realize that they have forgotten to choose an enemy (*Le Goûter des généraux*). Similarly, amid the ravages of a war involving the French, the Americans, and the Germans, a wedding is being prepared—that of a French girl to a German soldier, who is fighting a hundred yards away and is called to the wedding by telephone (*L'Equarrissage pour tous*). War being absurd, Vian improves on its absurdity; but his method consists essentially in treating it with nonchalance.

The spectator at such plays is, in a sense, struck by the horrors of massacre and the general incoherence, but far more by the absolute irreverence with which things are minimized—even those that in reality are the most shattering. In *L'Equarrissage,* for example, everything is set up for a torture scene, but the torture consists in tickling the victim. Vian's intention is to shock, but the shock comes less from aggressive provocation than from total disrespect in both form and substance. The tension in *Le Goûter* and *L'Equarrissage* is created by the enormous incongruity between bad jokes, intentionally superficial in nature, and the seriousness of the values involved. An antimilitarist and author of the well-known French song "Chanson du déserteur," Vian is subversive by way of frivolity. In the face of the universal phenomenon of death, the social and political problems melt away and are not even worthy of being attacked seriously.

As a final disrespectful and facile gesture, Vian does away with all his characters at the end of both plays. The generals and politicians of *Le Goûter* kill themselves one after another during a collective game of Russian roulette which they find highly amusing; the setting of *L'Equarrissage* having disappeared in an explosion, the few survivors kill each other to the sound of the "Marseillaise." Vian may well be saying that mankind, both military and civilian, entertains a death-wish for collective annihilation, falsely glorified by big words and noble pretexts. But his burlesque and spectacular finales are also a sign that he is the last to take his own creations really seriously: his game is altogether subversive in that it itself is an object of subversion.

In a third play, *Les Bâtisseurs d'empire,* Vian presents the reality in relation to which all human values and ambitions become equalized in their indignity and comic absurdity: death. *Les Bâtisseurs* approaches allegory but, as in Beckett and most of Ionesco, stops short of it to the extent that the equation between what is seen or heard and the concepts suggested remains ambiguous, polyvalent, and thus not intellectually translatable. The play as a whole follows a rigorous movement from progressive suffocation and isolation to final and complete obscurity. Taken literally, it is a nightmare of invasion from the outside: as a family flees from apartment to apartment, its members disappear one after another, until only the Father is left, and his last refuge is then invaded, in the dark, by the deadly enemies. Confronted by this mysterious destruction of the world, the characters try— very comically—to justify their existence or their achievements, using a language made up of clichés and paralogisms, and doing their best to ignore the invasion, the shrinking space of their successive lodgings, and the gradual disappearance of the members of the family.

With more obviously social and political implications, Georges Michel has recently picked up this theme in his *Promenade du Dimanche,* but Vian's play goes beyond that level of a "plague" à la Camus. It is also concerned with a metaphor of individual death and in this respect may be compared to one of Ionesco's later plays, *Le Roi se meurt.* While the family disappears and the living space gets progressively smaller and shabbier, one realizes that the Father's flight from room to room is illusory, for he is always accompanied by his Schmürz, an ignoble, bloody, and permanent witness-scapegoat. The Schmürz is sometimes ignored and sometimes—in fact, quite regularly—beaten up, but he is always there, silent. If he is meant to represent anything, it would be, in a very general way, an aggregate of outer and inner realities (evil, bad faith, sadistic impulses, and the desire to subject others, hence the shame and joy of being a master) which men sometimes recognize in distrust or hate and try to destroy or frequently prefer to ignore so that they may contrive to live with it in some measure of satisfaction. Scenically, the Schmürz is an embodiment of malaise—the malaise of reality, which is actually the unacknowledged awareness of future annihilation, of a death which keeps men from *really* living: a few seconds before the final obscurity, the Schmürz dies, but he does so just before the door is smashed in and the invaders at last make their entrance. The invaders are never seen, but they are "perhaps," says Boris Vian, "Schmürzes."

In fact, the Schmürz is the image that gives Vian's dramatic works their meaning. For the nightmare horror of *Les Bâtisseurs d'empire,* along with its implacable rigor, is what justifies the nonchalance and burlesque elements of his other two plays. None of this, however, excludes a touch of infinite tenderness, which is far more obvious in certain of Vian's poems or in a novel such as *L'Ecume des jours,* in which the heroine dies from a flower that grows in her chest, and the hero, in charge of "growing" guns, manages to produce them, but each with, at the end of its barrel, a rose.

In the nightmare that dominates the works of Fernando Arrabal, the fiend is not so much death as the powers of this world—judges, policemen, formidable mothers, torturers—who are always ready to detect the fateful flaw, punish it, or treacherously encourage it with an eye to even more severe punishment. Sometimes similar to Beckett's tramps, sometimes akin to the victims in Adamov's early plays, and colored by memories of Charlie Chaplin or the Marx Brothers, Arrabal's protagonists exist in a very special zone of their own: they have the mentality of children and the sexual prowess of adults—and hence a rather picturesque strangeness. The interests and somewhat perverse freshness of children are clearly shown, for example, in this dialogue between Climando and Mita in *Le Tricycle:*

| | |
|---|---|
| *Climando:* | Listen, Mita, where will we pee in heaven? |
| *Mita:* | You don't pee in heaven. |
| *Climando:* | What a pity. |
| *Mita:* | You'll get used to it. |
| *Climando (enthusiastically):* | Mita, you're so intelligent, you know everything. |

Being children, they are also, in a strangely innocent way, curious about gory or sexual acts. Above all, they have an intermittent sense of guilt and a fear of policemen, who are terrifying when they appear and just as quickly forgotten when their backs are turned. When these characters do something "bad," they are rarely conscience-stricken; rather, they consider it only a possible cause for punishment. Indeed, all the games they play are censured by the adult world, from the flagellation of dolls (*Le Grand Cérémonial*) to bloody murder (*Le Grand Cérémonial, Le Tricycle, Cérémonie pour un noir assassiné*).

In point of fact, however, the characters are adults. Although they commit their dread deeds while playing, they do commit them. Their sexual curiosity is actually voyeurism; they don't pretend to make love in coffins, they really do. And though they hide corpses as a child would hide broken toys, their corpses are real. Arrabal tries to portray sadism, masochism, necrophilia, and the taste for murder in all their horror but also in all their innocence.

The childishness of Arrabal's characters and their lack of any moral conscience evoke a kind of paradise lost forever. Responsibility for the fall is generally put on the mother image, which appears in many plays. Its cruel power is most clearly apparent in *Les Deux Bourreaux,* a play very similar in its rigor to certain of Adamov's early works. The mother is held responsible for the denunciation and torture of the father, whose screams are heard from behind the scenes, and whose corpse, hung on a stick like a dead animal, is carried across the stage by the two executioners; before the curtain falls, the two sons accept their mother's lies, give in to her, and ask her pardon. Here, added to the mother image, is that of police authority, the official executioners. In *Le Grand Cérémonial* the hero who whips dolls and murders a young girl is maintained in his psychotic state by the presence of an authoritarian and Machiavellian mother and her sentimental blackmail, while at given moments the sirens of police cars are heard offstage. This double prison of the protagonists—one deriving from Freud, the other from the police structure of the outside world—has its roots in Arrabal's private life and his memories of the Franco regime and its persecutions. His theatre is thus an extremely personal affair—the exploitation of an individual nightmare, which in itself is rich in possibilities.

On the other hand, Arrabal's presentation of nostalgia for a lost paradise is oversimplified, and the double game of innocence and guilt remains clinical. Throughout the show of generalized perversity an emphasis on horror and the whole baggage of devices that derive from the Grand Guignol or from a specialized brothel limit its scope to that of documents of pathological cases. The horror is too often simply horror in itself, so that the spectacle of a hunchback named Cavanosa who achieves orgasm by whipping a doll remains a mere curiosity. Original goodness and the Passion it leads to are the subject matter of *Le Cimetière des voitures,* where, with great imagination, Arrabal peoples the stage with a miserable and actively sexual community lodged in the graveyard's heaps of disabled cars. In their pitiful and comic midst there appears a "good" trumpet player, accompanied by two other musicians. This hero is of course a slaughterer whenever he feels the urge, but he is called Emmanou, is eventually betrayed and beaten up, and at the end is carried across the stage tied to a bicycle, a woman wiping his face with a cloth. The transposition of the Passion of Jesus is far too obvious, and the naïveté of the symbol lessens the power of the play, which is otherwise rich in invention and meaning.

In the past few years Arrabal has added a new dimension to the performance of his fantasies: the theatrical notion of ceremony. The intentions behind the rites in which his characters try to transcend their ambiguous game are clear from the very titles of the plays *(Le Grand Cérémonial, Le Couronnement, Cérémonie pour un noir assassiné)* and from the stage directions in the published texts (a ceremonial kiss, a sacrificial gesture, and so on). Crowns of thorn or confirmation dresses and staging that is meant to transform the acts of torture, sadomasochism, or necrophilia into a kind of Mass or sacrament are used in an attempt to make the spectator feel that during the performance he is committing the sacrilege of those who do not bow their heads during the high moments of the Catholic liturgy. Arrabal thus seeks to transform simple voyeurism of the psychoanalyst's-couch variety into mystical blasphemy. Indeed, the ambitious goal of these works is to damn us along with themselves, and to create *panic*—that is to say, the sacred horror that springs from the black sanctification, through ritual, of the evil within us.

Despite the recognizable echoes of Ionesco, Beckett, and others, Arrabal's theatre does have its originality. It is full of striking effects: an automobile graveyard, corpse-conveying bicycles, adult-conveying baby carriages, life-size dolls, strong suggestions of torture, the double image—both hated and adored—of oppression and unhappiness, and the Grand Guignol pathology of sado-masochistic ceremonies. Yet, while Arrabal shows great promise, he still fails to attain poetry, to absorb the spectator into the ceremony, or to transfigure unhappiness and personal fantasies into contemporary and universal situations—all of which has finally been achieved by that other fallen angel, Jean Genet.

The vision of life as absurd does not necessarily have to be conveyed through incongruous forms, the fantasy of improbable acts, or a scenic actualization of the phenomena of dreams and nightmares. A few playwrights in France today, seeking to assimilate and transcend the forms of Ionesco or Beckett, have tried to suggest that vision indirectly, by means of realistic surface effects. Foremost in the realm of what might be called a neorealism of the absurd is Marguerite Duras.

As a woman, Duras is of course very alive to the fate of women. One of a growing number of female writers of the past few decades, she has successfully avoided the traps into which feminine literature often falls: in her novels, her films, and her plays, she has spoken, not of lesbians or suffragettes or old-fashioned mistresses, but of women as such, in their very essence as women. This she has done in harsh, austere, and very modern terms, without ever going on coquettishly about the mysteries of her sex and her superiority in the matter of passion, suffering, and intuition, or else virilely about her hate for man and the equality of the sexes. For Duras woman is defined not as against, above, or below man, but as beside him.

Whether completely centered on dogs and the dangers of rabies *(Les Eaux et forêts)*, or alienated, being in domestic service *(Le Square)*, or distressed by a sudden divorce *(La Musica)*, or stricken by the plight of aging motherhood *(Des Journées entières dans les arbres)*, all her women are preys to an inner solitude, though her couples sometimes achieve a rare degree of complicity: in *Les Viaducs de la Seine-et-Oise*, two old people, in methodically cutting up a corpse and disposing of it by throwing the pieces into freight trains that pass under a bridge on their way to all the corners of France, almost manage to commit the perfect crime. Generally, however, her men and women never really meet: their fates may be parallel, but they are always separate. A man and a woman realize that both of them have failed to escape from the stagnation of solitude *(Le Square)*, or both members of a couple are aware that they are equally responsible for their misunderstanding and separation and are equally distressed by the barrier they have raised between them *(La Musica)*.

In *Les Eaux et forêts,* a comical farce built around a dog who has bitten a man in the street, one of the two women in the play —Woman 2, to be precise—says toward the end, "If you only knew how fed up I am." A bit later Woman I announces that she has "bloody well drowned [her] husband in the Marne to Rhine Canal." Actually, Duras' characters swing between those two poles —between being enormously weary of life and dreaming of some definitive act: murder, a great love, any form of escape. While the act is generally carried out, the results are never what the characters had imagined they would be, and no traditional type of escape is any help to them. The mother in *Des Journées entières dans les arbres,* having made a fortune in a former colony, returns laden with gold but with an empty soul—a pathologically hungry old woman—and the only way she manages to make contact with her son, a gambler and professional taxi dancer, is by letting him steal her bracelets so that he can gamble yet again. In *La Musica* Anne-Marie, who has been escaping from her husband first by going to the movies alone and then by divorcing him, sinks into an even deeper depression after her divorce, despite the telephone call from her lover.

This impossibility of giving meaning to their lives comes not only from within the characters but also from the "others." Just as bogged down in their own malaise, the men speak a language that is constantly out of phase with the women's, making the hopeful moments of possible contact even more pathetic. The maid and the traveling salesman who meet in the park (Le Square), the mother and son (Des Journées entières), and the divorced husband and wife (La Musica) often come close to some mutual understanding, but the understanding is either ephemeral or is simply based on a common awareness of irremediable separation. While for Sartre the "others" are hell, for Marguerite Duras they are the absurd.

Listening to a Duras play, one is reminded of a dramatic genre of the 1920s—Jean-Jacques Bernard's "theatre of the unexpressed," also called "the school of silence," which was characterized by the pauses, hesitations, and verbal reticence of its dialogue. Bernard's plays give the impression that the real drama lies in precisely what is not said, either out of reserve, shyness, or lack of vocabulary; similarly, Duras' characters are never sure they have found the right word and worry about whether the other person has really understood the nuances of what they say. Not that they have trouble conveying their feelings and the secrets of their hearts, as in Bernard; rather, it is their very being that they are struggling to express. Parallel to the constant effort of being, there is the constant effort of expressing that being. In fact, all her characters suffer from what Raymond Queneau comically calls "ontalgia"—the malady of being—making her plays poignant and philosophically modern little dramas.

Stubbornly in search of self-justification, possible only through a real contact with others (that is, with a man—husband, lover, or son), a Duras heroine is a kind of female Sisyphus who finds the strength to push her rock in telling how she pushes it. The tale may be farcical, as in Les Eaux et forêts, whose characters continue to exist by saying "just anything at all," as Duras herself explained during an interview on television in September 1965. Or a deaf ear may tragically be turned to the story, as in the case of the lonely and bitter maid in *Le Square* or the mother in *Des Journées entières dans les arbres,* consumed with love for her wastrel of a son. (Actually, the traveling salesman is a kind of Sisyphus in his own poor way, and the indifferent son, who manages to stay alive through the absurd game of alternately losing and winning, is yet another pitiful incarnation of the myth.) In *La Musica* the situation is both an end and a beginning, for the irremediable suggests the possibility of a new start, which would fatally lead to another impasse: always the same old story—or song, as it were.

In *Le Square, La Musica,* and *Des Journées entières* Duras has created an original theatre by adding to a vision of the absurd essentially akin to Beckett's a traditional but grating appeal to the emotions through elements of theatrical realism. Not that they are in any way related to those of the Théâtre Libre: even if the mother in *Des Journées* devours real mounds of sauerkraut and pork on stage; even if the setting of *La Musica* is a provincial hotel lobby, with its telephone, reception desk, and so on; and even if the dialogue avoids the madness, puns, and incongruity of Ionesco's or Beckett's—Duras' plays are always at a remove from reality because of their artificial language (painful repetitions and a profusion of conjunctions and adverbs, statistically different from those in ordinary spoken language), their lack of any decorative characters or objects to make it all "real," and their simplification of reality. By giving her characters a certain naturalistic dimension, however, Duras found a means for writing plays that are less metaphors of the absurd than intuitive grasps of it in the reconstruction of everyday life. She thus involves the spectators in a sympathetic relationship with the characters, making the absurd perceptible to the heart as well as the mind. Through the subtle balance of photographic realism and the unreality of modern theatre, Marguerite Duras would seem to have rehabilitated the "slice of life" by transfiguring it.

Also more or less a slice of life is Roland Dubillard's first real play, *Naïves Hirondelles*. An actor (whose stage name is Grégoire) and a poet (whose works Robert Kanters has related to Zen),[2] Dubillard began by writing and performing a number of poetic and absurd sketches for the radio. Then, after *Si Camille me voyait* —a very clever and extremely amusing fantastic parody of a symbolist drama, written in verse, where the heroine wanders about in a bathtub-carriage full of milk and finally escapes from her lovers by becoming the moon—he suddenly, with *Naïves Hirondelles,* emerged as a highly original and promising playwright of everyday realism and the absurd.

A summary of the plot will show to what degree the play derives from naturalism: A young man, Bertrand, and an older man, Fernand, rent a shop that belongs to Bertrand's aunt, Mme. Severine, a milliner; one day a young orphan named Germaine turns up to work as Mme. Severine's helper; after some time Germaine disappears with Bertrand, leaving Fernand and Mme. Severine to live alone. But this simple story is merely a pretext for innumerable variations on the themes of boredom, the absurd, self-justification, the vanity of man's efforts, and the curious mixture of weariness and obstinacy with which he carries out his wretched undertakings.

Part of the play's humor comes from simple gags drawn from the inexhaustible supply of everyday-life's little accidents: the characters pick the wrong bottle and drink *eau de Javel* instead of white wine; while making a cheese pie, they realize too late that they had mistaken a piece of soap for a piece of Swiss cheese; a shaky screen falls and knocks one of them out; an old table collapses right in the middle of dinner; or a fly, in a state of winter

2. In *Le Figaro Littéraire* (December 22, 1966).

grogginess, gets caught in a Kodak camera. Thus the universe of small misfortunes and the treachery of objects is presented in a minor mode and is made even funnier by the ludicrous behavior of the characters. While Mme. Severine persists in making hats, Bernard and Fernand continually change their plans but are absurdly stubborn about each of their little undertakings while it lasts, whether it involves cracking nuts, accumulating clocks they have no idea what to do with, or gluing together little un-matched bits of broken china. They energetically explain the great merits or the value of each of their undertakings and strongly believe in them, or want to believe in them, but they are at a loss when it comes to justifying them.

Here and there a few actual symbols also keep the play from falling into conventional realism. Bertrand's motorcycle, for ex-ample, is an object of annoyance to Mme. Severine and Fernand, since it is a threatening sign of his possible escape (indeed, it is on that motorcycle that he leaves with Germaine, never to return). Similar devices are the screens into which Mme. Severine closes herself up, as in a box, in the middle of the shop, thus completely escaping from the world for a few moments, and, above all, the giant vase that is hidden throughout the entire play and revealed just before the curtain falls—a "shapeless, unfinished vase" which Fernand has made bit by bit and on which he will continue to work ad infinitum. Furthermore, two or three somewhat strange details counterbalance the play's naturalism: the anxiety of the characters and the stage business provoked by a noise from behind a screen, all of which turns out to be for naught, since they never find the source of the noise and forget it; and the groggy fly which attracts as much attention as a character and which seems to obey the human voice.

Dubillard's originality is particularly striking, however, on the level of dialogue—a triumph of the shapeless and the incomplete. While in *Si Camille me voyait* he wrote a few verses that Jules Laforgue, Henri de Régnier, or Edmond Rostand would have en-vied, in *Naïves Hirondelles* he follows the undulations, hesitations, and alternating flow of spoken language, not as it would be recorded on tape, but as exaggerated by a poet who would seem to retain, above all, verbal punctuation ("let's see," "look here," "what a pity," "but really," "well well," "I mean that . . .") and manages to create a kind of incantation based on the difficulty of self-expression. Dubillard is thus in a class by himself, far from the systematic automatism of Ionesco and far also from the rigor and rhythms of Beckett.

In his second "big" play, *La Maison d'os,* the technique of dialogue is much the same, but its imagery is richer and sometimes frankly dreamlike. For in this play the naturalist anecdote is replaced by a metaphor. An old man (the Master) is dying in his house—a fantastic, Kafkaesque house, peopled by some forty servants and "higher Servants," such as a Doctor, a Priest, a Steward. The play should be "read" not as it unfolds in time but as art historians read a building—from the cellar to the attic or from the attic to the cellar, according to which visual line one chooses. For a performance the tableaux may be shifted around, and the final impression is one not of an adventure that progresses in time but of a visit to an architectural structure. For the spectator, of course, the visit is an irreversible phenomenon that begins at eight in the evening and ends at eleven, but the "memory" of the visit is not chronological. The spectator has seen and heard the shoe-shiner Valet before the Priest or the Doctor, but it is like saying that during a visit to the Louvre one saw the Delacroixs before the Corots: in fact, they coexist in one space. The title of the play indicates that the space here is the human body, and the play is a metaphor of the awareness of the simultaneous presence of all its members and all its organs, as they function and as they conflict—that is, an awareness of the multiple death that is constantly making its way through all the passages of the body.

Working with a subject related to Vian's in *Les Bâtisseurs d' empire* and to Ionesco's in *Le Roi se meurt,* Dubillard succeeds in superimposing the metaphor of simultaneity on a metaphor of progression. There is the past and the future (death) of an individual, yet life is a rumbling, an agitated gyration within the permanent present of the body and soul. This paradox is the source of both malaise and humor. At one point a servant, the Attendant, comments on this perplexing confusion of time and space: "History and geography? I never was very good at them." Elsewhere, a Valet asks himself questions about "what actually happened," and the only answer he manages to find is, "Uh . . . ," ending his monologue with "shit."

In *Naïves Hirondelles,* as in *La Maison d'os,* Dubillard creates characters who grapple with serious questions about time, the absurd, life, and death, and who are unable to answer them. They suffer these questions, as it were, amid all the agitation of daily life. They are constantly aware of them, and their drama is their incapacity to formulate them clearly as inner concepts or in language. His characters are thus both pathetic and extremely funny— pathetic because their dilemma is serious, and funny because they run aground, get bogged down in the details of life and language, and are reduced to shrugging their shoulders or exclaiming, "Oh, anyway, the heck with it," like respectable little Germaine in *Naïves Hirondelles.* Certain critics have judged Dubillard very harshly; and, indeed, his plays are a way of sadly but nonchalantly telling the spectator, "the heck with it."

The difficulty of being oneself and the awareness of being mortal (which leads both to a protest against the stupidity of war and to a lucid despair in the face of inevitable old age) are of course commonplaces. Expressed in new forms, however, such commonplaces are precisely what distinguish a large element of the new French theatre from that of other countries. The English or American "absurd," for example, puts more stress on the historical, social, and even national nature of the problem. Pinter's chief concern is England today, just as Albee's is the American myth. No doubt when Vian wrote his plays he was thinking of World War II and the colonial repressions of the Fourth Republic, Arrabal never loses sight of the "cop" and the tortures of the Franco regime, and

Duras' characters, whether servants or bourgeois, are imbued with the malaise of postwar France, as are Dubillard's shopkeepers. But the true concern of these playwrights is less with denouncing a time and a place than with stating a question about man's universal condition. Arrabal's *Guernica* could take place anywhere if only a few words (including the title) were changed, whereas Albee's *Who's Afraid of Virginia Woolf?* would be largely incomprehensible outside its American context.

Regionalism carried to an extreme does save the poets (Claudel, Lorca, Ghelderode) from abstract allegory and allows them to achieve universality. Yet for a theatre that aims at conveying a direct experience of everyday life, it could mean limiting the play's scope to that of a documentary. The modest but fierce playwrights that have just been discussed do "situate" their anecdotes, but they rarely expound on the specificity of the locale; when they happen to emphasize it, they mean only to bring out its strangeness (Marguerite Duras' Seine-et-Oise, for example, provokes as much wonderment in French spectators as Wyoming or Kamchatka). For the dominant tone of this theatre is classical: it concerns man in the world today, but any man at all—out of phase with his universe, whatever that universe may be.

# CHAPTER 10

# POLITICS AND EPICS:
# ADAMOV, GATTI, BILLETDOUX

Early in the 1950s any discussion of the current French stage was concentrated on three names uttered in the same breath—Ionesco-Adamov-Beckett—and in tones of surprised delight or indignation. The indignation was often chauvinistic: an avant-garde of foreigners! (What, one might ask, would Molière and Marivaux have been without the Italians, or the great French school of twentieth-century painting without most of Europe?) But the surprise was valid: here were plays which broke completely with the garrulity of the poetic or philosophical theatre, which used in amazing new ways the devices of the old avant-garde, the expressionists, and the surrealists, and which gave concrete form to the modern themes of the absurd and noncommunication without foundering in post-symbolist obscurity. Each of the three playwrights, in his own way, had found a means of astonishing the French public, as Molière had done in 1659 with his *Précieuses ridicules,* for *La Cantatrice chauve, Le Professeur Taranne,* and *En Attendant Godot,* despite

their differences in scope, were not only a return to the funda-
mentals of theatre but, like Molière's farce, an opening onto new
possibilities.

Today, however, the Ionesco-Adamov-Beckett trinity has lost
its meaning. To begin with, a native of France, a true Frenchman,
has entered the game—an abandoned child who developed into a
petty thief and a homosexual: Jean Genet. Then, of course, the
trio itself broke up: all that the Beckett of *Comédie (Play)* and the
Ionesco of *La Soif et la faim* now have in common is a surface neo-
expressionism used for entirely different purposes. Finally, and
most importantly, Adamov defected: after having written a few
plays comparable to those of Ionesco, situated in what he himself
calls the no-man's-land of the theatre of the absurd, he repudiated
the genre and moved in the direction of a Brechtian theatre. He
thus set himself up as the head of a new "critical" drama, whose
objective is the portrayal of a collective destiny, clearly situated in
history.

In a parallel way, but without Adamov's Marxist intransigency,
François Billetdoux branched out from the slice of life and
Kafkaesque metaphors to an attempt at epic theatre. And another
playwright, Armand Gatti, has devoted himself—from the very
beginning of his career and with varying success—to most auda-
ciously working in this new genre. These playwrights are not isolated phenomena, however, but part of a definite movement: just
as the playwrights of a private world of personal anguish, the passing of time, and the problems of communication continue to proliferate (Robert Pinget, Claude Mauriac, Nathalie Sarraute), so has
there been a recent wave of historical and/or critical dramas whose
notion of commitment extends from the Sartrean concepts of 1946
to pure and simple propaganda. Such plays have touched on all
types of political problems—the collaboration and Resistance of
the 1940s, the Korean and Algerian Wars, the Oppenheimer trial,
the Fifth Republic, and so on—and are meant to be both theatrical
spectacles and acts of collective demystification. Salacrou's *Boulevard Durand* is one example, Jean Cosmos' *Monsieur Alexandre*

(a transposition of *Volpone* to the world of modern high finance), another, and then there are the frequent adaptations of Sean O'Casey, John Arden, and, of course, Brecht, to cite only some of the more important productions.

Within this movement the Adamov case is the most significant and most original. The word "case" would seem suitable here, since the works of Arthur Adamov consist entirely of plays that surpass one another in a truly dialectical manner. Futhermore, he has written, parallel to his theatre, a body of texts made up of explanations, discussions, political and aesthetic stands—and remorse. His meditations on Strindberg, Chekhov, and Brecht, each of whom influenced him in turn, have the distinction of always being sharply critical, even when they are admiring and enthusiastic. In fact, the debate now dividing French playwrights into Marxists and anti-ideologists would be far more fruitful if Ionesco, in his theoretical texts, displayed as much intelligence as Adamov, who knows how to go beyond invective and self-defense and really come to grips with the basic questions concerning the future and essence of the theatre. What counts more than the debate, however, is the series of theatrical experiments—however unequal in value—that constitute Adamov's theatre.

Having begun with a theatre of dreams, Adamov moved off in the direction of documentary dramas (*Le Printemps 71* being an extreme example) and then reintegrated his dream world, or what he calls "neurosis," into works which "would be *forced* always to take place on the borders of individual life and collective life" and which would express "everything that . . . links man to his own ghosts, but also, but as well, to other men and hence to their ghosts, and all of this within a given era, which is not a bit ghostly."[1] Finding the no-man's-land of the plays during the 1950s too limited because it obliged the writers to go round in circles within their eternal commonplaces, Adamov wanted to give man a more com-

1. Arthur Adamov, *Ici et maintenant* (Paris, Gallimard, 1964), p. 240.

plete and more concrete image—that is, to restore his social and historical dimensions by means of a synthesis of the two visions, thus achieving a total portrayal of man's condition. Obviously, his evolution consists less in repudiating past experiences than in criticizing them, in order to recover them for use on another level.

For this reason, certain constants are characteristic of Adamov's works as a whole. The most striking is the use of fantasies—private fantasies, reconstructed fantasies, or fantasies borrowed from psychiatric works. In *Le Printemps 71* (1961) they are replaced by an objective form—political allegories inspired by Daumier's drawings—but this was merely an intellectual detour, reabsorbed into *Sainte-Europe* (1966, never performed), in which allegorical cartoons and the imagination's dreams are synthesized in the nightmarish behavior of characters who are at once Ubuesque monsters, medieval figures, and politicians of the Common Market. Essentially, Adamov's devices are drawn from the realm of dream, obsession, and delirium. He himself has explained[2] that a play like *Professeur Taranne* is hardly more than the transposition of a dream he really had, and *Les Retrouvailles* the transposition of a dream that he, as a writer, might have had. His later short play for radio, *Le Fiacre* (1962), is the reconstruction of the collective paranoiac delirium of three old maids who were confined around 1900, and he has also used a garbage psychosis in order to denounce apartheid in the play *La Politique des restes*.

Whether these plays belong to the traditional absurd or have some precise political significance, they are always objective representations of fantasy: the absurd, nonsense, nightmares, and madness are free of the blurred effects that would make them "ghostly." As in Ionesco, all that happens on stage is presented naïvely as a solid reality, not as a floating dream. *Le Professeur Taranne* is based on a shameful and very common fantasy—that of finding oneself suddenly nude or in some obscene posture in public. But the play relates the fantasy in terms of an event experienced in the

2. "Note préliminaire," in his *Théâtre, 2*.

waking state. When at the beginning of the play the protagonist, accused of exhibitionism in front of children, is not recognized by his friends, the universe of accusation and indifference surrounding him is presented with a feeling of evident and concrete reality. The spectator thus understands that there is as much reason for a character to say to Taranne, "I don't know you, sir" as the expected formula, "Good morning, Professor Taranne." Once this is taken for granted, the logic according to which Taranne is no longer what he was or what he thinks he is imposes a development on events that is as cold, calm, and convincing as the logic of permanent identity. Thus, beyond the impression of nightmare, yet because of it, the spectator—who has not been enchanted by any great display of poetic whimsey—is struck by an impression that reflects on the normal world: that of the instability of the real, the possibility of ordinary situations taking unforeseeable directions with the same apparent necessity as they are generally accorded, and the resulting terror.

Neurosis, then, has a double value in Adamov's theatre. Being real, it can be presented in terms that are used for other realities, but it is at the same time a reflection or, as it were, a way of living parallel to what is usually considered the normal world. Scenically, it legitimately represents that world, and by transposing a mental image into outer reality, the playwright both remains faithful to reality and presents it with a theatrical distance. Adamov was Brechtian before even meditating on Brecht.

Within this general phantasmagoria one particular motif persists throughout Adamov's works—that of the object. Here again comparisons can be made with the proliferation of things in Ionesco's plays (*L'Invasion,* for example, where Adamov's characters are drowned in piles of unreadable papers, the archives of a dead man, trying obstinately to give them some meaning), for Adamov is obviously haunted by objects—their unjustified presence, the meaning society gives to them, and questions as to their real meaning. *Le Ping-Pong* is entirely built around a pinball machine, which at the end is ironically replaced by a ping-pong table. *Paolo Paoli* groups representative members of French society in the years 1900–14 around butterflies and feathers. The protagonist of *La Politique des restes* is a madman convinced that the whole world is about to become a refuse pile and that a plot has been hatched to force all the refuse into his stomach.

Thus, while Adamov derided the metaphor in Ionesco's *Le Nouveau Locataire*,[3] he himself makes use of a similar obsession. He tries, however, to avoid the ontological stalemate created by it. Eliminating the absurd from the substance of his plays if not from the form, he *explains* the obsession in sociopolitical terms, relating it to a collective state of consciousness created by the modern world. In *Ping-Pong,* for example, the pinball machine is a product deliberately exploited by a consortium; in other words, if certain men founder in futility and the absurd, it is because they are the indirectly brainwashed victims of profiteers. In *Paolo Paoli* butterflies, those delicately beautiful natural objects, are shown to be the basis for a business, just as feathers, charming ornaments for ladies' fashions, were in 1900 the substance of the fourth largest industry in France.

On this level, *La Politique des restes* is perhaps Adamov's most modern play—not so much in form (the trial of a white South African who has killed a black man is presented through traditional flashbacks) as in his use of an object psychosis, which does not naïvely explain the protagonist's racism but is structurally parallel to it. Little is said during the trial to indicate that one is the cause of the other; there is simply a constant crisscross of the two themes—an obsession with the refuse of the world (cigarette butts, old torn-up tickets, kitchen peelings, and so on) and a fear of the expansion of the black population. It is not until the play is over that the spectator sees the significant relationship between the two and realizes that the racist murderer grasps the accumulation of civilization's refuse and the multiplication or political rise of the blacks in one act of consciousness, feeling equally and identically

3. See below, p. 221.

threatened by them both. Without foundering in a demonstrative
discourse, the play is a gripping metaphor of one vision of the modern world, in which a proliferation of refuse and a proliferation of
human beings leads to the same terror.

The two motifs also lead to a specific judgment. Most of
Adamov's plays clearly establish, deductively or structurally, the
equivalence of the profitable exploitation of objects and of man.
While in *Paolo Paoli* feathers and butterflies are profitably bar-
tered, between scenes phrases chosen from the newspapers and
documents of 1900–14 are projected onto a screen, announcing, in
their cynical innocence, the exchanges effected by the European
countries in regard to the colonies: France gives Egypt to England;
England in exchange gives France a free hand in Morocco (or vice
versa). Meanwhile, in the same terms—but alas at too great length
—the characters discuss (always profitably) feathers, butterflies,
feathered hats, buttons decorated with butterfly wings, and so on.
They also discuss the fate of a young man, and here Adamov points
out—not only from a Marxist but, more broadly, from a Kantian
point of view—the absolute disgrace of men considering man as an
object.

The theme of the man-object as a victim is the second constant
in Adamov's works. Once again his point of departure is an existential anguish typical of the theatre of the fifties. More expressionistic or Germanic in form than Ionesco's or Beckett's, his plays
point up the tragedy of conscious and irreplaceable subjectivity
being incomprehensibly massacred, humiliated, or mutilated by
the world. The form is more expressionistic because his imagery
not only is painted with bold strokes but suggests the world more
in terms of social universality than in terms of cosmic universality.
In Adamov's absurd plays, as in all the plays of that school, what
the spectator sees onstage is at first given as no more than what he
sees. The difference comes when the spectator tries to set up a
parallel with the perceived reality of his own life. With Beckett
the experience is complex, generally extrahistorical, and completely imbued with a poetry that assimilates the Greeks, Dante,

and the popular myths of the modern world. With Ionesco (except for the third part of *La Soif et la faim*) the mind comes up against the eternal problem of the individual confronted by outer reality—that is to say, solipsism (philosophically) or a naïve but shattering individualism (ideologically). With Adamov, however, one pole of the conflict is a social specificity, the other being the individual, of course, but the individual situated socially. If the individual is a victim, it is because the social system can be maintained only by an anti-Kantian procedure. Adamov's plays are all centered on that blind victimization (*La Grande et La Petite Manœuvre,* for example) or on a refusal of it *(Le Printemps 71)* as well as on an aesthetic revenge: the playwright himself transforms into objects—that is, into puppets—the social forces that feed on the dehumanization of man.

Adamov's theatre is thus committed and openly Marxist—and hence is unacceptable, on principle, to a great number of French critics. Their judgments, however, must be largely dismissed, for what really matters is Adamov's dramatic experimentation—the manner in which he began with the absurd and expressionism, absorbed them, and then went beyond them, without actually repudiating them. For him the absurd, which is concerned only with "eternal" situations, is idealistic in nature and thus futile. What really interests him is that the modern form of his theatre have a practical significance "here and now" (the title of his collection of critical essays). When the slogans and news items of 1900–14 are projected onto a screen between grotesque debates about the price of a rare butterfly, scenically using the fictional device of Dos Passos in *U.S.A.,* a double theatrical distance is created, so that the spectator may judge for himself the close relationship between two futilities—the one inoffensive for the most part, the other a source of collective massacre.

As we have said, Adamov is a "case." He is extremely ambitious and at the same time places too much confidence in his audiences. Needless to say, a certain bourgeois public, which automatically considers 1789, 1848, and 1871 as black dates in the history of

France, is absolutely closed to any attempt at an epic re-creation of the events of those years—indeed, is indignant at the very mention of them. On the other hand, the public which thinks of those historical episodes as glorious milestones and a source of political hope is far from having the knowledge necessary to understand the subtleties that Adamov is trying to communicate. One wonders, for example, whether Adamov, an intellectual and a finical historian, truly believes that the workers of East Paris know enough about the history of the Commune to understand the thirty-six possible attitudes he presents in *Printemps 71,* from cautious liberalism to the militant Marxism of the late nineteenth century. One wonders still more whether he truly believes that the working-class and even communist public at which he aims has a sufficiently detailed idea of the political vicissitudes of the Common Market to follow the complex adventures in *Sainte-Europe,* even if the Ubuesque figure of Karl immediately evokes De Gaulle (although, in fact, Adamov wants Karl to be *more* than De Gaulle). For while *Sainte-Europe* is a political cartoon expanded into a three-hour spectacle, the cartoon is inspired by *Le Canard Enchaîné,* a very subtle satiric journal for intellectuals of anarchist tendencies.

On the other hand, Adamov's plays are not altogether didactic. They are primarily a theatrical transposition of "mechanisms." In the early plays the universal mechanisms of the dream that paralyzes the individual and the totalitarianism that mutilates people or chooses scapegoats are not linear; their horror comes largely from the dialectic of the fallacious hope and the real despair that they impose on the individual, the better to crush him. At the other extreme, *Le Printemps 71,* which demonstrates the failure of the first proletarian revolution, is concerned not with a universal mechanism of society but with a specific event unique in history—the Commune. Indeed, all of Adamov's plays are haunted by the workings of human affairs. He shows how, mechanically (and dialectically), the individual is crushed as a Negro is killed, a revolution comes to grief, or a Holy Alliance is formed (an economic alliance, since this is the twentieth century). In fact, Adamov is the theatrical poet of mechanisms.

Adamov has been faced with a serious dilemma, however, for while each mechanism may have dramatic potential, it is primarily an object of science. Reconstruction—boring even during the period of Romanticism and local color (Alexandre Dumas père's *Henri III et sa cour*, for example)—requires a juxtaposition of details and a fidelity to all kinds of trifling vicissitudes that may be fascinating in a history book but are monotonous on stage. If the playwright transposes or poetizes, his only recourse is allegory, which may charm the imagination but which, since it reflects an intellectual study of the problem, obscures the historical event more than it adds the distance necessary for criticism. Adamov is still hesitant about the means to establish that distance: he has tried the contrast between an imaginary anecdote and the interjection of historical documents *(Paolo Paoli)*, the contrast between a fresco of revolutionaries' daily lives and allegorical interludes *(Le Printemps 71)*, the almost medieval transposition of a contemporary political mechanism *(Sainte-Europe)*, and, perhaps most successfully, the parallel that may exist between an individual psychosis and a collective attitude *(La Politique des restes)*. In the last case the double game of participation (we who belong to a world that is essentially racist are hypocritically urged to commit racist murder) and distance (the racist murderer in the play is mad by any standards—that is to say, a creature separate from us, who bears the weight of our intellectual and objective judgment) is convincing. Adamov simultaneously dissects two mechanisms, remaining faithful both to his own temperament and to his ideology. Influenced by Brecht—not as a disciple but as a critic— he might create a new and significant committed theatre if, beyond his defection from the no-man's-land of the absurd, he continues to resist copying Brecht and avoids the oversimplified and tortuous intellectualism of *Sainte-Europe*.

The objective of the new committed playwrights is to awaken the working-class public to its own interests and to provoke its self-criticism.[4] Using more or less Brechtian means, they create spectacles of past or imaginary collective adventures identical with or parallel to the current fate of that public. In other words, more than a theatre of revolt, theirs is a theatre of revolution. Whether or not one is in sympathy with its ideology, and despite expected and facile effects such as ending *Le Printemps 71* with the International, their theatre has considerable dramatic interest. Following Brecht, although disagreeing on certain points, the revolutionary playwrights have finally understood that form is inseparable from substance—that it is not enough to offer a traditional presentation of the conflicts between worthy proletarians and nasty bosses, but that the very structure of the play must also be a revolutionary act.

In this respect Armand Gatti, previously a journalist, has been even bolder than Adamov. Certain of his works are better overlooked. The banal *Le Crapaud-Buffle,* for example, is a burlesque allegory of a personal dictatorship; and *Le Poisson noir* is pretentious and obscure. Others, however, are remarkable for their architectural structure and their dramatic power.

One of Gatti's favorite methods is to base a play not on a chronological flow of time but on a meeting point of the past, present, and future. A striker mortally wounded by the police sees during his agony the events of his past reenacted, as well as one possible future event *(La Vie imaginaire de l'éboueur Auguste Geai)*. The meeting, in a fairground, of a former prisoner of a concentration camp and the widow of a man who had been shot provokes not only a confrontation of their respective pasts but a "murder" of those pasts and finally their unavoidable resurrection *(La Deuxième Existence du camp de Tattenberg)*. The story of Sacco and Vanzetti is simultaneously and currently performed in five theatres in different cities, and the fictitious spectators, each

4. Such playwrights and some directors have raised the question of an altogether new public. See below, Appendix I, pp. 319–20.

in his own way, relive the trial of the two anarchists, thus representing the trial's future *(Chant public devant deux chaises électriques).* All three plays are extremely complex in form (even if some of the dialogue is very elementary), for the meetings, parallels, and contrasts between groups of men, eras, expressionistic symbols, and levels of reality are multiplied. In *Auguste Geai,* for example, one sees onstage, sometimes simultaneously, Auguste at nine years old, Auguste at twenty-one, Auguste at thirty, Auguste at forty-six (the year of his death), and "ageless" Auguste. In *Chant public* the spectators from Boston, Los Angeles, Hamburg, Turin, and Lyons alternate or join together, and in *Tattenberg* there is a mixture not only of the camp's dead and survivors but of giant puppets and imaginary characters out of a Viennese parade. Thus, as a whole, Gatti's plays may be described as clusters built around a central adventure and radiating in space and time. Compared to such complexity, Salacrou's innovations in *L'Inconnue d'Arras* now appear somewhat mild.

Salacrou's works, however, have the distinct advantage of being clear. For a Gatti play, despite the author's orchestral sense, is absolutely dependent upon precise staging, based on a clear-cut handling of scenic space; otherwise, the themes are obscured, the opposing forces remain undefined, and the text itself seems something of a muddle. Indeed, Gatti depends upon his director (Jacques Rosner for *Auguste Geai*) and has himself proved to be most competent in directing *Le Poisson noir* and *Chant public.* Much of the complexity of his attempt at total theatre derives from the fact that the plays are great spectacles organized almost cinematically. Vast decors rising in tiers and embracing the world (or at least all the places involved in one lifetime), expressionistic film projections, photographic collages, sound effects, revolutionary songs, an alternation of realism and speeches directed to the audience—Gatti is willing to use any device whatever to evoke the totality of a particular experience and to alternately include and exclude the audience.

One of his most striking devices is the very special use he makes of theatre within theatre. While a reconstruction of the Sacco and Vanzetti trial by means of a play within a play is perhaps not original, Gatti's innovation was to multiply that play within a play by five, thus confronting the audience with some fifteen possible conflicts and simple tensions. More subtly, the characters in *Auguste Geai* first participate in a dance marathon, with a police-force orchestra, and then, at the end, in a film that Christian Geai will perhaps make about the life of his father. In *Tattenberg* the fairground milieu supplies, among other theatrical possibilities, puppet-soldiers who give a daily performance of the murder of the heroine's husband. And, in general, the characters' dreams, memories, or deliriums are distinguished from present reality by their obvious staginess. In all these examples the theatre within theatre has a twofold result: on the purely aesthetic level it is a source of the fantasy and poetry of terror or horror and, sometimes, joy, and on the ideological level it creates the critical distance so sought after by the neo-Brechtians.

Nevertheless, Gatti has not managed to avoid certain of the pitfalls of epico-political theatre. His language often consists of electoral-convention clichés, he tends to divide the world into innocents and villains, and his anti-Americanism is over-simplified and naïve. On the other hand, the portrait of a garbage collector's fate in *Auguste Geai* carries real conviction because of a richness in the character's inner and outer conflicts, an imagery devoid of any romanticizing of poverty, and the subtlety of the symbols: the dance marathon, on a collective level, and the double image of the Black Baron (a bum on whom Geai has concentrated his fantasies of childhood terror) and the White Baron (boss of the garbage collectors, thus an adult and socially objective terror). The aim of this kind of theatre is to neutralize the enemy and exalt the friend. *Auguste Geai,* utilizing all Gatti's theatrical skills, succeeds in much the same way as Brecht's *Caucasian Chalk Circle:* while the revolutionaries find in the play images of their own grandeur and their own shortcomings, counterrevolutionaries, at the end, begin to clap against their own interests.

Modern epic theatre is not necessarily a privilege of the working class, nor does critical theatre have to derive from orthodox Marxism. Indeed, the later works of François Billetdoux are a case in point. American audiences know Billetdoux's *Tchin-Tchin,* a rigorous, mathematical, and sober little play (despite its alcoholic content), with only two characters, which on Broadway was unfortunately blown up into a spectacular and burlesque star vehicle. Its theme was clearly defined, however, and from this first play to his later works, Billetdoux has raised questions about the relationship of the individual to society, his accomplishments in the outside world, and man's use of other men. While the suicides' inn of *Va Donc chez Thörpe* represents a kind of infernal paradise where men try to escape from such exploitation, the American suburbia of *Le Comportement des époux Bredburry* is the setting for an "absurd" variation—although, according to the author, based on an actual classified advertisement—of the individual considered as an object of commerce: a wife puts her husband up for sale at a price of $30,000. In his last two plays, *Comment Va le Monde, Môssieu? Il Tourne, Môssieu!* and *Il Faut Passer par les Nuages,* the theme has taken epic proportions on the levels of both content and form.

The form of *Comment Va le Monde* is extremely Brechtian. The characters move around in the world (from eastern Europe to the United States); the scenes are dated (from December 1944 to August 1945—the atomic bomb on Hiroshima and Nagasaki); the two "human" heroes are surrounded by mute figures (fellow prisoners, soldiers, civilians, customs officers, a wife, and so on) whose silence and pantomimes situate them on another level of scenic reality; and the scenes are interspersed with "meaningful" songs (a Nazi improvisation, a Jewish lament, a Negro spiritual, and a ballad in the manner of Boris Vian). But this truly Brechtian spectacle is primarily related to the German playwright's negative works, with the addition of a really French savor. The dialogue (only the two heroes speak, one a deported French soldier, the other an American prisoner) is midway between the language of

Paul Raynal's 1914 soldiers in *Le Matériel humain* (1935) and that of Louis-Ferdinand Céline. The subject matter itself is a common little Frenchman's cocky banter and gumption confronted by American pragmatism. The Frenchman uses the American, and the American uses the Frenchman, each in accordance with his "national character," throughout an interminable adventure that leads them from a Nazi concentration camp to an absurd murder in Texas.

During the long spectacle the two protagonists of *Comment Va le Monde* constantly oscillate between a recognition of the other as a person and the use of the other as an object. The American, for example, manages to convince his companion to sleep with a homosexual immigration officer in New York so that they can disembark illegally (the Frenchman, of course, rises to the situation by deciding to give the officer a thrill he will never forget). But the adventure, whatever its antics or horrors (the play opens on a suggestion of cannibalism in the Nazi camp), is stopped short with the murder of the American, and the curtain falls on the little Frenchman's solitude—not on his despair but on an absurd and absolute "beginning": "That's all very well, but how the devil do I begin?" These, the last words of the play, uttered by the Frenchman over the dead body of his American companion, in some indeterminate Texas, close this epic of survival. Man can survive only by exploiting man or allowing himself to be exploited. Men love or hate one another for their exchange value. Thus, in contrast to the Marxists' "open" tragedy based on economy, Billetdoux has written a closed melodramatic epic based on a parallel explanation of the workings of society.

Like Gatti, Billetdoux uses great scenic orchestrations to give the spectacle of everyday preoccupations the scope that Claudel, in *Le Soulier de satin,* gave to the conquest of continents and the crises of Christianity. His *Il Faut Passer par les Nuages* answers Gatti's gigantic glorification of the garbage collector Geai with an operatic amplification of individual revenge in a bourgeois milieu. Here again the underlying dramatic theme is that of the commerce or exchange of men socially sanctified by financial power. Actually, one might say that *Il Faut Passer par les Nuages* is a Salacrou Le Havre play—with its flashbacks, deceits, and caste prejudices, all deriving from naturalism—suddenly projected in cinemascope. Thus the play's originality lies not in the invention of characters, situations, or even the theme of its Samson-heroine, who brings the temple down on her own head as well as on those of the family who has been exploiting her, but in the proportions given to this woman who is mistress of a fortune. Though the anecdote may be called bourgeois and limited, it is no more so than the butterfly collection in Adamov's *Paolo Paoli*, because, on the one hand, it reveals just as powerfully the social crime of worldwide repercussion committed against the Kantian imperative and, on the other, the spectacle of an awareness of, and revolt against, that crime is equal to the very best in its genre.

Critical in manner and epic in form, Billetdoux's most recent plays may provoke some annoyance by their pretentiousness. His systematic use of the long monologue, for example, occasionally recalls the kind of bad literature that tries to be Greek tragedy. Furthermore, while the stage directions given in the printed text, emphasizing the author's orchestral intentions, are extremely useful, they are also inordinately pompous.

There is no doubt that certain of today's playwrights have been so taken by their epic ambitions that they see themselves as great eternal geniuses—as kinds of secular Claudels. More important than their megalomania, however, is their main objective: to get away from the idea of a "chamber theatre" and, through the very dimensions and complexity of their spectacles, to present a grandiose vision of the human drama. One is also struck by the underlying theme of all their works, which is finally independent of any precise political doctrine: man's exploitation of man. While the ideology behind the theme may be Marxist, it is not necessarily so. Though man's growing awareness of the fact that he is a product of commercial exchange is of course a cliché of modern times, when it is projected with all the scenic discoveries of the past fifteen years, as well as with the huge stages and machines of today, it becomes both an object of reflection and a way open to new techniques.

Up until now this kind of theatre has been walking a tightrope —with, on one side, the abyss of the old naturalism and the elementary psychologism of the "message" play and, on the other, the precipice of allegory. Nevertheless, it is truly experimental— both sociologically, since it aims at a new public which in some measure already exists but which must be largely created (especially in the case of Adamov or Gatti), and theatrically, since it transfers the experiments that were formerly carried out on small stages in the past onto the largest ones possible.[5] In fact, much of the experimentation done in little theatres has, in the past few years, become the new establishment and is now invading the large state theatres in the persons of Ionesco, Beckett, and Genet.

5. To be absolutely fair, the concept of an epic theatre does not exclude "small" plays. Georges Michel's *Promenade du Dimanche,* for example, is a kind of digest of such ambitions, created for a small stage. Michel has reduced the great epic space to a street along which one particular family walks back and forth. Society is symbolized by that family, the drama of the individual-as-object by a series of murders, and history by explosions of OAS bombs at the end of the Algerian War.

PART IV

THE NEW ESTABLISHMENT

# CHAPTER 11

# THE WEIGHT OF THINGS:
# EUGENE IONESCO

While the possibility of an epic theatre takes shape around the commonplace of man's exploitation of man, Ionesco, one of the pioneers of the "new theatre," is continuing to champion a non-political and nonideological form of the art. Altogether committed to noncommitment, he has multiplied the statements, articles, and interviews[1] in which he takes a stand against the theories of Sartre and Brecht, maintaining that their so-called demystification leads only to new mystification. In his theatre he has gone so far as to present certain ideologies merely to show the fragility of their mechanism (the scene of the clowns Tripp and Brechtoll in Episode III of *La Soif et la faim*). For Ionesco ideologies and works based on ideologies not only are transitory and contradictory but betray the true purpose of art, which is to present the invisible and eternal

---

1. Most of them are collected in the volume *Notes et contre-notes* (Paris, 1962).

aspect of man's condition. Albert Camus' phrase, "Men die, and they are not happy," might well be applied to his works, for, although the formula is intellectual, Ionesco's art consists in conveying its immediate and perceptible truth by embodying it in dreams, in obsessions, and in man's daily existence.

Early in the 1950s Ionesco's "absurd" plays performed on the small stages of Paris were condemned by the majority of French critics.[2] Today certain of them are included in the repertoires of the national theatres (the Comédie Française, the Théâtre de France), are produced throughout the world (including some of the socialist countries),[3] and have become classics for the use of American college students. Thus the fact that he is now one of the established playwrights of the twentieth century signifies that the avant-garde or "new theatre" or "antitheatre" of the fifties has quite simply become the theatre of our times. Sketchy characters being carried away by words, changing identities, having three noses, laying eggs, talking without communicating, becoming preys to organized disorder, murder, or the most grotesque cruelty, living out directed dreams, being transformed into rhinoceroses, flying in the air and disappearing into the hell of the future, being brainwashed by monks who are not really monks—none of that seems baffling any longer. Despite the direct language and the somewhat dreary settings, Ionesco's works are, above all, poetic, in the modern sense of the term. They present a concrete realization of metaphors and an immediate experience of existence, grasped in the individual's relation to himself and to the world that surrounds him.

Like many of the French poet-playwrights, Ionesco brings the intangible elements of his vision of the world to the stage in the concrete form of objects or acts. But by going beyond a representation of his private imagery, he succeeds in giving a metaphysical impression, elementary enough to have universal value, at least

2. With the exception of a few enlightened reviewers such as Jacques Lemarchand.

3. See Jan Kott, "A Propos des *Chaises* à Cracovie," *Cahiers Renaud-Barrault*, No. 42 (February 1963).

today. He confronts the spectator with a direct metaphor of the modern world, sending him back to his own anguish instead of merely drawing him into the mysteries of a privileged imagination.

Nevertheless, Ionesco's imagery does arise from his own inner fantasies. In giving the sources of many of the scenes in his plays, he himself has explained that his dreams, nightmares, childhood memories, and feelings while walking about in a big city are all part of his material. As his characters gradually take on more realistic dimensions—in particular, the figure of Bérenger (called Jean in his most recent incarnation)—his works become more and more a personal confession. Bérenger's incomprehension in the face of existence, his fear of death, and his "burning nostalgia" *(La Soif et la faim)* are three dimensions of Ionesco the man, now the creator of a rather neo-Romantic theatre—not in form but in substance—though the importance of his works is their "neo" aspect, in the fact of his having both transcended his purely private drama and given it a particular form.

Using a device that is now common to many playwrights of the absurd, Ionesco managed scenically to present his inner world, especially his dreams, with objectivity. The dreams' enchantment —sometimes joyous, usually frustrating or terrifying—is replaced by a factuality reminiscent of Kafka. The spectator may find the flow of events incoherent or disconnected, and the dialogue is often a series of paralogisms or automatic puns, but the characters— whether surprised, indignant, or frightened—accept such phenomena as real. While the growing corpse and the mushrooms in *Amédée ou Comment S'En Débarrasser* may be dream symbols referring to a guilt complex, or might even be considered as elements of a nightmare, they are eminently real to the characters, who are not dreaming but are terrified by real events and real dangers, not by fantasies or hallucinations. In *Le Piéton de l'air* Bérenger actually flies in the air while his family and a crowd of Englishmen look on and react in various ways but always as if it were a possible feat, finding it exalting, shocking, embarrassing, or merely contemptible. All that happens in the universe of these plays may be extraordinary or contradictory, but it never belongs to another order of reality. Ionesco himself stresses this point. When someone in *Le Roi se meurt* says of Bérenger I, "He was big. He was small," Ionesco wants the actor to pronounce both sentences in the same tone of voice, for the simultaneity of two contradictory truths is normal in the play's world. Although the transformation of men into rhinoceroses is in the nature of the unreal and verbal contradiction is in the nature of madness, when such fictions are presented onstage as a matter of fact, the spectator is confronted not with poetry opening onto some beyond but with a universe parallel to traditional reality. Ionesco uses dream not to reveal other worlds but to highlight the one we live in.

To begin with, by giving absurd fantasies the concrete and obvious properties of ordinary reality, Ionesco's theatre shows reality to be equally absurd. Our world is neither more nor less justified than what unfolds onstage and can be considered quite as ridiculous. The madly delirious conversation in *La Cantatrice chauve* and the fiancée's two or three noses in *Jacques ou La Soumission* are analogous to the facts of real life, and the destructive laughter they provoke reflects on their real correlatives. Thus, while Ionesco is uncommitted, his works are essentially satirical, for the device of objectivization results in a denunciation of the absurdity of man's behavior and his everyday good conscience.

Language was Ionesco's first victim—and continues to be, despite the fact that he has progressively given up the exercises of systematic demolition that constitute *La Cantatrice chauve*. In addition to tautological statements such as "The ceiling is up, the floor is down," man's conversation consists of contradictory affirmations expressed with such absolutely equal conviction that, when brutally juxtaposed in theatrical dialogue, they destroy each other. One of the many examples of this is the concierge's song in Act III of *Tueur sans gages:* "When it's cold, it's not hot,/ When it's hot, it's because it's cold!" If such contradictions are stated as obvious facts, their absurdity is so striking that the spectator begins to question his own "reality."[4]

Ionesco's satire has branched out into every possible realm since *La Cantatrice chauve*, and even there, he was exposing the shallowness of conversation and all the petty bourgeois behavior, beliefs, and values that it implies. Ten plays later, in *Tueur sans gages*, his hero Bérenger is led to a final scene in which the process of complete demystification is explicitly developed. Finding himself alone with a killer, Bérenger tries to convince him of the criminal and useless nature of murder in a long monologue that gives the arguments both for and against it. He discovers simultaneously that while there is no reason to kill, there is no reason *not* to kill. Happiness, the brotherhood of man, all the good reasons are destroyed even in Bérenger's mind by the Killer's silence or derisive laughter, especially when, getting no response whatever, Bérenger himself goes beyond the reasons he presents in order to find more convincing ones and, in fact, ends in confusion: "I don't know anymore, I don't know anymore. Maybe you're wrong, maybe wrong doesn't exist, maybe it's we who are wrong to want to exist . . . Explain. What do you think? I don't know, I don't know. *(The Killer sneers.)*" The Killer's "infinite energy of obstinacy" wins out over all the values, even over Bérenger's instinct of self-preservation, for Bérenger drops his gun and lets himself be knifed, muttering, "What can we do . . . What can we do."

---

4. Ionesco asks that his actors' performance be theatrical, of course, but mostly he wants it to be effective—that is, to bring out the "unreality of the real." If, for example, in the case of *La Cantatrice chauve* the actors succeed by performing the play as if it were Ibsen's *Hedda Gabler,* so much the better; or if they get the required effect by acting like the Marx Brothers, why not? What they must avoid, however, is disguising the contradictions by the use of tricks, such as making the spectator believe that the character, realizing that his first statement was false, seems to think better of it and then reestablishes the truth. (See Simone Benmussa, *Ionesco* [Paris, 1966], pp. 87, 104.) That is in fact what Robert Hirsch might be criticized for in the role of Jean in *La Soif et la faim,* for every time his language strayed from traditional logic, he gave the impression of apologizing.

By extension, the vision of the world presented in *Tueur sans gages* clarifies a significant aspect of Ionesco's plays. His initial irreverence about the daily routine of life, giving new form to a hackneyed theme, was in fact aimed at all action and all behavior. Indeed, the whole of his works is a cluster of metaphors illustrating Bérenger's final idea: "Maybe it's we who are wrong to want to exist."

While such generality may have enriched Ionesco's plays, it has also resulted in some confusion. Everything is finally brought into question, each statement ultimately negates itself, and all the absurdities are given equal importance—the presence of things, man's decisions, social disorder, the conventions of society, psychological impulses, old age, and the problems of city traffic. In a world seen simultaneously on all levels the main problem or subject does not exclude the other levels. Thus *La Leçon* is at the same time an almost surrealistic use of certain textbooks, a satire on teaching, and a terrifying psychodrama. *Tueur sans gages* combines a tableau of everyday life with the nightmare of organized disorder in a large modern city, a psychological study, and the tragedy of Bérenger in search of and then faced with the Killer; by thus juxtaposing themes as disparate as the satire of big city traffic and the failure of Bérenger's reason, a universe is evoked in which any hierarchy of levels is obliterated. While in *Le Piéton de l'air* the central theme is Bérenger's flight, which is at first exhilarating and then indicative of a future of universal horror, the playwright does not hesitate to move about freely among considerations as to the meaning of literature, examples of conventional language, and the metaphor of a higher judgment in the form of a dream involving a father image. Of course, the final apocalypse appears as the supreme truth, but the play equalizes all the other elements, from a bombardment and dreams of happiness to English dignity and family quarrels. In other words, Ionesco's theatre in general presents the image of a world where everything is equally important—and, by the same token, unimportant.

All that can be said for this universe is that facts, events, beings, and things exist. Indeed, they exist in abundance. One of the authentically dramatic dimensions of Ionesco's theatre lies in the tension between a superabundance of being and the absolute impossibility of justifying the *fact* of being. It is therefore metaphysical drama to the extent that it shows existence as having no reason to exist and the unjustified as existing in superabundance. In short, the world is superfluous.

This feeling is communicated visually by an overcrowding of the stage—an accumulation of objects or their increase in size. On the most elementary level, in *L'Avenir est dans les œufs,* the stage is gradually filled with millions of eggs until it finally collapses. In an ironic tone, the protagonist of *Le Nouveau Locataire* willingly imprisons himself in the midst of the countless pieces of furniture he has brought to his room. More subtly, the two old people's imaginary world in *Les Chaises* is overpopulated, with the crowd visually suggested by empty chairs that multiply onstage. Even *Rhinocéros,* in which all mankind is transformed into rhinoceroses and which ends with Bérenger's refusal to become one like the others, is less an attack on totalitarian regimes (obvious though it may be on one level) than a terrifying metaphor of the isolation of the individual in a world where even other human beings proliferate like things. As for *La Soif et la faim,* beyond the Romantic anecdote of an attempted but unsuccessful escape, and as a symbol of its failure, a striking contrast is set up between the great open space of the second episode and the closed room of the third, where from minute to minute additional characters—so-called monks—appear but are perceived as objects anonymously accumulating onstage, for they are merely human shapes depersonalized by monks' frocks. In addition to things and beings, there is a superabundance of words themselves. The dialogue is drawn out for no particular reason and filled with repetitions that ultimately produce a kind of incantation, as in the case of *Les Chaises* or certain scenes of *Tueur sans gages* and *Le Piéton de l'air.*

There are doubtless similarities between Ionesco's vision of matter and certain passages of Sartre's *La Nausée*. But where in Sartre the impression is qualitative, in Ionesco it is quantitative: the viscous substance of existence in Sartre is replaced by a numerical or measurable (the corpse in *Amédée*) superabundance. When Ionesco does allude to viscidity (there are several references in his works to the *mud* of being), he expresses it in terms of sinking—that is, of progression. Suggested in *Victimes du devoir,* mud dominates the whole first scene of *La Soif et la faim:* the apartment of Marie-Madeleine and Jean not only is muddy already but gets progressively muddier—even the drawers fill up—as it sinks into the ground. In other words, Ionesco's conception of the viscidity of opaque being is not stable, as it is in Sartre; rather, it becomes a growing cancer of consciousness.

Such quantitative imagery made it possible for Ionesco to devise a simple form of comedy corresponding to Bergson's definition of the mechanical imposed upon the living. When a mechanism is applied to the phenomena of daily life, insignificant activity, and the many domains one habitually thinks of in nonmechanical terms, the combination approaches the essence of comedy. For example, when in a conversation about members of a family—their births, marriages, jobs, and deaths—Ionesco gives all the members the name Bobby Watson (*La Cantatrice chauve),* he is certain to provoke laughter for two reasons: because of the contrast between what a family *should* be and the incongruity of the supposedly typical Watson family, and because the truth behind the accepted notion of the family is found to be rigorously mechanical.

To the mathematical rigor imposed on human phenomena Ionesco often adds a process of geometric progression or acceleration. The mechanisms are slow and regular at first (the corpse's growth in *Amédée,* the production of eggs in *L'Avenir est dans les œufs,* the repetition of dialogue in *Les Chaises,* the professor's nervous irritation and confusion in *La Leçon,* and the multiplication of rhinoceroses in *Rhinocéros*), but then the growth or accumulation gathers speed until it reaches a mad precipitation.[5] Indeed, the general impression is often that of a machine out of control. While pauses result from variations in speed, they are more comparable to a shifting of gears than to the slowing down of the mechanical process or the return to a more human perspective. And since the acceleration is always cumulative with regard both to the speed and the object's proliferation, the loss of control ultimately applies to the very phenomenon of being. Ionesco's theatre, then, is the comedy, both laughable and terrifying, of man transcended by being itself or, more precisely, by his increasing awareness of being itself.

In contrast to the so-called existentialist theatre, according to which man has the freedom and indefeasible power to make himself and make the world, Ionesco's theatre is one of disenchantment. His vision may be similar to the early phases of the existentialist philosophy—the isolation of the individual consciousness in our absurd universe, the unjustified presence of things, and the unbearable fact of existence itself (as in Sartre's *La Nausée* and Camus' *L'Etranger*)—but while both Sartre and Camus developed their themes into reasons for action, Ionesco, one literary generation younger, marks the failure of any such ambition. Indeed, his plays exemplify in many ways the nihilism of which existentialism has so often been accused. Those who have termed this type of theatre a "theatre of the atomic age" are right to the extent that any hope in an efficacious praxis has been considerably shaken by an awareness of the possibility of total destruction. Faced with that possibility, not only do the problems of modern naturalism (homosexuality, drugs, conflicts limited to the family and society) have little weight, but the theme of political revolution loses its acuity and is leveled to the rank of the others. Sartre and Camus needed great exemplary acts to describe the human condition more effec-

5. Here one senses the influence not only of gags like the Marx Brothers' but of the technical acceleration of the motion picture image.

tively in their plays. In the perspective of absolute annihilation, however, all acts are equalized, in Ionesco as in Beckett.

Not that the end-of-the-world atmosphere is always explicit. The setting of Beckett's *Fin de partie* may, of course, be interpreted as a symbol of the world after the Bomb, but in Ionesco there are only a few precise suggestions of it. One occurs in *Les Chaises:*

> The Old Lady:    Paris never existed, my dear.
> The Old Man:    It must have existed, since it collapsed. It was the city of light, since the light has been out, out, for 4,000 years.

Even if the image is a product of the Old Man's delirium, it does reveal the psychosis of A.D. 1,000—an obsession with universal catastrophe—but now there is no Last Judgment and therefore no hope of redemption in a beatific beyond. Indeed, Bérenger's shattering vision at the end of *Le Piéton de l'air* leaves little doubt in that regard. It is true that his daughter, Marthe, has the last word in the play: "Maybe everything will be all right in the end . . . maybe one day the flames will go out . . . maybe the ice is going to melt . . . maybe the abysmal voids will fill up . . . maybe . . . the gardens . . . the gardens . . .". She did not go along on the flight, however, and her enthusiasm and refusal of nihilism is in fact only an expression of Ionesco's wishful thinking.

Taken literally, Ionesco's latest works oppose the opacity of an unlivable world of things and beings to gardens, azure skies, and radiant cities. The green paradise of the English countryside *(Le Piéton)*, which makes Bérenger so happy that he begins to fly; the large platform high in the sky (Episode II of *La Soif et la faim*), which Jean reaches at one point in his escapade; the sunlit, ideal city in the style of Le Corbusier *(Tueur)*, which is visited by Bérenger—all these paradisaic images are just as real to the characters as their horrible misfortunes. Such enchanting places are of course in direct opposition to the others the characters have known: they are spacious and almost devoid of things. In fact, the sunlit city is itself so far from being a thing that it is never shown onstage: the hero is enraptured by an empty setting which consists only of light.

In addition to being traditional representations of an outer reality, these privileged places are closely linked to the characters' inner forces and are an element of the "new" psychology on which Ionesco bases his theatre. In *Victimes du devoir* the character Nicolas d'Eu explicitly states Ionesco's own intention of excluding any traditional psychology: "We shall give up the principle of identity and unity of character for the benefit of movement, for a dynamic psychology . . . We are not ourselves . . . Personality doesn't exist. Within us, we have merely contradictory and non-contradictory forces." This concept corresponds to the psychology in many contemporary French novels: the characters are defined both by the objects around them and by the inner play of those contradictory and noncontradictory forces. In *Amédée* the cancer of guilt is both represented objectively (by the ever-lengthening corpse and the mushrooms that grow in the parlor) and expressed in psychological terms. In *Tueur sans gages* Bérenger's desires not only take the form of a modern, sunlit city but are also conveyed in an analysis of his inner necessity. Both are combined in the remark:

> In short, inner world and outer world are bad expressions; there are no boundaries between those so-called two worlds. There is obviously a fundamental impulse, which comes from us, and when it can't be exteriorized, when it can't be objectively realized, when there is no complete accord between my inner me and my outer me, the result is catastrophe, universal contradiction, the final break.

The fact that Bérenger never succeeds in communicating this analysis to the Architect creates an initial drama or conflict, but, on a deeper level, his comments prefigure an adventure to come— one that he has already experienced within himself as an abrupt transition from joy to melancholy, a "kind of tumultuous vacuum

—like at the moment of a tragic separation, intolerable." Just as the new city is the hyperbolic realization of the force of joy within him, so the presence of the Killer and the final murder are the amplified and extreme realization of the opposite force. Indeed, what gives the play its value is Ionesco's skill in playing with the four elements of the drama—inner joy, inner vacuum, City of the Sun, Killer—inserting "breaks," as Bérenger calls them, at given points between the subjective and the objective, thus relating them not symbolically but concomitantly. Similarly, in the first episode of *La Soif et la faim,* Jean's inner self is concretized in the mud that fills his apartment. As soon as he leaves, the same apartment becomes the flower garden of Marie-Madeleine's love.

Ultimately—and this is what makes Ionesco's drama particularly somber—the "sunlit" force, in its inner and outer forms, is deceptive, for it always contains a seed of self-destruction. The City in *Tueur sans gages* harbors the Killer; the platform in *La Soif et la faim* becomes the embodiment of solitude; *Le Piéton's* silver bridge in the sky leads to atomic hell, to curtains of flame, to monsters. Though these beautiful places, of which the heroes dream with "burning nostalgia," do exist, they are precarious: visiting them means transforming them. The "Azure" to which one escapes from suffocation hides nothingness or the horror of annihilation. In fact, Ionesco's paradises cease being paradises as soon as one knows them, as if knowledge were a condemning sin.

Fundamental in Ionesco's theatre is farce—that is to say, a spectacle of beings whose existence is inferior to what the spectator considers his own. While serious theatre stylizes man, traditional farce partly humanizes objects. The spectator's laughter and satisfaction spring from the humanized object's failure to imitate life. The clown imitating a man of the world and the marionette aping a lover are merely silhouettes—inferior forms that never succeed in being equal to their own ambitions and never attain the consistency and weight of their human objective's existence. The puppet is constantly called to order by a continual resurgence of mechanical forces that limit his imitation, thus provoking laughter. The characters in *La Cantatrice chauve* are all little machines that speak without communicating and, as in seventeenth-century farce, never realize it: language eludes their grasp, breaks loose, and becomes gibberish. The Old Lady and Old Man of *Les Chaises* ✝ remain, for the most part, on this side of what the spectator considers true humanity because of their language as well as their uncontrollable inner mechanisms. Indeed, all Ionesco's works are marked by moments in which the characters find themselves carried away, unknowingly, by Bergsonian mechanical forces.

On the other hand, the farce is "dark," for even in those plays that are altogether farcical, the mechanism of the puppets is presented not as accidental, as limited to the passionate moments of life, for example, or to specific individuals or professions, but as universal. In *La Cantatrice chauve* it is language in general that is brought into question. In the other plays incoherency or the absurd is not confined to types but attributed to figures that represent all of man and any man whatever. Just as the character originally responsible for this extension, Jarry's Ubu, transcends the satire of the ambitious bourgeois and reveals the pitiful and terrifying Shakespearean monster within all men, so Ionesco's works imply the human condition as a whole.

From play to play Ionesco has made the human element more explicit to the extent that the puppet becomes increasingly aware of his defeat. As he does so, the laughter stops. In a traditionally Romantic world all laughter stops when the clown starts to cry; in Ionesco anguish takes the place of sentimentality. His clowns are nostalgic for the human element: suddenly, amid their farcical delirium or automatic responses, they begin to talk about it and appeal to it in the form of memories, dreams, or aspirations. The dialogue of the two old people in *Les Chaises,* alternating between communication and contradictory deviations, conveys that ambiguous situation in which man makes contact with man, only to be driven back to his solitude as a distraught and unwitting clown.

In his latest plays, and especially with his creation of Bérenger, Ionesco points up a particularly pathetic aspect of the dilemma. While Bérenger's language, his sudden bursts of enthusiasm, and his closed mind show him to be something of a puppet, his chief quality is his enormous good will, similar to that of Charlie Chaplin's Tramp. But, like Chaplin's Tramp, he is a mixture of both the comic and the tragic because of the fact that his good will ultimately turns against him. Also, by becoming humanized, he becomes increasingly isolated and discovers that he has been led to an impasse both within and without. This is exemplified by the defeat at the end of *Tueur sans gages,* the standstill at the end of *Rhinocéros,* the ghastly and apocalyptic bewilderment caused by the revelations at the end of *Le Piéton,* and the mechanical hellish society on which the curtain falls in *La Soif et la faim.*

In direct contrast to Beckett, Ionesco has need of great spectacles, for the universe in which he struggles is not empty but too full. Moreover, as Beckett's plays grow shorter, Ionesco's grow longer. In Beckett man *clings* to a few favorite, privileged, but exasperating objects (Winnie, in *Happy Days* [*Oh! Les Beaux Jours*], has trouble deciphering the trademark on her beloved toothbrush) and at the same time isolates himself in a void. In Ionesco man is *entangled* in things and thus requires an ever-larger stage, for the overbalance of his world—sometimes cumbersome, sometimes pleasurable, but always frustrating—must be represented. Entire cities, kingdoms, herds of rhinoceroses, and a host of monks are the current equivalents of the chairs, the mushrooms, and the eggs of ten years ago.

If Ionesco has evolved, it has been from "armchair" proliferation to cosmic proliferation. Compare, for example, *Victimes du devoir* (1953) with *La Soif et la faim* (1966). In the first, Choubert, who is curiously directed by a wife with changing personalities and by a policeman, takes a trip inside his apartment that leads him under the furniture and then up on a chair which has been placed on a table, thus sinking into the mud of memory and then discovering the Azure to which he nostalgically aspires; at the end he is forced to stuff himself with stale bread in order to stop up the holes of his memory. Jean's journey in the second play, the image of mud, and his obligation to remember as he is force-fed are very similar themes, but his adventure is spectacularly exteriorized on a world-wide scale. The same might be said of the conclusion of *Rhino-céros* as compared to the next to the last scene of *La Cantatrice chauve*. In other words, as the protagonist becomes progressively humanized, the "inhuman" pole of the inner conflict gains in-creasing independence, exteriority, and scope. Thus Ionesco, who began with a subtle interplay between the subjective world and the objective world, has become more and more allegorical.

Paradoxically, Ionesco's most successful allegory in the past few years is perhaps *Le Roi se meurt,* in which, instead of the world expanding and things accumulating, they progressively dis-appear. King Bérenger I is dying, and during his agony his king-dom shrinks, his people diminish, his cities sink into bottomless chasms, his following thins out, his two wives leave, his palace vanishes, he himself disappears, and the curtain finally falls on an empty stage bathed in gray light. This play clearly expresses the ultimate meaning of Ionesco's works, which amounts to the follow-ing: that the only real drama is the individual's, that everyone experiences it alone, that everyone is a universe rent by an un-justifiable contradiction between the weight of things and the drive of consciousness (or, to use the existentialist jargon, between the "in itself" and the "for itself"), and that, with the death of each one, things and consciousness are reabsorbed and annihilated —just as one imagines that planets are born in space, sustain civilizations in which the spirit desperately struggles against mat-ter, and disappear, leaving no trace.

# CHAPTER 12

# EXISTENCE ONSTAGE:
## SAMUEL BECKETT

Since the 1952–53 season, during which Samuel Beckett was in danger of being eclipsed by more established names, critics and a great majority of the public have almost unanimously recognized the importance of his first play, *En Attendant Godot (Waiting for Godot)*, which is now considered *the* play par excellence of the "new theatre"—the masterpiece of French (and perhaps English) postwar drama. It is original, it lives, it not only represents a true insight into a way of feeling typical of our times but formulates a definition of man that transcends our times, and it introduces a new form of dramatic expression. Indeed, *Godot* would seem the end result of a long and searching endeavor—through the bitterness of naturalistic plays, the mysticism of Catholic drama, and the transcendency of poetic theatre—to express man's fundamental drama.

Certain critics have described *Godot* as an "allegorical play," whereas it is in fact altogether symbolic without being traditionally allegorical. Allegory implies analysis, exteriorization, and a concrete representation of the elements of the analysis. In *Godot* the elements of waiting (psychological, symbolic, or metaphysical), which remain *within* the characters, are not even individually conceptualized but are continuously and synthetically experienced by the characters. Moreover, there are no personifications of the abstract or the imaginary: Vladimir is not the personification of the soul or of the thirst for God; Estragon is not the personification of material hunger. Although the subject of *Godot* is the waiting for what never comes, and although the play, from beginning to end, evokes that gaping emptiness within man which, according to the play, is his very condition, it does not contain the intermediary that is characteristic of allegory: the reduction to abstract elements.

The play also avoids the traps of expressionism and the dangers of the "play of ideas," since there is no question of abstract qualities or intellectual analyses. Although Vladimir and Estragon sometimes "philosophize," they are in no way like those profound and lucid tramps occasionally found in theatre or films. *Godot* does not imply that out of the mouths of tramps comes wisdom. What they say is not explicit and is immediately transposed into poetry; it is chiefly an effort in the direction of ideas, memories, and a crude intellectualization of feelings or impressions—so that the interest lies not in their reasoning but in the effort they make to reason. The vague ideas they express are not given for themselves, but have a purely dramatic function: they are one of the poles toward which the characters desperately strain. There is neither debate nor confrontation, as in Giraudoux, Anouilh, or Sartre, but merely a representation of the vacuum that separates the characters from what they want to attain.

The absence of any intellectual debate and the spectacle of a constant state of tension sets *Godot* radically apart from the "play of ideas" and recalls symbolist drama, in which intellectual content is not given a logical and discursive form of expression—a form unsuitable for treating a reality that in itself is experienced.

The late nineteenth-century symbolist playwrights were concerned with reaffirming the reality of the Idea as against ideas—that is, the totality of an Essence grasped by intuition in contrast to analytic categories. By the same token, Mood (*Etat d'âme*) was opposed to Discourse. Whereas Discourse gradually develops in time, advancing through the moments of an action, Mood is immobilized in order to evoke an eternity. To the naturalistic discourse, to the sequence of events linked together by the relation of cause and effect, moving ahead in time which is comparable to that of an office worker, a physicist, or even Darwin, symbolist drama opposed "moments, minutes that are eternal."[1] Almost Bergsonian in intention, it became "static drama"—a drama that does not move forward and in which nothing happens, similar to a "ball that seems inert" but is "charged with electricity."[2] In extreme cases it has been reduced to the presentation of a painting onstage.[3]

Rémy de Gourmont's description of symbolist drama would seem to anticipate *Godot:*

> Hidden in mist somewhere there is an island, and on that island there is a castle, and in that castle there is a great room lit by a little lamp. And in that room people are waiting. Waiting for what? They don't know! They're waiting for somebody to knock at their door, waiting for their lamp to go out, waiting for Fear and Death. They talk. Yes, they speak words that shatter the silence of the moment. And then they listen again, leaving their sentences unfinished, their gesture uncompleted. They are listening. They are waiting. Will she come perhaps, or won't she? Yes, she will come; she always comes. But it is late, and she will not come perhaps until the morrow. The people collected under that little lamp in that great room have, nevertheless, begun to smile; they still have

1. Rémy de Gourmont, *Le Livre des masques* (Paris, 1895), p. 21.
2. Ibid.
3. See above, Introduction, p. 7.

hope. Then there is a knock—a *knock,* and that is all there is: And it is Life Complete, All of Life.[4]

The play itself must flow; its time is that of the performance. But within the play, time is neither that of the scientist nor that of the watch-wearing spectator: it is a synthesis of the time of the performed anecdote and the time of "All of Life." Since waiting contains both of these dimensions at every moment, it is the same whether it lasts for one hour or for fifty years. Here the similarity with *Godot* is obvious. In each act there is an anecdote that takes place in the evening and continues for a few hours. The two evenings are consecutive, yet they are situated in different seasons, and "one day we are born, one day we die, the same day, the same second" (Act II). Moreover, the inaction characteristic of static drama is closely related to that of *Godot.* Gestures or words lose their inherent finality when considered in the light of eternity: they are leveled off by the waiting, by the consciousness of a missing transcendency. Experiencing great love or eating a carrot are two "adventures" that dissolve in the same grayness, the same hollow.

A transcendency can color the world in two contrary ways: it can enrich it (two pieces of wood become the Cross; a red rag embodies the liberation of man) or it can make it appear insignificant, as in Rémy de Gourmont's description or in *Godot.* The transcendency that strips the meaning or ordinary value from an action and substitues no glorification on any other level took a different form in Shakespeare: the sound and fury of Macbeth's adventures dissolve into a final nothingness, and life becomes no more than a tumultuous story "told by an idiot." Didi's and Gogo's clownish tricks and screams, like Macbeth's machinations, would not be insignificant were they given for themselves, but their meanings are reduced to zero by the waiting for Godot. While in *Macbeth* zero is reached at the end of a long trajectory, a long evolution, in *Godot* it is given in advance and is thus responsible for the play's

4. Ibid. As quoted by John Gassner in *Directions in Modern Theatre and Drama,* p. 101.

apparent inaction (despite all the activity), for the fact that it marks time, and for the impeccable constancy with which the basic tension is maintained.

*En Attendant Godot* is a new form of static drama in which three levels are constantly juxtaposed: the words and actions (poetry, clownish tricks, embryonic scenes), the direct significance of those words and actions (love, misery, hunger, the role of the intellectual, the dialectic of master and slave, the dimness and confusion of memories, fear, bad faith, even a certain "miserabilism"), and the waiting which levels everything off. As raw material, Beckett used comedy and the drama of the bum—an art similar to Chaplin's or to Fellini's film *La Strada,* a farce about poverty and solitude, based on realistic observation, in which the spectator is asked to recognize an image of his own condition. Although *Godot* has a more universal and profound meaning, Beckett used the same foundation, the same background of observation.

As the minutes go by, Vladimir and Estragon produce an unpretentious mixture of "sound and fury": they live, they eat, they suffer, they dance, they move about. Their activities are the stylization of a kind of tramp's slice of life: they make use of the objects they find, they eat the bones left by a rich picnicker, they are cold, and they are beaten by the "others." On a psychological level Vladimir and Estragon are much more coherent and individualized than the "characterless" characters of the first absurdist plays. They are characters in the traditional sense of the word, without appearing as neo-Romantic masks of the author (as, for example, Ionesco's Bérenger does). Each of them has a coherent and original personality, a body, and a past, yet they are often treated anonymously. They are called Vladimir and Estragon only in the cast list: the young boy calls Vladimir "Monsieur Albert," Estragon introduces himself as Adam (Catulle in the French version), and between themselves they resort to the childish nicknames Gogo and Didi. Although according to Edith Kern they are as anonymous as A and B in *Molloy*,[5] such anonymity would seem more comparable to that conferred, by the use of conventional theatricalist names, on characters in farce or in a Molière comedy than to the abstractions A and B or the numbered characters in certain expressionistic plays. Didi and Gogo are not interchangeable either between themselves or with the members of a collectivity. In fact, they strongly resemble the colorful, turbulent, and diversified fauna that desperately peoples the works of the Irish.

While in one of his radio plays, *All That Fall (Tous ceux qui tombent)*, Beckett showed his gifts as an observer in the traditional style, the setting in *Godot*—a vague platform with one lonely tree—is far less precise and can hardly be said to evoke an Irish landscape. Nor are Didi and Gogo as localized as Mrs. Rooney, Mr. Tyler, Tommy, and Jerry of *All That Fall*. As tramps, they have cut all attachments to their places of origin; they come from different backgrounds and met somewhere a long time ago. Indeed, it seems as if each one's absolute uprootedness was part of his individual definition—an uprootedness accompanied by partial amnesia, and perhaps even explained by it. Yet the fact that they only dimly recall their pasts does not mean that they have none. Their former lives are suggested in illuminating flashes. We learn, for example, that their youths were more promising than their present situations. "In the nineties," says Vladimir, "hand in hand from the top of the Eiffel Tower, among the first. We were respectable in those days. Now it's too late. They wouldn't even let us up." We also learn that Estragon was a poet, that he and Vladimir harvested grapes together, that Estragon threw himself into the Durance and that Vladimir fished him out—unconnected memories in a state of uncertainty which is in keeping with the characters' general psychological confusion.

The realism of Vladimir and Estragon is increased still more by their differences. The lines of one could not be spoken by the

5. Edith Kern, "Drama Stripped from Inaction: Beckett's *Godot*."

other. Vladimir thinks more, he is more cultured, his anguish is more intellectualized, he is more hesitant and more demanding in his choice of words. Estragon is more spontaneous and more lethargic, he is more childish, he sulks more, he is more eager for protection, he is more egotistical and more obstinate, he holds to his own vocabulary and refuses Vladimir's nuances. Vladimir is more restless, more active, Estragon more inert. Vladimir has the responsibility: he is in charge of the carrots, radishes, and turnips that constitute their meals. Estragon is more the victim: he is kicked by Lucky. While Vladimir tries to make conversation with Pozzo and to seem "well-bred," Estragon listens only because he is threatened or ordered to; otherwise, he independently follows the flow of his own thoughts. Didi and Gogo clearly recall the traditional vaudeville couples. In fact, their ancestors come directly from farce: the yokel and his sly partner, transformed in the modern world into the two soldiers of the nineties in French military *vaudeville,* the comic teams in American movies, Lemmy and George in Steinbeck's *Of Mice and Men.*

On the level of anecdote the difference between the two characters creates a dramatic tension. Vladimir and Estragon are bound by a relationship that subsists on their dissimilarities. Their dialogue is not only a kind of antiphonal chant of misery but also a theatrical dialogue in which the two characters attract and repel, possess or elude, one another. Essentially, like an old married couple, they need each other. Vladimir needs someone to talk to, a soundboard for his verbal digressions, and tension is created the moment Estragon refuses to "return the ball." Estragon wants protection, and in that respect he is the feminine half. He actually demands protection, reproaches Vladimir with singing in his absence, gets angry, leaves, then is afraid and comes back—a kind of coquettish friendship. What saves this study of two tramps from being merely grotesque or clinical is the fact that their friendship is profound. It provokes emotion and recognition in that its basic element, independent of needs or habits, is tenderness. They talk about a common past, they help each other, they kiss each other, and even when their actions are somewhat farcical, they are steeped in compassion.

While the play's ultimate objective obviously transcends the anecdote and characterization, *Godot* is made up of traditional elements despite its originality as a whole. In the first production of the play in Paris those elements were stressed, with the result that the spectator's participation was increased, the misery of the characters made more striking, and the tension between a life similar to ours and an indifferent and forgetful universe made more convincing and more poignant.

The spectator also participates because this slice of tramp life is charged with human suffering. Even if he does not identify with the characters, he is bound to be sensitive to the spectacle of misery in general, for although *Godot's* "miserabilism" (similar to Chaplin's) is one of the least important aspects of the play, it is constantly present.

In a broader sense Vladimir and Estragon symbolize man in general, and on that level the play presents a commentary on life and a definition of man. Edith Kern points out that Vladimir and Estragon are outside of society, that they are not what the existentialists would call *en situation*.[6] Actually they are *en situation* inasmuch as they are beaten, beg, and so on, but they are detached from the machinery of society, in which they no longer have any function, and also from the historical situation. Therefore they have the time to be men. They play at the kind of purity that the classics have bestowed upon certain tragic heroes.

The tramp, then, is the modern metaphor for universal man. The King in tragedy—risen above men, conducting his politics for himself, closed within his own glory, in direct contact with Fate and Values—represented man's condition in its pure state, without intermediaries and freed from bondage. When Voltaire and the Encyclopedists defined man by his function in and his relation to the world of objects (manufacture, commerce), the

6. Ibid.

bourgeois became representative of humanity. He was Sedaine's citizen of the world. By comparison, the royal hero, who did not transform either economy or materials, would seem like an abstraction. Now that bourgeois society has begun to doubt its own definitions, we have returned to the metaphor of man in the form of a detached character—the Proustian hero, for example, that bourgeois who does nothing. Leftist ideologies continue to define man by his relation to transformable materials but consider the bourgeois relation as abstract and take the proletariat as the symbol of humanity—a humanity *en situation,* defined both by its work and by the conquest of its freedom. If one believes, however, in the permanence of universal man, it is difficult to accept the proletariat as a satisfying metaphor, for at this particular moment in history the proletarian is no more than a "half-man" (Sartre). Beside him we have the tramp—a symbol of humanity considered as residue, stripped of its functions and plans for transformations, and left face to face with itself. The tramp has become the image of our condition laid bare, with everything else a mere secondary quality or anecdote. He is an image of humanity reduced to zero, about to start again from nothing. Here there are perhaps possibilities for a new classicism. A.J. Leventhal, for example, established a strict parallel between man according to Beckett and man according to Pascal.[7]

The tramp represents man as such, as detached from society. He is in some ways the symbol of the inalienable part of every man, the irreducible element that transcends particularities and remains aloof from social, political, civic, or ideological brigades. He marks the renunciation of bourgeois participation in common values, as well as the idea of humanitarian commitment. Indeed, man now seems better defined by his solitude and his estrangement than by his participation.

One of the signs of man's solitude is physical suffering. Where sympathy is possible in the case of moral suffering, physical pain

7. See his "Mr. Beckett's *En Attendant Godot.*"

would seem to isolate the individual. When Vladimir suffers, he is no more than a spectacle for Estragon. From the very beginning of the play each tramp remains outside the other's pain:

> *Estragon:* Help me!
> *Vladimir:* It hurts?
> *Estragon:* Hurts! He wants to know if it hurts!
> *Vladimir:* ... I'd like to hear what you'd say if you had what I have.
> *Estragon:* It hurts?
> *Vladimir:* Hurts! He wants to know if it hurts!

No one feels physical suffering *with* another. Here again a comparison can be made with man according to Pascal—the "Man without God," who cannot even use his suffering as a means to salvation. Pascal's idea of solitude as unbearable is also exemplified in the friendship of the two tramps, which shows man's inability to remain alone with himself. The drama of the human condition thus lies in the uncertainty of each man's relationship to others. Existentialist theatre derives its basic drama from a Sartrean analysis of the "others." Similarly, man in *Godot,* in a perpetual series of rebounds, is constantly thrown back into his solitude. At one extreme there is the idea of a kind of "togetherness" in common action, thanks to which emptiness and solitude seem to be filled:

> *Estragon:* We don't manage too badly, eh Didi, between the two of us?
>
> . . .
>
> We always find something, eh Didi, to give us the impression we exist?

In contrast to Estragon's "we" is the other extreme—a total absence of communication, even an absolute rejection of the other, as when Estragon, in a moment of brief but cruel betrayal, closes his eyes and, in the depths of solitude, calls to another, infinitely more powerful than Vladimir:

> Estragon: *(Stopping, brandishing his fists, at the top of his voice)*. God have pity on me!
> Vladimir: *(Vexed)*. And me?
> Estragon: On me! On me! Pity! On me!

Man's situation should be defined not by his communion with others, nor by an absolute absence of relations with others, but by a fluctuation between the two extremes, by his attempts at communion that are perpetually broken off, by a shifting synthesis of permanent solitude and the effort made to emerge from it. The fluctuation is characteristic of our activities and brands them as futile. Vladimir and Estragon do not act: they try to act. They invent games and then quickly tire of them. Their agitation is a kind of Pascalian diversion practiced by characters who know that they are only amusing themselves. What Beckett's man has that Pascal's freethinker lacks is lucidity, the consciousness of his own condition. Pascal's King who hunts continues to hunt because he does not know why he hunts. Vladimir and Estragon know that they act in order to avoid thinking about their condition. One acts merely to fill up a vacuum—a fact of which the King is unaware. The tragedy of their condition is circular: man's condition is unbearable, but the only apparent means of escape are illusory.

Suicide is twice considered as a possible solution. In the first act, presented as a sinister form of amusement on the same plane as the others, it is attractive only momentarily (for the sexual consequences of hanging) and then rejected because it may separate the two tramps should one of them fail to die. The idea is renounced merely because it means complications. At the very end of the play they come back to it, but they still do not commit suicide—now because of a technical accident: the cord breaks. Yet they never give up the idea, and the dialogue shows that suicide might be a solution when, at the end, Estragon declares that he "can't go on like this," suggests to Vladimir that they separate, and Vladimir answers that they will hang themselves next day. Nevertheless, there is no suicide; there are only two attempts. Here again, even in the case of suicide as a last possibility, the true condition of man is not in the realization but in the effort made toward it. Since the attempt miscarries, it makes suicide an action like any other. Moreover, it represents what is most theatrical in any action —the moment when the character tries to act and seems immobilized between two modes of being: this time, the being he is and the nonbeing he envisions. The drama is neither in the "to be" nor in the "not to be" but in the "or" that links them. Thus another tension is established in *Godot* between the importance one ordinarily attaches to the "or" and the character's apathy toward it. "Why don't we hang ourselves?" is a proposition that has neither more nor less importance than: "We could do our exercises."

Suicide is parodied in a way by the characters' inactivity or desire for inactivity in the scene in Act II in which, once they fall down, they remain lying down. That kind of "Oblomovitis"—the lethargic irresponsibility of man lying down—is made impossible by Pozzo's agitation. The world of the others, who beat Estragon, also condemns him to getting up and acting.

An intrusion into the monotonous flow of the tramps' gestures and comments is provided by the entrance of the couple Pozzo and Lucky. This type of intrusion, so frequent in theatre—the arrival or passing through of an apparently different kind of person— makes the spectator wonder whether the intruder will succeed in transforming the play's universe or whether his difference will prove to be no more than illusory. For the two tramps, Pozzo and Lucky constitute a fantastic spectacle offered by the society of men from which they are excluded. By the same token, they are treated less realistically than the two heroes, for they are a sort of metaphor of what the tramps see in the society that is foreign to them.

Their nature and the nature of their relationship are immediately clear to the spectator. Pozzo, dressed like a country gentleman, carries a whip and holds, at the end of a rope, a pale and thin creature wearing a valet's vest and heavily burdened. One is the master, the other the slave. They enter shortly after the following exchange of words:

> *Estragon:* (*His mouth full, vacuously*). We're not tied?
> *Vladimir:* I don't hear a word you're saying.
> *Estragon:* (*Chews, swallows*). I'm asking you if we're tied.
> *Vladimir:* Tied?
> *Estragon:* Ti-ed.
> *Vladimir:* How do you mean tied?
> *Estragon:* Down.
> *Vladimir:* But to whom? By whom?
> *Estragon:* To your man.
> *Vladimir:* To Godot? Tied to Godot? What an idea! No question of it. (*Pause.*) For the moment.

Almost directly, Pozzo appears onstage holding the rope to which Lucky is *tied*. Is Lucky's rope similar to the bond that might possibly unite the tramps to Godot? Are they not in fact waiting for the opportunity to give themselves up to bondage? They are waiting to be taken over by Godot, they hope to be, but they never explain what they want of him. All that Vladimir and Estragon say is that they are waiting to be "saved." The idea of salvation without any concrete content is suddenly actualized by the rope that ties Lucky to Pozzo. If salvation consists in being possessed by Godot, the desire to meet Godot and the repulsion provoked by the rope would be the two poles of a fundamental hesitation, a movement back and forth comparable to that which attracts the two tramps to one another and then separates them. Here again is the tragic circle, similar to that in existentialist drama: the vacuum of freedom calls for something to fill it, for the nothingness is unbearable; but when total commitment or possession is realized, the resulting state is just as agonizing. Man is caught between the vacuum of waiting for Godot and the bondage of a Lucky (the lucky one who has found his Godot).

Neither possession nor bondage, then, would seem to be solutions. The friendship between the two tramps and Pozzo's and Lucky's rope are only sketches or parodies of a true union—both desired and feared, yet never realized. They seem to imply that we never achieve more than a pitiful or grotesque approximation of a union, just as, through action, we achieve no more than the "impression we exist." In other words, our lives are farces of Life.

The master-slave relationship and Pozzo's acts represent one aspect of the farce—the most ordinary and the least lucid. The rope is meant to reassure Pozzo, just as through his comments Estragon reassures himself by dwelling on the friendship that ties him to Vladimir. But where Vladimir and Estragon make a pretense at acting, fighting, or playing, Pozzo takes his actions seriously, and the least of his gestures becomes a whole spectacle glorified by noble language. In exaggerating the simple processes of life—having Lucky serve him his lunch, sitting down again after having got up, describing the sky, lighting his pipe—Pozzo tries to drown his life in a general atmosphere of ceremony so as to cover up its insignificance. Either man waits for Godot or he clutters up his life with all the outer signs of importance.

In the second act Pozzo is blind. For Edith Kern, Pozzo's blindness and Lucky's muteness are signs of the inevitable degradation of the master-slave couple. Actually, Pozzo's blindness leads to a partial reversal of the relationship. He no longer drives Lucky, he follows him, and the rope has become shorter—a kind of parodic and concrete sketch of the master-slave dialectic. Besides, although the rope is shorter, Pozzo's blindness throws him into the shadows of his solitude. He thus grasps more accurately the horror of his condition, which has now become an amplification of Vladimir's and Estragon's. For even more than having doubts about time and his situation in space, Pozzo is in complete ignorance or total confusion.

Indeed, it would seem that truth lies in the depths of the confusion. Pozzo's definition of life, implied by the play as a whole, is drawn from his darkness: "One day we are born, one day we die, the same day, the same second." Since the days are all alike, they merge into one indefinite day. There is no flow, only a state. Yet the words are spoken by a character who is in perpetual motion. Beckett plays with contrasts and creates a whole network of subtle tensions between the *state* and the *effort*. Pozzo, who passes by, clings to his state. The tramps, who remain, are always making an effort to get up and do something. When Estragon almost reaches a state (the deathlike state of man lying down), it is Pozzo who, also fallen down, makes an effort to get up. That scene, in which Vladimir and Estragon call themselves "men" and Pozzo "all humanity"—with all the characters who have fallen down now trying to get up, now refusing, going from immobility to effort and vice versa—is the most developed metaphor of the human condition. It has an echo in *All That Fall,* when Mr. and Mrs. Rooney, he blind, she lamed by her obesity, try not to fall.

Pozzo tried to give his life a structure by his possession of Lucky and the visible sign of his possession—the rope. By the same token, Lucky is "saved" by that bond, by his function and his state of servitude. Servitude, however, leads to a mechanization that crushes the individual. Lucky is reduced to basic reactions: he trembles, he cries, he kicks. He has a past: he had been a better dancer, he had been Pozzo's "thinker," he had been, and still is, his valet and his jester. Lucky is more than a servant in the ordinary sense of the word. He represents other servitudes, principally that of the intellectual and the artist. He thinks *for* Pozzo, he dances *for* Pozzo. Vladimir and Estragon think and play, or try to think and play, for themselves. Their efforts are perhaps ridiculous, but Lucky's are inhuman and abstract—at least they have become so in Pozzo's service. Ultimately, both situations—independence (or solitude) and service (or union)—result in grotesque failures. Moreover, the complexity and incoherence of Lucky's long speech[8] show his

8. Lucky's speech recalls that of the Doctor in ancient farce and the Pedant's in classical comedy, both represented as buffoons of a given society.

situation at that moment to be a farcical satire on the condition of professional intellectuals. Supported by a society for whom they are all valets, they "produce" thought, as they are asked to do, but exasperate their masters by their verbal delirium. The result of such deteriorization is silence: in the second act Lucky has become mute.

This new state introduces a usual notion of time. We are born and die the same day, but still the change indicates that we are born *before* we die (in *All That Fall* there is mention made of a little girl who dies because she has not been born). Pozzo and Lucky have changed from one act to the other, from one day to the next, from winter to spring. The amount of time is undetermined, but the direction of time is preserved. In the compressible but irreversible time that Vladimir and Estragon fill up in their monotonous way, the Pozzos and the Luckys "evolve":

> *Vladimir:* How they've changed!
> *Estragon:* Who?
> *Vladimir:* Those two.
> *Estragon:* That's the idea, let's make a little conversation.
> *Vladimir:* Haven't they?
> *Estragon:* What?
> *Vladimir:* Changed.
> *Estragon:* Very likely. They all change. Only we can't.

Where the two tramps are immobilized by their waiting for Godot, the couple Pozzo-Lucky, who are not waiting for anything, deteriorate in time. If they were meant to represent a society entirely concerned with itself, a kind of prophecy can be seen at that level. Desperately clinging to its present structure (the master-slave relationship) and its rites, amused by an abstract and anguished art (Lucky, who formerly danced the jig and the fandango, breaks out into a symbolic pantomime of "the net"), society, by means of an intellectual delirium that no longer has meaning, will evolve into a world of blind Pozzos and mute Luckys—or toward the world of Hamm and Clov in *Fin de partie (Endgame)*.

The scenes that include Pozzo and Lucky show the meeting of two living durations in different modes that merge: the perpetuation of waiting, a monotonous flow experienced by men who ask for happenings and change (*Estragon:* Nothing happens, nobody comes, nobody goes, it's awful!), and the transition, change, and deteriorization experienced by men who cling to their state, although conscious of the speed of destruction and the unexpectedness of events (*Pozzo:* . . . night is charging and will burst upon us—pop! like that!). In contrast to social and historic man, who is in a hurry to be something or thinks he is, in the brief decrescendo that makes up the duration of a life or a civilization, the play offers a portrait of man as withdrawn from history and society, left to his existence, and continuously yawning in the indefinite flow of monotonous time.

In both cases the activities and effort are vain and serve only to pass the time. What maintain and reinforce this particular meaning of the play, keeping the spectator from attributing an inherent finality to any one activity, are the constantly repeated references to Godot, who is awaited but never comes. Pozzo and Lucky come up to us like the person who stops and tells us the story of his life while we are impatiently awaiting a friend. The fact that we are waiting takes away all real finality from his words and relegates them to a negative universe marked by the absence of the friend we are awaiting. In the same situation the drink we are having is not drunk for itself; it is drunk-while-waiting. And it is the *waiting* that permeates all of the tramps' gestures and comments and relegates their acts to a background of nonbeing such as Sartre analyzed in *L'Etre et le néant*.

Of course, besides the agitation invented to pass the time, the moments of life marked by hunger, blows, fear, or physical suffering are real and are experienced in horror. Yet even that reality is finally reduced to insignificance. It, too, becomes the negative background marked by the absence of Godot. Thus the transcendency by which suffering is negated is itself no more than an absence. In the symbolist drama the Idea—mysterious, obscure, or chaotic as it may be—is reality. In *Godot* the real remains at the level of what is directly experienced, and Godot is systematically absent; his very existence is uncertain: he is the fantasy that is satisfying because it gives content to man's desire for a frame of reference. Man is unable to accept insignificance, unable to understand that his misery and his existence are themselves devoid of meaning. Godot is that by which man both justifies and confirms the insignificance of existence. He is the Hypothesis that explains a negative phenomenon. He is the Yes dialectically necessary for life to be the No that it is. The question is not to justify being but to justify nonbeing. The development in *En Attendant Godot* consists of three movements: awareness of insignificance, the assertion of a meaning (Godot) in relation to which it is possible to conceive of an absence of meaning, and the strengthening of insignificance through an awareness of and the waiting for something that *has* meaning.

On the level of anecdote Godot is a character just like the others. His absence makes him more blurred and more uncertain, yet enough details are given to form a sketchy but concrete image. He has shepherds, agents, a family, and a bank account. He even has a beard. He is distant, capricious, and powerful, like the Masters in Kafka's world. Exactly who is he and whom does he represent? Edith Kern suggests God plus the ending "ot" of Charlot, the name given to Chaplin's Little Man by the French. C. Chadwick, on the other hand, sees a relation between Godot and certain French pejoratives, such as *godiche,* implying clumsiness or stupidity.[9] In fact, the meaning of the play does not lie in explanations of what Godot symbolizes. Whether he signifies God[10] or any other belief or illusion is of secondary importance. The subject of the play and its drama is not the identity of Godot but the waiting itself.

9. See Pierre Mélèze, *Beckett.*

10. Beckett sometimes does use Christian symbolism as a literary device. The tramps, for example, compare themselves to the two thieves crucified with Christ, implying that one might be saved and not the other. The tree might be interpreted as an empty Cross and Godot as the absence of God.

Therefore the play does not fall into any of the established categories of religion or ideology, which in themselves would suggest a definition of Godot. It represents a reversal of the Romantic attitude: instead of God coming first and then the *vague à l'âme* (a rather indefinite anguish and melancholy) as a sign of our desire for God, the desire for Godot to arrive comes first. Godot is a positive element created to correspond to man's feeling of emptiness and insignificance, which alone is real and experienced.

The play reveals a universe of insignificance, its tension created by the conflict between that insignificance and man's effort to give himself meaning despite everything. The metaphor of waiting is the best form of expression for that conflict, which is Beckett's definition of man. *En Attendant Godot* is not an allegory, an unfinished *Pilgrim's Progress,* but a concrete and synthetic equivalent of our existence in the world and our awareness of it.

Whatever Beckett's evolution in the past years, *En Attendant Godot* remains the most satisfying of his dramatic works. The others, all in the foreground of today's theatre, pick up and develop particular aspects of *Godot,* Beckett's basic play.

On the scenic level, *Godot* was written for the Italianate or picture-frame stage, and it is within that stage frame that Gogo's and Didi's endless adventure must be seen and heard. The set consists of a platform, with an audience seated in front of it and a curtain hung at the back of it. Both audience and curtain are incorporated into the play, for Beckett uses the convention of the fourth wall or breaks it at will. In *Godot,* by unexpectedly destroying the conventional illusions, he produces unoriginal but surprising effects: in Act I the audience is taken for a "bog" or is ironically considered as "inspiring prospects," and in Act II (French version) the background itself, suggesting a space alongside a road, suddenly becomes a stage set again when Estragon, in a moment of panic, rushes headlong "toward the backdrop, gets entangled in it, and falls." For his other plays as well, Beckett demands a conventional stage. It is very important, for example, when he tries to produce a full-face effect: in *Fin de Partie* Hamm in his armchair must be seen from the front, just as the figures in Giacometti's paintings, looming out of a space enclosed on three sides, are prisoners of their frames, or like one of Francis Bacon's horrifying apparitions. The play can thus be performed only in a box set, strictly limited by its frame. Both *Krapp's Last Tape (La Dernière Bande)* and *Happy Days (Oh! Les Beaux Jours)* must also be played on the conventional stage if Krapp is to disappear into the background to drink in obscurity, and if Willie is to remain hidden behind Winnie's sandpile. For *Play (Comédie)*, too, an Italianate stage is absolutely necessary for not only the facial alignment of the three characters in urns but the lighting effects.

Indeed, it is not at all surprising that Beckett became interested in the screen—of both television and the cinema. While these relatively new media allow certain writers complete freedom of movement, they may also be conceived as limiting frames: the power of Beckett's *Eh Joe (Dis Joe)* lies in the closeup of a face that is prisoner of the frame of a television screen, while his film *Film* is the story of a character who flees until finally a frame (of both a mirror and the screen) reveals his true face to himself and to the viewer.

In other words, for Beckett the tradition of the Italianate stage, like that of the rectangular screen, offers possibilities for profoundly theatrical effects. While others seek theatricalism in complexity, in the systematic multiplicity of points of view, and in spectacular movement *around* the action, Beckett is satisfied with the elementary artificiality of a stage frame and exploits it to a maximum. Instead of merely forgetting it, as is done in realistic theatre, he makes it not only obvious but obsessing. An immobile eye is fixed on the characters—that of the spectator. They perform facing him, on occasion they acknowledge him, and sometimes they identify him with some imaginary witness. On television, as Joe listens to a woman's voice coming from nowhere, he has no choice but to stare with horror at the eye of the camera.

In explicitly confronting an audience with actors who perform for it, Beckett is not returning to the naïve devices of the Renais-

sance prologue or the improvised conversation with some particular spectator in the manner of the English music hall, but he never
hesitates to address the spectator directly and with varying degrees
of complicity. Certain lines are not only a direct expression of the
character's thoughts but also comments addressed to the spectator by the playwright himself:

> *Vladimir:*   This is becoming really insignificant.
> *Estragon:*   Not enough.

In *Fin de partie* the asides to the audience are more obvious. The
play begins like a nineteenth-century bourgeois comedy, with the
servant's pantomime of his domestic duties followed by several
remarks explaining the situation. More frequent are comments to
the audience on the meaning of the play itself, such as Clov's last
declamatory speech. In *Happy Days* Winnie's entire soliloquy is
addressed to the spectators: just as she is prisoner of a sandpile, so
are they her captive audience, whether they like it or not.

Beckett's characters are like children who can act only if they
feel they are performing. A child never really acts without a witness ("Look at me, daddy," "Don't look now, daddy") by whom he
wants to be seen or from whom he is hiding. While Beckett's characters are adults and in no way similar to Arrabal's infantile
creatures, they do exist and want to exist in that state of relativity
called "play." The master in *Fin de partie,* for example, is named
Hamm, and since his partner's name is Clov, the image of the ham-
mer and the nail *(clou* in French) was immediately suggested to
certain critics. Nevertheless, Hamm's first words in the play, after
he is unmasked by Clov (who removes the bloody handkerchief
covering his face), are: "Me—to play." Once he emerges from the
immobility conferred by the mask, he begins to live—that is, he
becomes a ham actor. Moreover, the characters know they are playing. All of them feel they are giving a structure to their lives by
choosing particular events and telling about them in an affected
style with rhetorical effects, aware not of reliving but of replaying
them. "How did you find me?" asks Pozzo after his description of

nightfall. Hamm demands an audience and constantly interrupts to comment on his own style: "Nicely put, that . . . A bit feeble, that." And Mr. Rooney asks, after an interruption, "Where was I in my composition?"

Such composed narratives are part of a system of rites by which Beckett's characters try to give form to life, fitting it into a framework of beautiful language or deliberately masking its horror. In *Krapp's Last Tape* the hero records the narrative of his life as it unfolds, and he listens to himself. While Proust's hero set about saving his past by making it eternal through art, Beckett's heroes try to save their lives from insignificance through narrative. On the other hand, Pozzo and particularly Hamm are aware of the vanity of their attempts, and Krapp's tape turns silently at the end of the act. Literature, then, is not necessarily salvation; it is merely an effort to save oneself, perhaps as futile as any other. Yet Beckett himself makes the effort.

Presented as theatrical "numbers," the narratives—and, by extension, literature and theatre—are games. Conscious of the aesthetic quality of their monologues, Pozzo, Hamm, Mr. Rooney, and Krapp play and watch themselves play. And just as Winnie, in *Happy Days,* interrupts her monologue to comment on her own language ("old style"), so the Man in *Play* constantly apologizes for ruining his monologues with burps. Of course, Vladimir and Estragon never succeed in taking their own actions seriously; they rapidly become aware of the fact that they are actors and spectators at the same time. Life consists in pretending to live—just as children pretend that they fly or are animals—yet we have nothing more than our lives. Thus there is a correspondence between our lives in the world and the essence of theatre, in which, paradoxically, what is performed is both reality and a game and requires both participation and detachment. Clearly, Beckett's vision of life is made for the stage.

Using all the devices involved in the art of theatrical language, Beckett has always written three-way dialogues: character 1, character 2, the spectator. The triangle may be Gogo-Didi-the spectator, Hamm-Clov-the spectator, Krapp-his tape recorder-the spectator, the Man-two Women-the eye (or spectator), or Joe-the Voice-the television camera (or spectator). Thus two clearly drawn but closely linked dramas are created—one between the characters, the other between the characters and the spectator.

While the former is obviously traditional, Beckett has given it new power by reducing it to essentials and building his whole theatre around the couple. The characters are bound two by two in varying forms of solidarity. Even the character of *Acte sans paroles I (Act without Words I)* is in contact with a kind of invisible and superior being who plays with his desires. With the greatest simplicity, each character rebounds against another; each one acts now with, now against, that other. Indeed, the relationship with another would seem necessary to the effort of playing at living, dialogue being one of the forms of the tension that constitutes man's existence. Tenderness, need, and hate are the psychological components of the bond and are always treated with a rather touching irony, for while the characters are bound by the recognition of their common misery, the bond remains unworkable, never transforming the misery, and each one uses the other, pretending to communicate with him. When Nell and Nagg *(Fin de partie),* for example, reminisce about a boat outing on Lake Como, they realize that, for different reasons, they had experienced the happy moments each alone, and their so-called common past had not saved them from final agony in separate garbage cans. The couples Pozzo-Lucky and Hamm-Clov, aside from their affective ties, add another dimension to the drama—the master-slave relationship, as conceived since Diderot's *Jacques le fataliste* and especially since Hegel.

Beckett's language and staging has given this drama of the couple such rigor and such new form that it could well stand alone. Since it is altogether permeated with systematic theatricalism, however, the spectator is drawn in as a participant. Not only, as mentioned earlier, is he addressed directly, but he clearly becomes a witness to the characters' conflict. For the characters speak into an ear and act for an eye—both situated beyond the footlights. While the suggested or related adventures may be close to certain slices of life, as in *Happy Days* and *Play,* they are not the subjects but the objects of the plays, the real drama being that of the evidence *clamata in deserto*—that is to say, addressed to spectators who thereupon become actors. Through an obvious but subtle form of theatricalism, Beckett's plays make the entire theatre into a stage, on which man discovers that he has no witness but man.

Since life is no more than the comedy of life, no more than an attempt to play at living, no more than an embryonic farce, the often childish or capricious "games" that represent life onstage must necessarily be borrowed from genres in which the spectacle consists of failure, stumbling, and the resistance of objects—that is, circus and vaudeville sketches and their outgrowth, the motion-picture farce. Among others, the hat business in *Godot,* Mrs. Rooney's difficulties with Mr. Slocum's car in *All That Fall,* and Winnie's struggle to decipher the trademark on her toothbrush in *Happy Days* clearly establish the equivalence between daily life, made up of obstacles, repetitions, and failures, and the most elementary and crudest forms of theatrical comedy. Farce of this kind is grating, precisely because the equivalence is made so obvious and because the spectator's life is directly concerned. Beckett's characters are constantly caught between their own clumsiness and the resistance of objects (shoes that are too narrow, hats too small, car doors too low, windows too high), including their own bodies (prostate conditions, hemorrhages, itching). Moreover, they forget necessary objects or misplace them, especially in *Fin de partie* and *Krapp's Last Tape.*

In fact, Beckett's universe is one of perpetual irritation, in which nothing works—a universe of imperfections, in which things would seem to have been created not for man, nor actually against him, but merely in order to exist in a state of passive resistance to his efforts. In *Actes sans paroles, Happy Days,* and *Play* Beckett is more explicit. Objects literally slip away from the character in the pantomime *Actes sans paroles,* while the noticeable atmosphere of concrete uneasiness that pervades his spoken plays is replaced by an abstract notion of frustration. Winnie is prisoner of a sand-pile into which she is gradually sinking, and the three characters of *Play* are reduced to immobile heads and invisible bodies compressed into urns: here the physical world is not only irritating but altogether paralyzing.

In the plays in which the characters enjoy a relative freedom of movement, all the small obstacles of daily life cause men to make a series of efforts that represents, in a way, the more general attempt to give a structure and meaning to life. The various attempts made are given a theatrical quality by means of techniques borrowed from the art of clowns and which result in pure theatricalism. In *Godot* Beckett uses a twentieth-century myth—that which best expresses man's attempt to live decently in a world of hostile objects and social groups: Charlie Chaplin's Tramp. In Act II of *Godot* the curtain rises on Estragon's boots placed "front center, heels together, toes splayed," and Lucky's bowler hat thrown somewhere in the background. Chaplin's cane is missing, as if the tramps, relatives of Chaplin's Little Man, had not managed to achieve his elegance.

Chaplin's Little Man is a modern myth and, apart from Hitler, the only modern myth sufficiently distant and individualized. Hollywood, the Party, the middle-class American and Frenchman, and the capitalist are all institutions, collectivities, or abstractions raised to the level of myth. Chaplin's Little Man emerged directly as a myth, with his own individuality and his own past. His universality is guaranteed in part by his generality. He is known, recognized, and loved by about everyone. In suggesting Charlie Chaplin, Beckett is using a contemporary tradition to give a visible sign of the play's universality, as well as to show that the universal is in the present.

In *Godot* Beckett multiplied the Little Man's family. The character closest to the source is Vladimir, with his attempts at playing a certain worldly game: "Never neglect the little things in life," he says as he buttons his fly, and when he is asked his opinion on Lucky's dance, "There's something about it . . . ," he says, "squirming like an esthete." On the other hand, Estragon's shoes most clearly recall the Little Man's classic attributes, and it is Estragon who kicks like him in order to have his revenge. All the characters, however, wear bowler hats as a sign of their participation in the myth, for Chaplin's Tramp is the myth of man who, despite everything, *plays* at being a man.

Although Beckett's other dramatic works are not concerned with the myth itself, the idea of life as a game and of man's attempt to play it remains a central theme. The titles *Fin de partie* and *Play* are themselves indicative of it. On the other hand, the physical agitation and narratives that represent those attempts to play are constantly countered by images of release through annihilation. Just as in *Godot* there are the motifs of Estragon's Oblomovitis, the characters' supine positions, and suicide as a possible solution, so in *Fin de partie* the characters waver between play and a desire for annihilation, in *All That Fall* Mrs. Rooney wants to be transformed into a "big fat jelly" or disappear into her comfortable bed, and in *Happy Days* Winnie's gradual sinking into the sand, while apparently not her fondest wish, is nevertheless representative of the theme of fusion with inert matter, of a final repose that has already been accepted by her body.

The struggle between an attempt to play and the wish for self-destruction is always accompanied by an awareness of life's absurdity and brevity: "The same day, the same second . . . ," as Pozzo says; or Mrs. Rooney's "Just one great squeak and then . . . peace. They would have slit her weasand in any case," after Mr. Slocum had squashed a hen with his car; or Hamm's "Moments for nothing, now as always, time was never and time is over, reckoning closed and story ended," which concludes *Fin de partie*. *Krapp's Last Tape* ends in a kind of stupor, with the tape recorder turning silently after Krapp's last words on the best years of his life: "I wouldn't want them back." Beckett's great feat is to make the spectator experience simultaneously the interminable series of

minutes that make up his life—a game that never stops ending
and in which he exists in a state of permanent tension, perpetually
headed for defeat—and the somewhat objective awareness of life's
brevity. "The end is in the beginning and yet you go on," says
Hamm parodying T. S. Eliot. Life is a bad play performed for
nothing, yet it is the only one we have. Mrs. Rooney dreams of
annihilation but continues nonetheless to appreciate the landscape and makes every effort to walk without falling. Hamm and
Clov call out for the end to come but continue to play the hateful
game of the man who cannot sit down and the man who cannot
get up.

Although the same themes and theatrical devices are found over
and again from play to play, and although Beckett's general vision
of life and definition of man are relatively unchanging, each play
is situated in a different and shrinking universe. *All That Fall,* for
example, takes place in the peopled and known world of realism:
Mrs. Rooney has gone out, regrets it because of the dangers of the
outside world, but persists in following the road to the station
amid people, animals, and flowers; while the point of view
is always hers, the people she meets are treated with an objectivity
in the manner of Maupassant. If *Godot's* universe is also that of
the outside world, its space is subjectively interpreted by the characters and becomes a kind of desert shot through with rare and
unjustified happenings. In *Fin de partie* the characters never go
out at all, remaining voluntary prisoners of their own private
dramas. The outside world, which continues to interest them, can
be seen only through a telescope: it is an end-of-the-world landscape in which life has almost disappeared and the sea itself has
become immobilized. "To hell with the universe," says Hamm as
he resumes the interminable quarrel that binds him to his servant
Clov. Just as the indefinite space of *Godot* becomes, in *Fin de
partie,* a closed room, so the open image of waiting for salvation
has been replaced by the closed image of waiting for annihilation.
In *Krapp's Last Tape* the room itself shrinks to a shadowy hole,

while in *Happy Days* and *Play* the characters' living space is reduced to almost nothing, for they exist immobilized in their containers.

Parallel to Beckett's evolving toward ever-clearer images of physical paralysis is the increasing emphasis he puts on the weight of the past. The characters in *Godot* are, on the whole, turned toward a problematic future, as those in *Fin de partie* live in relation to an end that never comes. But with *Krapp's Last Tape*, *Happy Days*, *Play*, the radio plays *Embers (Cendres)*, *Cascando*, and *Words and Music (Paroles et musique)*, and the television script *Eh Joe*, reminiscences, vague memories, and difficult plunges into the past gradually take on greater importance and create an atmosphere of general discomfort, not only because of lapses in memory, but because of the relatively obscure guilt feelings that are disclosed. Indeed, the more immobile they are, the more Beckett's characters speak about their pasts or are confronted with them by the voice of another. The language itself—difficult, hesitant, and spellbinding in its rhythms, breaks, and resumptions —is the embodiment of the tragic condition implied by Beckett's works: it signifies the effort to live and at the same time discloses the absurd sin that consists in living. As Pierre Mélèze points out in his *Beckett*, this is a theatre of impossible redemption: since Godot never came, there is nothing to be done but contemplate the fundamental sin, which is to have been born and to live.

Using certain grotesque gestures of everyday life, the buffoonery of clowns, and, above all, language, Beckett—in the wake of the successive demystifications of the postwar playwrights—attempts the supreme demystification: he attacks life itself. He does it without lengthy rationalizations and without contradictory debates. He merely places existence onstage. Existing, for Beckett, means watching oneself try to exist and, by the same token, either being fully aware of the effort it takes or attempting to blind oneself to it. The dogmatism of the Cartesian *cogito* is transformed into a skepticism tinged with Eastern philosophy: "I see myself trying to exist, therefore I exist." And, as Pozzo says, "Sometimes I wonder if I'm not still asleep." In fact, the drama that constitutes the substance of Beckett's theatre is the ironic duality of demystified man.

Beckett's characters silently struggle toward forms of being or structures that are suddenly disclosed by a gesture or in words. Lyricism, eloquence, invectives, and clichés are like fixatives, making existence intelligible and temporarily "saving" it: the words that hesitatingly move on from image to image toward the greatest possible precision or toward an enrichment or transformation of reality are punctuated by screams and swearing that also "fix" some gesture or some impression. Yet while the poetry of the language lies in its precision, in the music of intersecting voices, and in the calculated alternation of pauses and transparent words, the fixatives are ephemeral and the words fall back into silence, as water subsides to form a new wave. The pulsation of effort, forever repeated and forever vain, gives Beckett's works their rhythm, their balance, and their form. When all of life is a game, theatre, the game par excellence, has the last word.

# CHAPTER 13

# THE GLORY OF ANNIHILATION:
# JEAN GENET

While Beckett continues to sing, in muted tones, of the desperate effort to exist and to voice an obsession with the irremediable past, Jean Genet, in a great flourish of lyricism, has gradually become the master of ceremonies of a frenzied plunge into annihilation. Seemingly paradoxical, his theatrical works give the impression of a sumptuous structure, huge and complex—an ornate temple, baroque in its way and sometimes even "pop," whose saint of saints, both the pretext for such extravagance and the goal of the characters, is quite simply nothingness. From play to play this has become increasingly clear, until today a formula that might be applied to the whole of Genet's works is Archibald's description, at the end of *Les Nègres,* of the spectacle that has just unfolded: an "architecture of emptiness and words."

At the roots of this venture is a dual assumption, which Genet initially expressed in a letter appended to his first performed play, *Les Bonnes.* To begin with, and closely related to Artaud's theories, is Genet's disgust with Western theatre, especially its frivolity and triviality: at most a quality entertainment, such theatre is nonetheless mere entertainment. What Genet would like is something similar to Oriental theatre, or at least what we know of it—theatre in which ceremony would replace the masquerade, and symbols the characters. Or, as he writes, "there is nothing more [theatrically] effective than the elevation" during Mass. Religious mystery and communion are the two necessary components of true theatre. Beauty would replace faith, but a beauty that "must have at least the power of a poem—that is, of a crime." Together with this aesthetic mystique is a second principle, that of theatre as a vanishing dream: "A performance that does not act on my soul is vain. It is vain if I don't believe what I see, which will stop—which will never have existed—once the curtain falls." This is an extreme expression of theatricalism and of the paradox of two simultaneous states of consciousness, assimilating the spectator to the regular customers of Irma's brothel in *Le Balcon:* during their visits, each customer, by means of a sumptuous disguise, becomes his own ideal of social and sexual grandeur, but during the ceremony, "they all want it to be as real as possible . . . except for some indefinable thing making it all not real." To his higher demand for mystical— or magical—effectiveness Genet adds an equally unyielding demand for illusion and the negation of reality.

Critics have put great emphasis on the ritual aspect of Genet's theatre. And, indeed, his plays are both the presentation of a rite and a rite in themselves. First of all, Genet uses theatre—and often the novel—as an instrument for evoking or exorcising his most private fantasies. Adorned with all the marvels of lighting, make-up, and theatrical costuming, the inhabitants of his sexual imagination assume shapes, are objectified, and become real. The beauty of the prisoners in *Haute Surveillance,* the incarnation of Blood, Tears, and Sperm in three young men in *Le Balcon,* the muscled femininity of Arthur in the same play, the steely eye and disarray of the handsome Sergeant of *Les Paravents,* all show that the universe of Genet's plays is, as it were, his private Hollywood, where he can be both the creator and the prey of his own gods. On this level the ceremony is elementary and similar to the secret rites of adolescents who seek satisfaction by making obscene drawings, thus conferring "existence" upon imaginary, ideal, and forbidden creatures. Yet Genet's method transcends childishness because of his awareness of the ambiguity of such incarnations: he knows that they are merely theatrical figures, performed myths, not living realities. The statue of Galathea remains a statue, and Pygmalion has merely an illusory satisfaction.

On another level the plays tell a story, in which the characters take part in a ceremony that is meant to procure for them some particular satisfaction. In Genet's first play, *Haute Surveillance,* the rite is very primitive, since the symbol is inseparable from the act: seeking to identify with great criminals and thus commune with them in love, Lefranc commits a murder by strangling young Maurice. In *Les Bonnes* the situation is more complex: the murder of Madame by her two maids Claire and Solange never takes place, and the play ends with the suicide of Claire, who is "playing" Madame—a suicide that is the equivalent of both an expiation and the symbolic murder of Madame. Similarly, at the end of *Le Balcon* the defeated revolutionary, Roger, dressed in the costume of the Chief of Police, castrates himself, thus symbolically mutilating the man responsible for his defeat. In *Les Nègres,* where the purpose of the ceremony enacted onstage is to free the Blacks not only from the Whites but from the image they have of themselves because of the Whites, the symbol ends by dispensing with even the vicarious act: the black actors who, masked, represent an image of the Whites are sent off to hell, but they are presented to the audience as actors and quite simply leave the stage. Thus, from *Haute Surveillance* to *Les Nègres,* Genet has gradually changed the ceremony into a symbol, going from the realism of a ritual murder to a metaphor that is openly offered as a metaphor.

While this gradual evolution might appear to be a weakening of dramatic force with increased recourse to abstraction, it in fact has given Genet's works greater theatrical power. Despite the rhetoric and *préciosité* of the dialogue, *Les Bonnes* and *Haute Surveillance* are dramaturgically no great departure from traditional theatre (for which reason Genet almost repudiated *Les Bonnes*). When it was first performed, *Les Bonnes* could easily have been taken for a social protest against the oppression of servants or for a high tragedy of serving maids. As for *Haute Surveillance,* it might well have been seen as, above all, a documentation of the stranger aspects of prison life. With *Le Balcon* and especially *Les Nègres,* phantasmagoria and masquerade eliminate the realism and at the same time address the plays directly to the audience. In her final monologue Mme. Irma, speaking to the spectators, puts them on the same footing as the characters and declares that the illusions of her brothel are merely a reflection of the illusions of our own lives, which are made up of rites that we take seriously but that are even more deceptive than those of the Balcony. In *Les Nègres* the spectator finally becomes an actor who does not witness a ceremony but actually takes part in it: at least one white spectator must be seated in the theatre so that his reflection may be seen onstage in the form of the grotesque masks of the Queen, the Missionary, and so on. The black actors who are not masked play constantly with their two audiences—the white masks and the spectators. They mock them both, threaten one by way of the other, and frankly insult the spectators by obliterating their image when they send the white masks off to hell. The play ends with all the black actors grouped together, apparently freed and separated from the spectators, who, after having been "used" throughout the play, are relegated to a solitude in which nothing any longer offers them the satisfaction of being reflected, of being set up as formidable images.

Although Genet's plays differ with regard to the spectator's degree of involvement in the theatrical rite, they have this in common: that the performed rite or rites, whatever their purpose, are always based on the acting out of a role, on the characters' attempt at identification with what they want to become or want to destroy. Lefranc plays at being a great murderer by strangling Maurice, in order to belong to the world of Yeux-Verts and perhaps to that of the supermurderer Boule de Neige. Claire and Solange, making ready for the murder of Madame, play at being Madame and Claire. The regular customers of the Balcony play at being a bishop, a general, and a judge. The Blacks play at being Whites and also at being Blacks such as the Whites imagine them to be. Thus the characters become reflections, images of something other than themselves—but no more than reflections, for there is always that distance of unreality required by the customers of the Balcony. On the other hand, these reflections have a real effect when the identification has actually been achieved in the eyes of others: when they are really taken for the Bishop, the General, and the Judge, the customers of the Balcony—led by the Chief of Police and Irma, who has become the Queen—make possible the defeat of the revolution; and Claire, who has become Madame in the eyes of Solange playing the role of Claire, is really poisoned. But the characters or actors never completely take the place of those whom they reflect or symbolically embody. The real Madame doesn't die from Claire's poison; at nightfall Irma is still the head of the brothel, and Roger, the revolutionary who castrates himself, castrates only himself: "I still have mine," cries the Chief of Police with satisfaction; "though my image is castrated in all the brothels in the world, I remain intact. Intact, gentlemen." One can only conclude that in the long run the rite is ineffective and vain.

As early as *Haute Surveillance,* Genet showed the ritual murder to be a failure. Of course Maurice is really killed, but Lefranc, objectively a murderer, does not manage to correspond to the image of himself that he wanted to have in the eyes of Yeux-Verts. Genet recognizes that a rite, by definition, is trickery, since it is a deliberate representation of something other than itself. Hence the "tragedy" of *Les Bonnes* is that the gesture of the two maids, seeking desperately to identify with their mistress so that they can manage to kill her, must result in suicide for one of them and in prison for the other. In a different tone, *Le Balcon* can end only in mockery, since, in an offhand manner and by way of Irma, both spectators and characters are dismissed and sent back to their daily illusions. As for *Les Nègres,* the play is frankly presented as a deception: the game of mirrors, insulting to all, is ultimately shown to be merely an entertainment without any real significance; all the sumptuous imagery and the whirlwind of language and gestures actually have been not only a warning but, essentially and taken as a whole, a masque meant to conceal some obscure event that was truly happening offstage and that was the concern only of the Blacks in the mystery of their drama and their rebellion. A divertissement in the etymological sense of the word—that is, an action designed to turn away or distract—*Les Nègres* recalls those royal betrayals in which, while the jesters were dazing the guests by amiably mocking them, outside the palace a massacre was taking place. Faced with this particularly complex game, the spectator is tempted to wonder whether it is true that every evening, during the performance, a real act is committed by the Blacks while the white audience lets itself be taken in by the sorcery of a sham ceremony in a theatre. But, obviously, the act committed offstage is real only in relation to the spectacle; it is another sham, more threatening than the spectacle but just as imaginary.

Thus this most ritual of all theatre remains theatre. That is to say, contrary to true ritual—or, as it were, a true Mass, however black—the symbol does not represent a transcendent and actual reality but becomes an aesthetic absolute in itself. Having proclaimed his dream of a theatre-Mass—that is, a ceremony during which the bread would veritably become divine flesh—Genet is the first to acknowledge the inevitable failure of that transubstantiation. His plays as a whole, and not merely the beautiful and sordid sexual objects in which they abound, are wishful thinking and are presented as such. Genet may have once dreamed of what a Mau Mau theatre might be, but he well knows that the magic it implies can be only imaginary in the world of today. Our world is such that when we stick pins in the effigy of an enemy, he doesn't necessarily collapse of a deadly disease. Genet is not an enchanter, a surrealist magician, or an illuminist. His works—fictional, poetic, or dramatic—have little to do with a primitive attempt at working magic. They are quite simply a search for personal salvation—his own and that of his characters—and while the terms are very special to him, it is a really modern salvation: asserting one's authenticity within the social and political world.

In Genet's universe that outside world always remains essentially the same, even though it sometimes changes color, as it were. Madame sips champagne with her lover, who has just been released from prison, while Claire poisons herself. The Chief of Police, still "intact," closes himself into his sumptuous tomb "to wait for 2,000 years," while Roger castrates himself. The colonists in *Les Paravents* and the Whites in *Les Nègres* may have fled or been sent off to hell, but the principle of authority remains unchanged: the Arab soldiers in *Les Paravents* have set up their own police state; the Blacks in *Les Nègres* foresee the coming of a "black" state. Both states—the overthrown and the new—are necessary and hateful. They interest Genet only to the extent that they allow his chosen (that is to say, wholly cursed) characters to define themselves.

*Les Nègres* and *Les Paravents* clearly show the stages involved in that search for an authentic definition. The first stage is the liquidation of authority as it exists in the world of established Good: for the Blacks, the Whites, and for the Arabs, the colonists. Here Genet is in a sense cheating, for he portrays those established groups by way of expressionist masks representing a historically dated reality: his queens, his missionaries, his generals, his big landowners, English or Dutch, are in fact allegories of nineteenth-century colonialism, contemporaneous with Queen Victoria or Lyautey. Their kind of oppression is of course a reflection of ours today, but a degraded reflection, out of phase with the times, showing ours as nothing but a dying memory of past conquests. In *Les Nègres* Genet's portrayal of the Whites as a cliché of anti-

colonialist liberalism allows him to point up not simply the Blacks'
revolt against authority, but, more importantly, and on the periph-
ery of White authority (which is so easy to satirize), the *inner*
drama of the black rebellion; for the mysterious and threatening
act committed offstage is a drama between Blacks.[1] In short, the
drama is less the rebellion than the inner life of the rebellion. Similarly, while *Les Paravents* shows first the elimination of nineteenth-century colonialism and then the gory battle against the
present reality (the Foreign Legion and soldiers of repression), its
real tragedy has to do with the Arabs themselves. True, it is in relation to the missionaries, the big landowners, the academicians, the
Foreign Legion, and the police that the revolt is made possible, but
what the play really suggests is the question of how not to re-
produce what one hates. Revolt, for Genet, is valid only if it remains a revolt—hence the tragedy. In the end, one order is replaced by another, and authority and oppression remain or merely
take on new forms: Madame alive, the Chief of Police immortal in
his tomb, and the Algerian rebels in their new roles of judges and
organizers are all necessary to his thesis. For it is only in the
negation of success—that is to say, in defeat or renunciation, in
suicide instead of murder, in the vicarious mutilation of the hated
image, or in the most extreme realization of baseness—that the
protagonists achieve the authenticity which Genet calls "glory."

Glory is a word that occurs frequently in the works of Genet,
and one which has innumerable connotations for the French.
Among other things, it evokes, on the one hand, the fate of the
Christian martyrs and, on the other, the ambition of Corneille's
heroes. And these two connotations are closely linked: glory results when a being has completely achieved his destiny, his inner
purpose, or the demands of his faith, in his own eyes or in the
eyes of God or man. It means that a radiance emanates from his
person, and Genet's imagery ("shining," "radiant," "illuminating")

---

1. The ambiguity of the whole thing lies in the fact that Genet speaks
forcefully to the spectator, only to say that it is actually none of his business.

is not far removed from that which bestows a halo on the saints or from the "glow" and "brightness" by which the heroes and heroines of Corneille make themselves visible. The only ambition of Genet's protagonists is to be seen or to see themselves in that dazzling light conferred by self-realization. It is their definition of salvation. It is also Genet's. And what better means is there than theatre for imposing that image of himself on larger and larger crowds—an image that finally becomes his truth through having been relentlessly asserted.

A play by Genet may be a ritual, but the purpose of that ritual is not to prod us into action in order to improve the lot of maids, blacks, or Algerians (Genet is hostile to all liberal reform, finding it an insult), or to strike us down magically in order that the oppressed may more easily win their freedom. Its purpose is to bestow halos on the oppressed and, by the same token, on him around whom oppression has crystallized—Genet himself. For Genet is Genet, and his intensely personal works are, above all, a description of the author's destiny. While Genet sings of the evil and misery of an entire antisociety, it is upon himself that his song confers glory or himself that it annihilates.

Genet and his characters are, of course, all prisoners of definitions or humiliating images that have been imposed on them from the outside, and their prison provokes in them the angry rebellion through which they transcend such definitions. At the very start, however, *Haute Surveillance* showed that to transcend one's lowly state and rise to the level of a great hero required more than just wanting to, or even performing acts similar to those of the heroes; one had also to be marked out by a kind of grace. It was in *Haute Surveillance* that Genet disclosed his personal dilemma. Rejected by established society, who saw him as a pariah, a petty thief and homosexual prostitute, he accepted that rejection but only to go beyond it toward a more grandiose state of evil or misery. Yet such glory through excessive evil was also refused him. Genet is not and never could be a hero of crime, but he has discovered still another possibility: the acceptance of both rejections and a continuous effort to sink ever deeper into a social and moral no-man's-land—the realm of absolute negation.

It is doubtless from this perspective that Genet's most recent play, *Les Paravents,* should be considered. And, retrospectively, that play throws light on his earlier dramatic achievements. Men, as seen by Genet, aim at dazzling the world with a powerful and beautiful image of themselves. If the image fits in with the established Good, Genet holds it up to ridicule, although he pays poetic tributes to certain killer-images of that established order: the Executioner, Chief of Police, Soldier—those who destroy in the name of Good being both the adored and hated brothers of the criminals branded by Evil. If such an image is at war with the established Good, in the name of crime or destructive revolution, it is glorified by Genet through lyricism and all the resources of the imagination. In both cases Genet is the savage or ecstatic bard, but he can be only a bard: he himself is out of picture; he is the cursed poet, doubly cursed, and his poetry is of one substance with his malediction. Having, at the end of *Haute Surveillance,* revealed that double curse in Lefranc's cry, "I'm really all alone," it would seem that from play to play Genet managed to "assume" his double solitude and out of it finally created the main character of *Les Paravents,* Saïd, whose long pilgrimage is a difficult and rigorous descent into the zone of dual rejection and, in the end, complete annihilation.

Indeed, Saïd's glory in *Les Paravents* is not that of the great criminal, king of the prison, whose walk to the guillotine is an apotheosis. His glory is that of the traitor. Presented from the very beginning as the poorest and most abject of all, it is by forcing his abjection to the very extreme that he ends by "shining"; it is because he is finally executed by his own people that he, more than any other character, has completely achieved his destiny. When the curtain falls, the dead are waiting for him to arrive; but he will not arrive, for his death is an absolute death. Ironically, the dead themselves say that he is "among the dead": on earth as in heaven or hell, absolutely nothing of him remains, except the legend of his achievement.

*Les Paravents* has over ninety characters but is entirely organized around the great adventure of Saïd and his wife-shadow, Leila, the ugliest woman in Algeria—so ugly that she has to wear a hood to hide her face. It is in relation to this adventure that the numerous events of the play—crimes, rebellions, repressions, revolutions, murder—all drawn from the substance of the recent war in Algeria, take on their meaning. There can be no doubt that on a certain level the play is on the side of the rebels and includes a vicious, although rather ambiguous, satire of the colonists. That the French Army and the Foreign Legion are handled too roughly[2] is open to question: Genet raises the Lieutenant and the handsome Sergeant to a level of poetic heroism that shows how both attracted and repelled he is by his own characters. He glorifies them, but for their almost Nazi nihilism or for the foul things they do, and he poeticizes them in the name of Evil. However, he rejects the Algerian revolution as soon as it sets up its own order. In other words, by using but transcending a political issue that is still an extremely sensitive subject among the French and Algerians, Genet deliberately situates his play in the living reality of the most current collective passions, thus, beyond any ambiguity, pointing up the stand he takes, or what might be called his personal heroism. Well anchored in the present historical reality, he describes his ethic—a refusal of the world.

In this respect the play is both the outcome of a search that has abstract philosophical depth and the integration of an individual drama into concrete reality. In all probability the intellectual exchanges between Sartre and Genet contributed to this development; in fact, one sometimes gets the impression that Genet is becoming what Sartre said that Genet was aiming to be. But whatever the influences that came into play, Genet has arrived at the

2. For this reason the performance was interrupted by violent manifestations in May and September 1966.

historic embodiment necessary for a theatre "of ideas" to evolve
from abstract allegory to living drama, a process to which we have
already alluded in the case of Claudel.[3] Thus with *Les Paravents,*
and within the framework of history, the philosophical implications of Genet's works become clear: they lead straight to nothingness, but a nothingness *hic et nunc.*

There is, at the outset, Genet's desire to exalt an antisociety
through poetry, describing it in all its horror, but with the flour-
ishes of a rhetoric that gloriously parodies the French "beau style."
This antisociety is necessarily relative to our own society and is, so
to speak, a negative of it. It is the world of thieves, murderers,
perverts, prostitutes, rebels—or of blacks, since *we* are white, and
of slaves, since *we* are masters. "Going into a brothel," says
Carmen in *Le Balcon,* "means rejecting the world." That is to say,
going into crime is like going into holy orders: it is a sign of
renouncement. Carried a step further, renouncement becomes not
only social but universal: from *Haute Surveillance* to *Les
Paravents* (and no doubt with all the "whirligigs" Sartre speaks of
in his *Saint Genet*) one moves into that more complete negation.
While society and antisociety reflect one another as photograph
and negative, within each of the two groups there is also a play of
reflections in which everything is merely appearance—that is, in
which the real dissolves. This is the general meaning of *Le Balcon,*
where not only is the General, for example, reduced to "nothing
[nothing other than the image of what he is not, since he is not
really a general] reflected ad infinitum" in the mirrors of one of
the studios at Mme. Irma's, but the play itself is presented as an
illusion that merely reflects, in the form of a reverse image, the illusion of our own world. As for *Les Nègres,* once the ceremony is
over, even if the Whites have been symbolically eliminated, the
curtain falls on the group of Blacks contemplating the white cata-
falque seen at the beginning of the play: if they continue to exist, it
will be in relation to their revolt against the Whites. And even if

3. See above, pp. 69–70.

the dialogue and final reunion of Village and Vertu have been considered "the first gleam of hope in Genet's dark theatre,"[4] their dialogue emphasizes the fact that the existence of the Blacks remains
relative: Vertu reproaches Village for being like all men—that is,
for "imitating"—and concludes by saying, "There's at least one
sure thing: you won't be able to wind your fingers in my long
blond hair"—as if she can't manage to picture herself except in relation to a kind of Mélisande. Turning one's back on someone, even
as a sign of liberation, means taking him into account. The identity
of antisociety can be affirmed only in contrast, by means of reflection, even if that reflection be rejected. Hence there can be no absolute identity or authenticity. In fact, the only "reality" is nothingness—a nothingness, as Sartre points out, perhaps not very
different from Mallarmé's Void while he was in the process of
composing his incompleted text *Igitur,* and indeed Mallarmé
needed a mirror in which to look at himself in order to be sure he
existed.

Genet's last works are filled with symbols of emptiness: the
tomb (no doubt recalling Franco's) into which the Chief of Police
disappears at the end of *Le Balcon;* the sheet stretched over the
chairs in *Les Nègres* ("architecture of emptiness"), under which
the expected coffin is missing; and, most of all, the many absences
that punctuate *Les Paravents*—the suitcase of wedding presents
that turns out to be empty, at the end of Tableau 1 and, again, the
gendarme's empty suitcase in Tableau 13; Saïd's empty pants
dancing alone in the third tableau; the giant empty glove in the
fourth; the nonexistent farmyard of Leila and Saïd's mother in the
third; and Leila's blanket reduced to a single hole in the ninth.
Actually, all of Genet's works move in the direction of emptiness,
but especially *Les Paravents,* which picks up devices, motifs, and
even characters from his earlier novels and plays. In the sixteenth
tableau of *Les Paravents* (when one discovers that nothing of
Leila is left on earth, and that only her hood remains among the

---

4. Martin Esslin, *The Theatre of the Absurd* (New York, Doubleday
Anchor, 1961), p. 163.

dead) there is one of the most violent metaphors of this theme: in a long speech the dead Sergeant tells about how he died and describes the moment when, with "vacuous eyes," he evacuated into a hole. The scatological metaphor may be unbearable for many spectators—indeed, it is meant to be—but it is no less valid for all that: at the very moment that, empty-eyed, he empties his bowels, the Sergeant loses his power, "the beauty of [his] warlike gestures," in the same way that at such moments a general would lose his stars. The glow of the image of the hero as hero dies out not only for himself but for others. Since the end of this play reveals a glory of another kind, however, Genet pays his character the tribute of killing him off then and there, without giving him the time to become again the mythical Sergeant haloed by his murders and bloody deeds.[5] One might say that the Sergeant died a "beautiful" death, its beauty being not that of the guillotine or torture but that of emptiness. That is why, in death, he makes contact with Saïd, who of course is much farther along the road to annihilation than he is, for annihilation is the result not of some final circumstance but of a long progression.

During *Les Paravents* the main characters are destroyed one after another, and while the survivors manage merely to replace a hateful order by one equally hateful, the dead find themselves in a common limbo, where they are all smilingly reconciled. Only Saïd and his wife succeed in going even beyond death to nothingness. Just as there is a hierarchy of established society and a hierarchy in the world of crime, so there is a hierarchy in death, the summit of which is complete absence. Situated directly under that glorious spot is Saïd's mother, for it was she who did her very best to help her son in his journey toward nothingness, foreseeing

5. For the performance Roger Blin and Jean-Louis Barrault didn't hesitate to give the Sergeant's speech the marvelous theatrical setting Genet was after: the two greatest ladies of French theatre today, Madeleine Renaud (playing the fantastic prostitute Warda) and Maria Casarès (playing Saïd's mother), both among the dead and in extravagant costumes, serenely transformed themselves into sumptuous armrests to hold up the squatting Sergeant while he told and mimed his story.

and summoning that nothingness, which is the cause of her bark-
ing like a dog and her wild laughter that fills the Algerian night.
She herself remains this side of the final achievement—as one
might say that Mary does not have quite the perfection of Jesus—
but among the dead she has the right to a throne. Thus, after having sung of an antisociety, Genet, with *Les Paravents,* managed to
impose the image of an antitheology.

"I know of no other criterion for the beauty of an act, an object, or
a person than the singing it arouses within me," said Genet—or,
rather, wrote Genet, since the quotation comes from a speech
written for the radio but never delivered. This statement may not
be the key to Genet's works, but it does clarify them: Genet sings,
and he calls what he sings *beautiful.* In fact, all the philosophical
"whirligigs" in his works add up to an aesthetic. In the wake of
Baudelaire and Rimbaud, Genet renames the world through his
song—that is, through his words—thus creating beauty.

Among thousands of examples of his aesthetic theory, consider
the flute player in *Les Paravents,* who at one point appears playing
his flute with his nose. A rather banal metaphor of poetic alchemy,
this episode illustrates an idea that has been well known since
Baudelaire, the Romantics, and, even before them, Boileau (with
his "odious monster").[6] Here "the air breathed out of two holes in
a dirty nose" becomes sweet music. But elsewhere in the play, and
more precisely, Genet affirms the power of semantics itself: in
Tableau 9 Leila almost drops a glass, keeps it from falling, and
says, "Stop being an ass or I'll break you. . . . And what will you be
then? Bits of glass . . . bits of broken glass . . . little fragments . . .
little pieces of glass . . . debris. *(Solemnly)* Or, if I want to be kind,
chips . . . sparkling splinters." Genet discovered (or rediscovered in
the wake of the *poètes maudits*) that beauty is a question of vocabulary; he also saw that the trouble Baudelaire took in *La Charogne*
or Rimbaud in *Les Chercheuses de poux* was unnecessary, that one

6. *Art poétique,* Chant 3, line 1.

has merely to give the name "glory" to all that is ignoble and the transformation is complete. Shakespeare and Corneille knew all about the trick, although they used it in their own ways and less systematically. But since they lived in a pre-Sartrean and pre-Lévy-Straussian period, they were unable to take Genet's short cuts.

If Corneille comes to mind apropos of Genet, it is not only because the two are linked by a particularly glorious vocabulary, but also, and above all, because the characters of both playwrights achieve their personal integrity through a systematic *abuse* of the vocabulary they use to describe themselves. In both writers language is baptism—that is, name-giving: the spectators or listeners must give in when a character says, "I am thus and so" or "this object is called thus and so," even if what they perceive is quite the opposite. Of course, another comparison is also suggested: "this is my body . . . this is my blood." The Gospel, Corneille, Claudel, and Genet all use the same hocus-pocus, in which madness, quackery, and mysticism meet, but which is fantastically effective, even after three centuries of rationalism. In short, one might say that Genet, for his own special purposes, reaffirms the reality of the Word.

An early nineteenth-century caricature shows Victor Hugo and the whole Romantic school on the back of a Pegasus-dragon, under the banner, "Nothing is beautiful but ugliness." Today the engraving may seem ridiculous, yet Hugo's assertion of the beauty of the grotesque was no less contradictory than Genet's exaltation of the beauty of crime, sordidness, and abjection. Leila in *Les Paravents,* who is so ugly that she is not allowed to live without covering her face, is worthy of the same homage as Quasimodo in *Notre Dame de Paris.* Saïd's thefts and betrayal are worthy of as much "admiration" as Cleopatra's revenge in Corneille's *Rodogune.* In all civilizations ugliness and crime have often been the object of poetic glorification. In this respect Genet is a traditional writer; he merely draws the extreme inferences of that tradition.

Genet's very language is comprised of both ugliness as such and traditionally poetic elements which paradoxically affirm the beauty of that ugliness. As Jacques Lemarchand remarked in his review of *Les Paravents*,[7] "the dirty words used by Genet," which shock the spectators, are spoken "by the very people who should use them, and if they spoke in any other way, we would no longer believe in them." In other words, much of Genet's vocabulary and syntax is borrowed directly from the violent slang used by the models for his characters, and such slang may be said to have its own beauty. But sometimes the characters suddenly stop using those realistic words and change to an artificial language, eloquent or poetic, which seems to be a parody of a lofty French style. In this way the characters themselves become the bards of their own crime, baseness, or misery. They steal from the world they reject, or which rejects them, a language that is not their own but with which they adorn themselves—just as they physically deck themselves out in stolen clothing or in shoes they happen to find. For Genet adorns his antiworld with more than language. The entire spectacle (costumes, makeup, decor) is meant to dress his characters and his favorite themes in their Sunday best, as it were.

The contrasts in color and the garish lighting of *Haute Surveillance,* like the Louis XV furniture, the lace, and the profusion of flowers in *Les Bonnes,* add to those sort of "No Exit" plays a feeling of chapels—one austere, the other very chichi—which serve to enshrine the murders. The brothel and costumes of *Le Balcon* are so extravagant that what might have been merely picturesque becomes a monument to universal illusion. With *Les Nègres* and especially *Les Paravents,* the scenic festivity becomes even more original and significant. In honor of the rebels or the crimes, an architecture rising in tiers is constructed onstage, the various levels serving not only to grade—that is, to promote or demote—actions and groups of characters, but to put them really on display—a display of the worst possible taste: black suits and yellow shoes, grotesque masks, excessive makeup in the expressionist manner, clashing and gaudy colors, an overabundance of rags and tatters, the mismatched motley of patched garments.

7. *Figaro Littéraire,* April 28, 1966.

The screens themselves, in *Les Paravents,* savagely and sketchily painted, are more than a mere functional device for quick changes and stylized decor: they give the play its title, and since, in their naïve fakery, they enshrine each action, they "unreal-ize" the whole play by reducing it to a decoration. In fact, the play itself is basically a setting (the screens) plus a song (culminating in Ommou's cry at the end of the play, "Long live the song!"). It is presented to the spectator as nothing more than a great architectural and verbal decoration, a huge façade, a gigantic creation of the imagination, like the illusion of a cathedral built in honor of nothingness.

In the middle of *Les Paravents* unfolds one of the most shattering scenes in today's theatre. Right after Kadidja, the leading woman revolutionary, has been killed, she invokes Evil: "Evil, marvelous Evil, you who stay with us when everything else is shot to hell, miraculous Evil, you're going to help us. Please—standing up, I beg you, Evil—come and impregnate my people. And they'd better not be idle!" Then one after another the Arab rebels arrive, and Kadidja asks each one what he has done. Briefly they answer: one has picked up weapons, another has raped the daughter of a colonist, a third has screamed "kill the bastards," a fourth has torn out a heart, a fifth has ripped open a stomach, and so on. They spread out onstage and each one, with a color-spray gun, quickly draws on one of the white screens what he has done. In a very short time the stage is decorated with horrible, improvised pictures representing weapons, fires, torn limbs, and other atrocities. This gigantic "happening" points up the general meaning of Genet's works: ritual invocations, hate, crime, and evil are all hurled at the spectator, but the frightful acts recalled by the Arabs are twice removed, in the form of images, for, more than the acts themselves, there is the beauty that emerges from their horror. In other words, the real massacres fade out behind the spots of color that represent them. And those spots of color are, in the end, merely spots of color.

If Genet shocks, it is certainly because he has set himself up as the poet of our possible collective massacre,[8] and also because he cries out his hatred of our well-being, affirms the presence of Evil within Good and of antisociety within society, and identifies us with what we prefer to ignore or repress. But his works transcend mere provocation or denunciation. Rejected from all sides, Genet rejects the world; or, rather, he empties it. Caught up in the frustrating mirror-play of reflections ad infinitum, haunted by the most personal fantasies, Genet, in *Les Paravents,* while keeping all the elements of that private universe, moves beyond them toward an authentic heroism or, as has often been said, toward a kind of saintliness: "I want you to refuse the brilliance of darkness, the softness of flint, and the honey of thistles," says Leila to Saïd in Tableau 13. And this going even beyond evil and misery is probably Genet's cruelest insult of all, for we realize that the great flourish of glory and heroism and the harsh poetry of renunciation have only one purpose—to conjure us away altogether, characters and spectators alike.

8. Indeed, Robert Brustein believes that Genet "may well go down as the dramatic artist who presided over the disintegration of the West" (*Theatre of Revolt* [Boston, Little, Brown, 1964], p. 411).

# CONCLUSION

# THE GAPING MASK

Not only are there some fifty-five theatres in Paris, with an average of three to four openings a week from September to July, but, as the result of a ten-year movement of dramatic decentralization, suburban and provincial theatres as well as dramatic festivals have been rapidly multiplying throughout France and seriously rivaling Paris in their productions of new plays. This abundance of dramatic centers has encouraged the creation of an impressive number of truly original works, which have reflected the important trends in thinking over the past forty years, opposing nihilism to political or religious optimism, earnestness to the victory of irony and humor, a world of fixed essences to a free or absurd world, and aestheticism to praxis. Such diversity has, of course, given rein to the individuality of writers, for while the outstanding playwrights are representative, they remain distinctly unique. Each has his signature—a mark that can be recognized at every level of his work, from surface effects to a fundamental vision of man and the world.

Indeed, each playwright presents a veritably different universe, for, according to the prologue of Apollinaire's *Les Mamelles de Tirésias:*

> His universe is his play
> Within which he is the god creator
> Who disposes as he will
> Sounds gestures gait masses colors
> Not with the sole objective
> Of photographing what is called a slice of life
> But to bring forth life itself in all its truth
> For a play should be a complete universe
> With its creator
> In other words nature itself
> And not only
> The representation of a small fragment
> Of what surrounds us or what once took place.

Because of such variety, the modern spectator is led, more than ever in the history of theatre, to consider each play as a possible metaphor, an objectivized hypothesis of man's and the world's condition. Not only is each adventure exemplary, as in all theatre, but the play's universe itself is a metaphor of the hidden structure of a possible universe, proposed among others. While writers of the past—that is, of a time when everyone had more or less the same general vision of the world—simplified, discovered, or poeticized what they accepted as the real universe, modern writers invent their own systems. Although an occasional playwright, such as Claudel, may consider his particular world as the only truth for all eternity, the spectator must think of each as a *possible* system. In other words, the modern spectator must regard his playwrights as poets, as makers of metaphors, tangible symbols of a truth that is always transcendent and always essentially controversial.

One basic feeling is obviously common to all the playwrights, and each work is an illustration and a concrete explanation of it. This can be expressed in the most general terms and is the condition sine qua non of all truly dramatic works: the very nature of man is to be torn apart within himself, and it is an irrecusable fact. In the nineteeth century the dramatic hero was often shown in contrast to a world of harmonious individuals at peace with themselves or at least without conflicts. In today's theatre the inner struggle is considered not to be exceptional or caused by circumstances but to constitute the very definition of man. When harmonious individuals are shown on the modern stage, they symbolize not, as before, a happy norm but, rather, blindness and bad faith.

The scenic metaphors expressing man's dramatic nature are doubtless part of a general evolution. Although the lack of historical perspective makes it difficult to define precisely, certain aspects of it are evident enough today to be isolated. Of course, the transition we indicated from the supernatural to man does not correspond exactly to a chronological evolution of French theatre. For example, the definitive acceptance of Claudel by the public at large and the success of Bernanos' *Dialogue des Carmélites* more .or less coincided with the rise and renown of Sartre and Camus. (Similarly, on an international level, Claudel and Brecht have been lumped together as the two great geniuses of the twentieth century.) Yet, while both tendencies are somewhat parallel in time, the new plays since the war show a definite return to man in his isolation. The idea of the divine may sometimes be apparent in Montherlant or in Beckett, for example, but never the divine itself. Such plays express the conflict between man and his own idea of the supernatural, not the conflict between men and the gods. And although the return to man has occasionally led to forms somewhat similar to the old naturalism (in Salacrou, Sartre, or Anouilh), more recent playwrights have avoided the danger by exteriorizing and concretely representing elements of their inner worlds and reintroducing scenic fantasy in more or less allegorical form.

There is no doubt that the current twofold movement extends, in modern times, the continuous debate in French thinking that follows the dialectic line Montaigne-Pascal-Voltaire-Rousseau-etc. —from humanism to Jansenism, Jansenism to rationalism, rationalism to vague Romantic mysticism, Romanticism to positivism, positivism to Baudelairean and Rimbaldian symbolism, and continued on into modern dialogues such as that between Gide and Claudel. What characterizes the present state of the debate is the fact that, although it is generally no longer between forms of rationalism and a Christian vision, both factions claim the notion of transcendency, one as residing in an outer reality (God, cosmic forces, a possible "kingdom"), the other as residing in man alone—in the solitary individual or in the society of men, presented as either an eternal or a historical phenomenon.

Thus it is sometimes difficult to distinguish between the symbol of an element or dimension of an inner world and the tangible symbol of an outer reality or another order. While there is no doubt as to the meaning of Claudel's symbolism, there may be some concerning certain of Giraudoux's fantasies. And while it is obvious that Sartre's Jupiter represents no more than a satirical allegory of the idea of God, Audiberti's monsters and Beckett's Godot are ambiguous.

Despite the productions of plays like Georges Neveux's *Le Voyage de Thésée* (1943) or André Obey's *Une Fille pour du vent* (1953, an adaption of the myth of Iphigenia), another movement today would seem to be a progressive indifference to the traditional material of professors and diplomats. Although Giraudoux and Cocteau drew freely from ancient mythology, Sartre used it in only one play, Camus as a playwright touched on it only through a historical character, and the poets either turn toward national and regional folklore or invent new myths and legends. Ionesco, Adamov, and Beckett deliberately move away from traditions of culture, and their myths are rather the modern ones, such as Charlie Chaplin, the Marx Brothers, or current political entities. Indeed, the gods of Olympus have been gradually replaced by clowns in modern dress. The fact that the process had become a convention can be seen from Anouilh's *Antigone,* in which the use of certain of Cocteau's and Giraudoux's devices is particularly obvious, despite the play's style and power, and Sartre's choice of Greek myth for

*Les Mouches* is quite clearly a deliberate and topical answer to Giraudoux's *Electre*. Moreover, the new playwrights prefer to start from zero or, rather, to base their theatre primarily on a direct experience of individual or collective life, not on bookish culture. In considering only the front line of important discoveries or contributions, the movement of humanization without recourse to academic humanism is an important characteristic of the French theatre's evolution in the past thirty years.

Even more essential in regard to an *idea* of theatre is the influence of Antonin Artaud, which has become increasingly vigorous during the last decades. Although in general Jacques Copeau was the main artisan of the return to integrity on the French stage, Artaud's spirit has progressively restored theatre's disrupting power.

Artaud is "an influence more than a presence, a presence more than a work."[1] He belongs to that breed of seers who leave trails of fire behind them as they pass through the world. Artaud might be said to have been part of the surrealist movement, to which he belonged from 1924 to 1927. But after a great row, he gave up the surrealist experiment and his works clearly transcend it. In fact, he was a unique phenomenon of the French literary world of the thirties. In the realm of theatre alone, he was an actor of both stage and screen, founder of the Alfred Jarry Theatre in 1927 (with Roger Vitrac) and the "Théâtre de la cruauté" in 1933, and author of a group of essays, begun in 1931 and published in 1938 as *Le Théâtre et son double*. When he died in 1948, the poetry review *K* published a testimonial issue including articles by Charles Dullin, Arthur Adamov, Henri Pichette, Audiberti, and Roger Blin. Since then, Gallimard has published his complete works; the *Cahiers Renaud-Barrault* and the *Tulane Drama Review* have devoted entire issues to him; and he is mentioned in all studies of the new theatre, from Robert Brustein's *Theatre of Revolt* to reviews of such plays as Peter Weiss' *Marat/Sade*. Indeed, his influence has

1. André Frank, in *Encyclopédie du théâtre contemporain*, 2, 54.

extended beyond that testimonial issue of *K* to the whole movement of theatrical evolution.

Artaud tried to totally redefine theatre. Using the now well-known metaphor of "le Thèâtre et la peste," he claimed that theatre is very much the same as the plague in that both provoke liberating and revealing "frenzies." Just as during the plagues of the Western world men were rid of their Western character (order, reason, morality) and restored to their true powers, great theatre not only presents the spectacle of individuals restored to those powers but awakens them in the spectator. The acts committed onstage, just as those committed by the inhabitants of a plague-ridden city, are both monstrous and gratuitous. True theatre, like the plague, should rid life of its "utility" and bring back the prelogical, non-civilized world that has been suppressed by the Western "conspiracy":

> Like the plague, theatre is the time of evil, the triumph of dark powers that are fed by a power even more profound, until extinction.
>
> . . . and if these powers and possibilities are dark, it is the fault, not of the plague, nor of the theatre, but of life.[2]

Moreover:

> Theatre, like the plague, is a crisis which is resolved by death or recovery. And the plague is a superior disease because it is a total crisis, after which nothing remains but death or an extreme purification. . . .
>
> The action of theatre, like that of the plague, is beneficial, for, pushing men into seeing themselves as they are, it causes the mask to fall and reveals the lie, the moral inertia, baseness, and hypocrisy of our world.
>
> . . . and in revealing to collectivities their dark power and hidden force, it invites them to take, in the face of destiny, a heroic and superior attitude they never have had without it.[3]

2. Antonin Artaud, *Œuvres complètes, 4,* 37–38.
3. Ibid., pp. 38–39.

Artaud thus goes back to a definition of what tragedy actually is—
but a definition that is nonrational, stripped of Aristotelian concepts, and restored to the feeling of magic found in the works themselves, not in the theorists. For Artaud was concerned with a magical operation and not with the resolution of "conflicts of a human
and passionate nature" through rational ethics or psychology.

Theatre is a delirium—similar to Rimbaud's *dérèglement*—
which restores man to the inhuman. Artaud, who believed that he
himself was "really not in the world,"[4] refused what is "human" to
the extent that such humanity is merely the artificial creation of
Western thought. Before leaving for Mexico in search of the secrets
of the Indian tribes, he wrote to Barrault: "Stop looking for human
characters, Man is what annoys us the most, and come back to the
subterranean gods, that is, to the enemy forces which become embodied as soon as we want to grasp them."[5] There is no contradiction between his rejection of man and the idea of a theatre that
reveals man to himself, since, according to him, man's true destiny
lies in that which is beyond him.

Among his concrete examples, Artaud chose, as a play to his
taste, John Ford's *'Tis Pity She's a Whore*. And, indeed, it does
express and provoke "the exteriorization of the underlying and
latent cruelty by which all the perverse possibilities of the mind
are localized in an individual or in a people."[6] The "cruelty" in
question here is seen not as a psychological phenomenon but as a
method. In the name of that method Artaud founded his "Théâtre
de la cruauté" and wrote his own play, *Les Cenci* (performed in
1935), based on the tragedy by Shelley and Stendhal's *Chroniques
italiennes*. The anecdote, made up of incest, parricide, and execution, was performed at a frantic pace, with moments of pantomime,
accompanied by a kind of concrete music, and played in a setting by
Balthus. The production was greeted with much reserve on the part
of the critics and lasted only fifteen days. As a first experiment in
"total theatre," as Barrault understands it today, it seemed hardly

4. Ibid., p. 40.
5. *Lettres d'Antonin Artaud à Jean-Louis Barrault.*
6. *Œuvres complètes, 4, 37.*

to have any future at all. Artaud's draft for another play, *Montezuma ou La Conquête du Mexique,* exists only in outline form.

Artaud's actual dramatic works are few, yet his concepts would seem to have permeated much of today's theatre: the powers that break loose and become embodied in Audiberti's plays; Adamov's characters, considered as the playthings of forces; Jean Genet's fantasies; the attempts in Sartre, Camus, Pichette, Vauthier, and Ionesco to produce theatrical shocks—all are closely related to Artaud's theories. In a more general way, an atmosphere of the whole helped create a shattering theatre which not only deeply moves the spectator but disturbs his very being. Almost all the great modern playwrights try to prevent the spectator from drowsing in a peaceful definition of man. While few, of course, go as far as Artaud in rejecting Western thought as a whole, all question the basic values of our world, its conception of good ond evil, and the satisfactions of rationalism. Although, except for certain poets, they do not invoke the return to a totally magical and mystical vision of the world, they do use violence, cruelty, derangement, and crime as *methods* for awakening in the spectator an awareness of his possibilities and for trying to bring out, beyond the falsifications of civilization, what is truly man—man being situated at a level that would traditionally be called inhuman.

In his preface to *Les Lettres d'Antonin Artaud à Jean-Louis Barrault* André Frank mentions, in connection with Artaud's theories, *Le Partage de midi, Le Procès* (Kafka/Gide), *L'Etat de siège,* and *Malatesta*—all plays directed by Barrault, whose pantomime of Faulkner's *As I Lay Dying* was acclaimed by Artaud in 1935. Although the inclusion of *Malatesta,* in which the portrait of an individual dominates the symbol, is questionable, all the works show not only a common use of passion, violence, and horror as a means of shaking the spectator out of his complacency but the same idea of destiny as a battle among forces that transcend the individual. More recently, Brustein, in his *Theatre of Revolt,* emphasized the fact that Jean Genet, whose play *Les Paravents* was finally produced in Barrault's theatre, is Artaud's most right-ful heir. Even far from the hotbed of Artaudian activity represen-ted by Barrault, however, the same spirit can be found in varying forms and with increasing frequency.

While in many cases the influence is obvious and direct—on playwrights such as Audiberti, Pichette, Adamov, Camus, and Genet—others, such as Ghelderode or Arrabal, have written plays that, by their very nature, just happen to coincide with Artaud's theories. Influences independent of Artaud are of course at work —for example, Aeschylus, the Elizabethans, Büchner, and Strindberg—but they have become incorporated into the same movement. In other words, while Artaud is not the only influence, he is the center of an increasingly generalized movement toward creating a theatre intended, more than ever, to shatter the spectator.

In order to reach his objective, Artaud, influenced by oriental theatre, suggested the use of a theatrical sign language, in which language itself would play but a secondary part. Thus a real meta-physics would be directly experienced in the symbolism of gestures, postures, lights, bodily rhythms, and sound patterns. Giraudoux reacted strongly against that type of spectacle, likening it to a German conception of drama. And, of course, French theatre has remained a theatre of language. Even in the Barrault-Claudel idea of "total theatre," the Word is on the same level as the Gesture. Indeed, the language of the French stage has, on the whole, con-tinued to be literary: all the great playwrights are great stylists, and, despite its incantatory quality, language still serves its normal functions.

In fact, as André Frank points out in his preface to the correspon-dence of Artaud and Barrault, "Anouilh, Sartre, Achard, Aymé, and many others have consolidated the position of that Western theatre 'of a human and passionate nature' against which Artaud rose up in revolt."[7] For, indeed, Artaud's dream was not of a sen-timental theatre, a satiric theatre, an intellectual theatre, or an

7. *Lettres d'Antonin Artaud à Jean-Louis Barrault.*

elegantly theatrical theatre, intended to amuse or satisfy "the intellectual's exasperated sensibility." Neither Marcel Achard's
Boulevard kind of sentimentality nor Marcel Aymé's violent, fantastic, or humorous satire questions the definition of man in any
disconcerting way. And the role of language and the appeal to
Western intelligence found in Anouilh and Sartre remain traditional.[8] Neither Anouilh nor Sartre are mystics; both believe that
everything comes from man and men: there are no Mexican gods,
no powers in the tarot cards, no magic spells, only attitudes of consciousness. The return to man, as a dominant tendency of the theatre in the 1940s, is obviously contrary to Artaud's belief in a *real*
presence of spiritual or subterranean powers, whether possessive or
destructive.

Artaud's major contribution, then, would seem to lie not so
much in form itself as in a basic intention—that is, a theatre of
shock intended not to awaken the public to current problems but to
use such problems or go beyond them to reveal man's metaphysical
reality, hard as it may be to take. In other words, the modern
French theatre wants to be metaphysical, and such metaphysics can
be effectively presented only through shocking violence, causing
extreme bewilderment.

When Sartre and Camus use traditional or "Western" forms of
thought and structure, their idea is to transcend them in an attempt
to emphasize both the topical value of the subject or problem *and*
the terrifying metaphysics it implies. And while Anouilh's plots
are resolved in human terms, the fundamental question transcending the plots is stated. In all three playwrights, although any
suggested attitude to action (social, political, or moral) is meant for
the present, the opening onto a metaphysical substructure is never
closed and the terror of existing is powerfully communicated.

While continuing the trend of a return to man, Jean Genet and
the trio Adamov (first period)-Ionesco-Beckett are even closer to

8. Audiberti's Joan of Arc is probably closer to Artaud's intentions than
Anouilh's, one being the creation of obscure powers within man and outside
men, the other considered as free will, an individual negating power.

Artaud. In the place of Sartre's anecdotic demonstration, they have resorted to the shock of direct images and the elimination of "utilitarian" elements. Moreover, the characteristic dreamlike quality of their works escapes traditional psychologism as well as surrealism. In fact, they would seem to comply with Artaud's statement:

> I propose to renounce that empiricism of images, which the unconscious produces at random and which we throw out also at random, calling them poetic images . . . .
> I propose to return, through theatre, to an idea of the physical knowledge of images and the means of inducing trances.[9]

For their imagery is often more physical than verbal, and although taken from the depths of dream or the subconscious, it is always planned with an eye to a shock effect or organized into a series of impressions more tangible than intellectual and comparable to the punctures of Chinese medicine, as Artaud had suggested. The shattering violence and shock-images taken "from an inner world" that is both personal and "an ancestral legacy . . . the universal language,"[10] a psychology based on the play of inner and outer forces, and a science of the effects produced by the very rhythms of the general structure and scenic movements make such plays part of a "theatre of cruelty."

In many cases the resemblance stops at that level. Most of the plays lack the gigantic or epic dimensions, the collective intent, the mysticism, and the true ritual aspects of Artaud's ideal. Furthermore, in some of them the intellectual distance inspired by Brecht would seem opposed to the emotional involvement sought by Artaud. Still, a synthesis of the two principles may take place within the living complexity of a spectacle. Just as Beckett's *Godot* successfully combines spellbinding poetry and metaphors of the master-slave relationship, and as Genet's *Les Paravents* at once assimilates and transcends both visceral shock and an appeal to the

9. *Œuvres complètes*, 4, 96.
10. Eugène Ionesco, *L'Impromptu de l'Alma*.

intelligence, so writers such as Adamov and Gatti—with their epic vision, their use of dreams and neuroses, and their historico-political awareness—may perhaps one day achieve the same type of synthesis. In any event, it is the spirit of Artaud that has given the French theatre of today its power and its greatest originality.

Since the beginning of the century, French theatre has managed to "cause the masks to fall"—the masks behind which man was hiding the fact that he is a metaphysical and tragic being. Whether he is, from a mystical perspective, always elsewhere or, from a purely existential perspective, in a state of constantly transcending himself, and whether such contradiction or absurdity is expressed in actualized metaphors or in intellectual debates, man's situation in today's theatre is always that of a creature, if not without hope (for there is Claudel's salvation, Sartre's action, and the Red flag often waved by Adamov and Gatti), at least without illusion. The time of what Artaud called "human conflicts" is over in true the-atre.

Yet man has been thrown back more and more upon himself, and the rebound has provoked a burst of laughter—that of modern farce. It is special laughter, in no way related to the detachment of the past. For the climate created by Artaud, as well as by the times themselves, would hardly authorize frivolity.

The new laughter initially sprang from an awareness of the old idea that life is, or has been made, a farce: the mask worn onstage is symbolic of another mask. To this cliché, modern theatre has added a terrifying qualification: the farce is acted out for nothing and for no one. While Claudel's comic characters dance about under the eye of God and act out scenarios that have meaning, Beckett's and Ionesco's are seen only by men like themselves. Artaud's vision of a dual universe of dark powers and spiritual redemption[11] is re-placed by the dizzying emptiness of unjustified existence. His method drives the spectator out of himself as it should, but toward

11. Although after his conversion in Ireland in 1937, he denied ever having been Manichaeist.

nothingness. More than a failure of metaphysics, the new trend might be seen rather as a metaphysics of failure. The irony goes to work on itself and Satan dominates: Satan falls because he laughs, and laughs because he falls. When we laugh at the farces of today, we are toppling over into the chasms of our own mouths.

> We sail over a vast sphere, always uncertain and floating, pushed from one end toward the other. Whatever point we think we can fasten onto and steady ourselves breaks loose and leaves us; and if we follow it, it eludes our grasp, slips away from us, and flees in eternal flight. Nothing stops for us. It is our natural state, and yet most contrary to our inclination; we burn with the desire of finding a firm foundation and a last and unchanging base to build a tower reaching to Infinity; but our whole foundation cracks, and the earth opens up to unfathomable depths.[12]

So Pascal tried to evoke reason's failure to explain man's situation in the universe. Today, after the bankruptcy of all great ideologies, including rationalism, the anxiety of an "earth open[ing] up to unfathomable depths" is at the central point of modern consciousness. The multiplicity of theatrical worlds proposed by various thinkers and writers constitutes a group of poetic hypotheses, while the idea of an "answer" is replaced by the dual idea of lucidity and creative power. One can hope that today's "dark" theatre, having furnished perfect metaphors of the metaphysical abyss and modern tragic terror, will go on to complete the tragedy by adding the necessary dimension, not of happiness and facile solutions, but of that higher exaltation Yeats called "tragic joy."

12. Pascal, *Pensées,* Sec. II, Frag. 72, of the Brunschvicg edition.

APPENDIXES


I. DIRECTORS AND PRODUCTIONS


II. FIRST PERFORMANCES AND
IMPORTANT REVIVALS

# APPENDIX I

# DIRECTORS AND PRODUCTIONS

*Before Jacques Copeau*

The theories of André Antoine were influenced by a general climate of naturalism and the discovery, in 1884, of foreign stagings (Henry Irving, the Meiningen Players). Antoine did not invent scenic realism; he carried it to an extreme. As early as Romantic theatre, emphasis was put on a search for exactitude in painted decor, combined with the use of real props. But even when the decor was scrupulously detailed, it was used for every play of the same period, and the attempt at illusion was paradoxical in the juxtaposition of painted canvas and the real volume of objects. In his Théâtre Libre, founded in 1887, Antoine's first objective was to do away with the paradox and establish a consistency in the decor by placing the real objects within a real construction. His second objective was to create a unity between the decor and the play's content—in other words, its psycho-sociological implications—decor being "the milieu which from now on varies with the movement." But most important of all, he revolutionized acting. He replaced the stylized declamation and conventional posture with a direct copy of man's speech and behavior.

Acting, decor, lighting effects, and text were all subordinated to the whole, which is life as we perceive it. Only at that price would theatre correspond to Stendhal's wish and Ibsen's formula: a removal of the fourth wall. And only at that price would a play stop being a pretext for the recitations of well-known actors and become a living work, whatever its limitations.

The dangers of scenic verism have often been pointed out: the audience is transformed into a group of Peeping Toms, the general interest is in surface effects, and the suggestion of what cannot be perceived is either eliminated or reduced to a minimum. Indeed, while Antoine brought Ibsen to the French, he saw and emphasized only the plays' naturalistic dimensions.

After his Théâtre Libre closed, Antoine modified his theories. Although he never betrayed the principles of scenic verism and unity of the whole, he moved from an excessive to a simplified realism and, in decor, with his productions at the Odéon, to a reinvention of the real rather than an imitation of it. In his productions of Shakespeare he tried to solve the problem of quick changes of decor by using curtains and mobile sets.

On the whole, the French naturalist experiment had a lasting influence on the basic principles of theatrical production, but it was immediately transcended—because of both an absence of great naturalist playwrights and the violent symbolist reaction.

ANDRÉ ANTOINE *(1858–1943):* Outstanding Productions

At the Théâtre Libre
Tolstoy's *The Power of Darkness* (1888)
Ibsen's *Ghosts* (1890)
    *The Wild Duck* (1891)
Courteline's *Boubouroche* (1893)
Strindberg's *Miss Julie* (1893)
Gerhart Hauptmann's *The Weavers* (1893)

At the Théâtre Antoine
Jules Renard's *Poil de Carotte* (1900)
Shakespeare's *King Lear* (1904)

At the Odéon
Shakespeare's *Julius Caesar* (1907)
Molière's *Tartuffe* (1908)
Shakespeare's *Coriolanus* (1910)
*Romeo and Juliet* (1911)

The history of theatre reproduced the general intellectual conflict of those years: positivism, psychologism, and a deterministic, naturalistic vision of man and his universe as against a certain Protean idealism, partially inspired by German idealism, but particularly indicative of an impatience with the limitations of positivism as a vision of the world. In France the reaction was successfully expressed in the realm of literature and the arts by a form of Wagnerism and by symbolism. Barely three years after the foundation of the Théâtre Libre, an antinaturalistic theatre made its appearance: in 1891, after the experiments of the Théâtre Mixte and the Théâtre Idéaliste, Paul Fort, aged seventeen, founded the Théâtre d'Art. It was inspired by Verlaine, Mallarmé, and Maurice Denis, as the Théâtre Libre had been inspired by Emile Zola and Paul Alexis. Stage sets became "ornamental fictions." Antoine's unity and consistency of spectacle was kept, but in the sense of a suggestion, an opening onto "poetic truth," which was in fact never really defined. Symbolist poems were produced, as well as Marlowe's *Doctor Faustus,* Shelley's *The Cenci,* and Maeterlinck's *L'Intruse.* Indeed, the Théâtre d'Art was more literary and decorative than theatrical. Taken over by Lugné-Poe in 1893, it became the Théâtre de l'Œuvre and continued the same type of productions but with greater scope.

A member of Antoine's company but also a friend of young painters and poets, Lugné-Poe tried to formulate a theatrical program of antinaturalism, but it remained vague—a theatre of ideas, with everything subordinated to the idea. However, decor became simplified and the painted backdrop took back its rights, not to create an illusion of the perceived real, but to eliminate it and, rather, to suggest a hidden idea or bring out the "soul" of a place. Some of his innovations have been picked up by today's theatre: the elimination of footlights, a sloped stage, actors performing behind a transparent curtain, extras playing the parts of doors. He also replaced realistic acting by a kind of chanted diction that was to be suggestive of the "inhuman" sources of language.

Lugné–Poe opened the door to antirealism, which from then on dominated the French stage. He was the first to present Jarry, Claudel, Crommelynck, and Salacrou to the French public. And he made possible the victory of painters (Maurice Denis, Pierre Bonnard, Odilon Redon, Edouard Vuillard) over set designers—that is, the victory of plastic imagination in direct relation to the text over the indifferent routine of specialists.

Yet Lugné-Poe 's attitude was not rigid. He often went back to more realistic devices. Ibsen's theatre was a case in point. Antoine saw it as pure naturalism, whereas Lugné-Poe thought of it initially only in terms of symbol and produced *An Enemy of the People* in the same way as he had produced *Pelléas et Mélisande.* However, his appointment of the Danish writer Hermann Bang as "scenic adviser," followed by a meeting with Ibsen himself, convinced him that less fantastic techniques and acting were in order. After having been the champion of symbolism in the theatre, Lugné-Poe remained audacious and original but very eclectic.

AURÉLIEN LUGNÉ-POE *(1869–1940):* Outstanding Productions

Maeterlinck's *Pelléas et Mélisande* (1893)
Ibsen's *Rosmersholm* and *An Enemy of the People* (1893)
    *The Master Builder* (1894)
Oscar Wilde's *Salome* (1896)
Ibsen's *Peer Gynt* (1896)
Jarry's *Ubu Roi* (1896)
Shakespeare's *Measure for Measure* (1898)

Gide's *Le Roi Candaule* (1901)
D'Annunzio's *The Daughter of Jorio* (1905)
Gorky's *The Lower Depths* (1905)
Claudel's *L'Annonce faite à Marie* (1912)
Shakespeare's *Hamlet* (1913)
Claudel's *L'Otage* (1914)
Crommelynck's *Le Cocu magnifique* (1921)
Jean Sarment's *Le Pêcheur d'ombres* (1922)
Salacrou's *Tour à terre* (1925)
Stève Passeur's *L'Acheteuse* (1930)
Anouilh's *L'Hermine* (1932)
Salacrou's *L'Inconnue d'Arras* (1935)

## *Foreign Influences*

During the 1880s and 90s the scenic reform was not restricted to France. In Germany, Russia, and England directors, writers, and theorists were raising their voices, founding theatres, and publishing manifestos—first in order to fight against outdated traditions and commercialization, and then either to carry on the realist experiment or to create a new poetry of the theatre. Several important events might be mentioned: the reform of the mise-en-scène of historical dramas by the Meiningen Players and their stage manager, Ludwig Chronegk; the reform of acting by Henry Irving (whom Antoine saw in London in 1888); George Bernard Shaw's articles in *The Saturday Review* in favor of Ibsenian realism(1895–98); the first essays of Adolphe Appia (*Die Musik und die Inszenierung,* Munich, 1899); the founding of the Moscow Art Theatre by Stanislavsky and Dantchenko in 1898; the beginning of Gordon Craig as director for the Purcell Society in 1899; and the beginning of the Irish Dramatic Company and Max Reinhardt's Kleines Theatre in Berlin in 1902. However, the first years of the twentieth century are essentially marked by the rise of Stanislavsky and the development of Adolphe Appia's and Gordon Craig's theories.

The importance of Stanislavsky's contribution lies in the breadth and flexibility of his conception of realism. Forsaking surface realism, he used Chekhov's plays to bring out, scenically but chiefly through acting, the "underlying text" of a play. His symbolist experiments (Maeterlinck's *L'Oiseau bleu*) made it possible for him to complete his "inner realism" by a rediscovery of theatricality. Stanislavsky transcended the conflict between realism and antirealism, creating a totally human theatre, with a naturalistic surface, but an increasingly transparent one.

For Gordon Craig (*The Art of Theatre,* 1905), if theatre was to be an art, it had to be absolutely controlled by aesthetic intelligence. Everything accidental and unexpected had to be eliminated. The actor was to be replaced by a "super-marionette," whose acting had to correspond absolutely to the most precise orders of the "author." Decor was to be an intellectual construction, in which lines, colors, and lighting effects contribute, with uncompromising precision, not to a representation but to a revelation. Where Stanislavsky stressed the actor, Craig stressed the design of the production. Theatre became a movement in itself, independent of the other arts, with its true "author" the director.

At the same time, in Switzerland, Aldophe Appia developed closely related theories, starting with a reform of the Wagnerian mise-en-scène. His objective was to "express a thought plastically" in space and in time. Although acting remained the vital element, it was only effective when rigorously subordinated to a rhythm of the whole, based on the text (spoken or musical). His most important idea was the conception of a three-dimensional architectural decor, set up in free space.

A fourth influence, bearing primarily on decor, was that of Diaghilev's Ballets Russes, first produced in Paris in 1909—a triumph of color. Gradually, the Ballets developed in the direction of constructivist techniques, with emphasis on the depth of space and vertical planes made visible by a succession of structures on several levels. And just as the Théâtre de l'Œuvre used certain Impressionist painters, the Ballets Russes worked with the Fauves and the Cubists; Picasso, Matisse, Braque. While their decors were reproached with crushing the ballet itself, they did show the possibilities of color and construction.

The major foreign discoveries were incorporated by Jacques Rouché into his book *L'Art théâtral moderne,* published in 1910. Short but clear and synthetic, the book was equivalent to a manifesto—the first really coherent and revolutionary work on the subject published in France.

### Jacques Copeau

In 1913 a second manifesto was published and served as a basis for almost all of French theatre today: Jacques Copeau's article, "Un Essai de rénovation dramatique: Le Théâtre du Vieux Colombier," in the September issue of the *Nouvelle Revue Française.* The intransigent critic of *L'Ermitage,* then of *La Grande Revue,* Copeau kept a careful watch on Parisian theatre, judged it severely, and demolished Hervieu, Bernstein, Bataille, Rostand, and the commercial spirit, which had remained a sore spot. In 1911 he gave Jacques Rouché, for the Théâtre des Arts, an adaptation of *The Brothers Karamazov,* and it was performed in the spirit of an "imaginary Russia."

From 1909 to 1913 Copeau was literary director of the *NRF,* which he had founded with André Gide and Jean Schlumberger. In 1913 he founded the Théâtre du Vieux Colombier. Although he recognized and praised the foreign antirealist experiments, he was on his guard against pedantry and any "extravagant systematization." A suggestive art can become vulgar and naïve through a too obvious use of material symbols. Overemphasizing them means sidestepping theatre:

> Being in favor of this or that decorative formula always means being interested in theatre by way of its side-issues. Being enthusiastic about the inventions of engineers or electricians always means giving usurped importance to canvas, painted cardboard, lighting arrangements—always means

falling somehow or another into tricks. Old or new, we repudiate them all. Good or bad, rudimentary or perfected, artificial or realistic, we intend to deny the importance of all machinery. [*NRF,* September 1913]

Copeau refused to believe that "the future of our theatre is bound to a question of machinery." What he wanted was, in some way, a return to the very essence of the stage:

The tyranny of the stage and its gross artificiality will act on us like a discipline in forcing us to concentrate all of truth in the feelings and actions of our characters. May the other marvels vanish and, for the new works, leave us with a bare stage. [Ibid.]

His principle of absolute simplicity, after the experiments of preceding reformers, was justified both by the continued existence of commercialism ("the monopolizing of most theatres by a handful of entertainers in the pay of shameless merchants") and by the confusion that reigned among the different schools, misleading the public and often resulting in no more than surface effects.

To reform theatre, Copeau wanted to reinvent it, starting from the most elementary principles. To his "bare stage" he added what might be called "bare actors." As early as 1913 he tried to strip them down and discipline them by what he called "exorcisms": "If I have the patience and the strength, in two or three years these actors will have almost become men" (Letter to André Suarez, July 14, 1913, quoted by Georges Lerminier in his *Jacques Copeau*).

Copeau knew about the attempts of Stanislavsky, Appia, and Craig. On many questions his work was parallel to theirs, at least in spirit. Like Stanislavsky, he stressed the actor and an inner realism, leading quite naturally to a transposition. Like Appia, he wanted a stripped and functional decor:

[Appia] sacrificed attractiveness to rigor, virtuosity to an inner law. [He replaced *trompe l'oeil* decor] by a three-dimensional architectural decor, purely practicable—in other words, purely dramatic or dynamic. The major reforms of the contemporary stage sprang from there.

[*Encyclopédie Française*, 17 (1936)]

And from there, in great part, also sprang "le dispositif fixe" or permanent set—a concrete architectural whole, with several levels, a projecting apron, and an arch at the back, framed by two stairways, all very Elizabethan in feeling, invented by Jacques Copeau and Louis Jouvet, and built in the Vieux Colombier in 1920, after having been tried out in the Garrick Theatre in New York. From Gordon Craig, Copeau took the idea of an independent theatre, completely devoted to its own unity and its power of suggestion in space and in time. All his life Copeau was suspicious of theorists' "systems," but he acknowledged his agreement on basic principles with Appia and Craig, whom he met in 1916, as well as with Stanislavsky, whom he entertained in Paris in 1922.

From the very beginning, Copeau's art was marked by the greatest simplicity. His bare stage remained almost bare, and when the "dispositif" was built, he used it for all plays, making it almost sufficient unto itself. Of course, the lighting was skillful, the costumes and decorative elements were calculated with care, and the taste for spectacle of his stage manager, Louis Jouvet, sometimes dressed up the bareness. But the text always came first. All the theatre arts were subordinated to it with a maximum of discipline and a minimum of means. Copeau wanted to bring out the direct reality and poetry of the text without misrepresenting or stifling it. The play itself was to be the focus of interest rather than merely a pretext for exhibitionists. Critics occasionally reproached Copeau for his too great austerity, but they always acknowledged the value of his work.

For Copeau was more than just another theorist or just another bold director. He represented a philosophical position in France that involved not only the dramatic arts but all of man. He was similar to Charles Péguy (whom he knew well) in his refusal of a world in which the relation of man to what he makes was becoming more and more abstract. He felt that mass production and gaudy luxury should be replaced by craftsmanship, with man giving himself completely to the one object he makes with his own hands, starting from zero. Similar to Péguy also was the mystical atmosphere surrounding his work. Jacques Copeau was the first in France to conceive of the director-actor as a priest, a conception currently embodied by Jean-Louis Barrault.

This conviction required a total reeducation of both the public and men of the theatre. And it was on the theatrical world in particular that Copeau left his mark. Indeed, he was the leader of a whole generation of directors and actors. In 1913 Copeau took his entire company to La Ferté-sous-Jouarre:

> There, every day, for five hours, they studied the plays of the repertory. In addition, two hours were devoted to reading aloud out of doors, as an exercise in intellectual flexibility and vocal articulation, also to analyses of texts and to physical exercises. ["L'Ecole du Vieux Colombier," *NRF* (November 1921)]

In 1921 he founded the Ecole du Vieux Colombier, where he trained actors to be as good singers as reciters, as good dancers as improvisers. While a sculptor taught them to make masks, the Fratellini clowns taught them mime and acrobatics. In 1924 Copeau retired to Burgundy, disgusted by the compromises he was forced to make in Paris, and his students followed him. There were gymnastics, acrobatics, and exercises in mime every morning; sewing, modeling, painting, then improvisation and rehearsals every afternoon. The objective: "The renewal of theatre . . . which seems to me essentially to be a renewal of man in the theatre." Gymnastics were meant to create "an obedient body"; dance and mime, "the idea of inner rhythm." At first the instruction was the same for all, then specialized, so that poet, dancer, mime, and actor all emerged "from the same tree," "not artificially regrouped and polished, but inspired from within, organically united." In fact,

Copeau finally replaced the idea of the *vedette* or star, plus just any group of actors casually brought together, by an "organic" conception of the theatrical company. Although in 1929 he closed his school, it continued on its own as "La Compagnie des Quinze."

Since the 1930s the French stage has been dominated by men who were more or less trained by Copeau as collaborators or students: Charles Dullin, Louis Jouvet, Jean Dasté, Michel Saint Denis, Jean Vilar, the mime Decroux, the actress Valentine Tessier, and, indirectly, André Barsacq and Jean-Louis Barrault. In the United States the postwar little theatres and the Theatre Guild owed much to Copeau's stay in New York from 1917 to 1919; in Belgium the Théâtre du Marais was based on the spirit of the Vieux Colombier and trained the director Raymond Rouleau; in Italy, where Copeau worked for the 1933 and 1935 Maggio Fiorentino, the Piccolo Theatro di Milano was founded in 1947 according to his principles.

Copeau's own career was difficult. The Vieux Colombier grew in reputation from 1913 to 1914 but was closed by the war. During the seasons of 1917–18 and 1918–19 in New York, Copeau was overwhelmed with work and often humiliated, having been forced into rush jobs and made to produce plays he despised. Despite the Vieux Colombier's success from 1920 to 1924, Dullin and Jouvet left him and financial difficulties piled up. Disgust, illness, and religious fervor led to his retirement in 1924. From then on, besides his teaching, lecturing, and some directing in Paris and outside France, he spent his time meditating on the theatre and on his past. He dreamed of a great outdoor theatre and admitted that the Vieux Colombier experiment was necessarily limited to the "little theatre." From 1936 to 1940 he had the opportunity of directing a few productions at the Comédie Française. He died in 1949.

Copeau never succeeded in creating the great modern poets he dreamed of. With a few exceptions, he was forced to draw either from naturalistic (Renard, Becque) or poetic (François Porché) works whose scope fell short of his ambitions. Nor did he manage to create an ideal public. Since the Vieux Colombier, in its day, was an avant-garde theatre, reserved for an elite, his students and successors were the ones who finally made greater contact with the public. They invented their own styles, were influenced by others, and even repudiated certain of his principles. But Copeau's experiment was situated beyond styles and schools and therefore was more far-reaching. It gave the French stage its spirit—in other words, a *mystique* and an ethics.

JACQUES COPEAU *(1878–1949):* Outstanding Productions

At the Vieux Colombier
Heywood's *A Woman Killed with Kindness* (1913)
Molière's *L'Amour médecin* and *L'Avare* (1913)
Claudel's *L'Echange* (1914)
Roger Martin du Gard's *Le Testament du Père Leleu* (1914)
Dostoyevsky's *The Brothers Karamazov* (1914)
Shakespeare's *Twelfth Night* (1914)

At the Garrick Theatre in New York (out of more than
      forty plays in two seasons)
Molière's *Les Fourberies de Scapin* (1917)
Mérimée's *Le Carrosse du Saint Sacrement* (1917)
Corneille's *Le Menteur* (1919)
Maeterlinck's *Pelléas et Mélisande* (1919)
Molière's *Le Misanthrope* (1919)

At the Vieux Colombier
Shakespeare's *Winter's Tale* (1920)
Vildrac's *Le Paquebot Tenacity* (1910)
Mérimée's *Le Carrosse du Saint Sacrement* (1920)
Molière's *Les Fourberies de Scapin* (1920)
Jules Romains' *Cromedeyre-le-Vieil* (1920)
Jean Schlumberger's *La Mort de Sparte* (1921)
Musset's *Un Caprice* (1921)
Beaumarchais' *Le Mariage de Figaro* (1921)
Molière's *Le Misanthrope* (1922)

Gide's *Saül* (1922)
Goldoni's *La Locandiera* (1923)

At the Comédie Française
Molière's *Le Misanthrope* (1936)
Racine's *Bajazet* (1937)
Mauriac's *Asmodée* (1937)
Corneille's *Le Cid* (1940)
Shakespeare's *Twelfth Night* (1940)

### Copeau's Contempories and Successors: The Cartel

At the same time that Copeau was working in austerity and for an elite, one of Antoine's collaborators, Firmin Gémier, launched the great spectacle of the masses, for the masses. Gémier, whose career was somewhat confused and ambitious, went from the Théâtre Libre to Lugné-Poe's production of *Ubu Roi,* from melodrama to *vaudeville,* from the play of ideas to Grand Guignol. But his major contribution lay in his attempt to set up a people's theatre, one appropriate for performing national epics. As against those who particularly tried to manipulate souls, Gémier tried to manipulate crowds. Outdoor theatres, theatres in tents, theatres in amphitheatres—any great space was to his taste. After 1916 he eliminated footlights and had extras performing in with the audience, all in a frenzy of great collective movements. Gémier's experiments, picked up more coherently today, have given rise to both the dramatic decentralization in France and the basic principle of the Théâtre National Populaire, such as we know it.

Another name stands out in the years following the war: Georges Pitoëff. Trained in Russia at the time of Stanislavsky, director of plays by Molière, Musset, and Becque, which he performed all the way to Siberia, Pitoëff settled in Geneva in 1915, came to Paris for the first time with Lenormand's *Le Temps est un songe,* and settled there permanently in 1922. He produced Pirandello,

Shaw, O'Neill, Molnar, Chekhov, Lenormand, Cocteau, and Anouilh on various stages and with often very reduced means. His contemporaries were especially struck by his acting, despite a rather frail physique, and even more by that of his wife Ludmilla, a combination of infallible skill and inspired amateurism. They were also struck by the ingenuity of his mise-en-scènes. He designed his sets himself, with a particular bias for modernism: three-dimensional structures on several levels, with a touch of expressionism or cubism and special emphasis on color and the succession of planes in depth. Not only was his objective to reach a strange and inner poetry that would move the modern soul, but he tried to bring out "a reflection of our thinking" and "the stirring questions of our times." The coherence of the spectacle and its power was to stem from the rhythmic construction of the whole—a harmony in the rhythm of text, movement, and decor.

What Pitoëff, more than any other theorist, brought to the French stage was an awareness of the fact that theatre is part of an evolution similar to that of the other arts. Form, content, and spirit had to be contemporary. He therefore produced Pirandello, who posed the problem of truth in modern terms, and Lenormand, who posed that of the subconscious. Yet, like Copeau at the end of his career, he was disappointed by writers and admitted that he had not found "the writer who could express the modern soul."

GEORGES PITOËFF *(1887–1939):* Outstanding Productions

In Geneva
Tolstoy's *The Power of Darkness* (1917)
Claudel's *L'Echange* (1917)

In Geneva, then in Paris
Lenormand's *Le Temps est un songe* (1919)
                *Les Ratés* (1920)

In Paris
Lenormand's *Mangeur de rêves* (1922)
Chekhov's *The Sea Gull* (1922)

Pirandello's *Six Characters in Search of an Author* (1923)
Ramuz and Stravinsky's *Histoire du soldat* (1924)
Pirandello's *Henry IV* (1925)
Shaw's *Saint Joan* (1925)
Cocteau's *Orphée* (1926)
Chekhov's *Three Sisters* (1929)
Gide's *Œdipe* (1932)
Schnitzler's *La Ronde* (1932)
Ibsen's *The Wild Duck* (1934)
Pirandello's *Tonight We Improvise* (1935)
Anouilh's *Le Voyageur sans bagage* (1937)
Shakespeare's *Romeo and Juliet* (1937)
Claudel's *L'Echange* (1937)
Anouilh's *La Sauvage* (1938)

In 1927 Pitoëff, an independent, founded the "Cartel des Quartre" along with Louis Jouvet and Charles Dullin, Copeau's prodigal sons, and Gaston Baty, one of Firmin Gémier's disciples. Despite their differences, although all antinaturalists, the members of the Cartel set up an organization for the defense of theatre and for mutual aid on a financial and on an ethical level—a defense against newspaper boycotts, such as the boycott of Dullin in 1929, and against commercial pressures. Indeed, the four directors were the unquestionable leaders of the French stage in the 1930s.

Charles Dullin, a friend of Antonin Artaud, left the Vieux Colombier in 1919. He founded his first "Atelier" in 1921 and, with Copeau's help, opened a second in 1922, where he remained until World War II. A great actor in spite of his rather puny appearance and weak voice, Dullin emphasized the sincerity of a theatrical vocation and scrupulously careful work on diction, vocal expression, and breathing. His construction of a character from the inside, the deep honesty of his work, his rejection of naturalism, and his conviction that the play comes first and that, without a great text, scenic inventions are merely music-hall techniques, all were a continuation of the Copeau tradition. Moreover, he felt that the mission of actor and director was to clarify the text itself and bring out its essence.

CHARLES DULLIN *(1885–1949):* Outstanding Productions

At the Atelier
Calderón's *Such Stuff as Dreams are Made of* (1922)
Pirandello's *The Pleasure of Honesty* (1922)
Cocteau's adaptation of Sophocles' *Antigone* (1922)
Achard's *Voulez-vous jouer avec moâ?* (1923)
             *Le Joueur d'échecs* (1927)
Aristophanes' *Birds* (1927)
Ben Jonson's *Volpone* (1928)
Salacrou's *Patchouli* (1930)
             *Atlas Hôtel* (1931)
Aristophanes' *Peace* (1933)
Shakespeare's *Richard III* (1933)
Calderón's *Physician of His Own Honor* (1935)
Balzac's *Le Faiseur* (1936)
Salacrou's *La Terre est ronde* (1938)

At the Comédie Française
Pirandello's *Right You Are If You Think You Are* (1937)

At the Théâtre de Paris
Molière's *L'Avare* (1941)

At the Théâtre de la Cité-Sarah Bernhardt
Sartre's *Les Mouches* (1943)
Corneille's *Cinna* (1946)

Louis Jouvet, stage manager and actor at the Vieux Colombier, left Copeau in 1922 to act as director at the Comédie des Champs-Elysées and then changed to the Théâtre de l'Athénée in 1934. Jouvet's success with a much greater public than his friends of the Cartel was due largely to a less revolutionary attitude. His demands for acting were much the same as Copeau's, but the ground had already been broken by his predecessors, and to their discoveries he added a spectacular theatricalism in good taste. The elegance of his great sets in perspective and Christian Bérard's fantasy were hardly avant-garde, and machines filled up the "bare stage." Still, his elegant theatricalism was perfectly suited to Cocteau's *La Machine infernale* and Giraudoux's plays. Jouvet may have been less revolutionary than others, but he was the symbol of the victory of modern theatre, now at ease in the midst of its discoveries.

LOUIS JOUVET *(1887–1951)*: Outstanding Productions

At the Comédie des Champs-Elysées
Jules Romains' *Monsieur Le Trouhadec saisi par la débauche* and *Knock* (1923)
Crommelynck's *Tripes d'or* (1925)
Vildrac's *Madame Béliard* (1925)
Gogol's *The Inspector General* (1927)
Giraudoux's *Siegfried* (1928)
Achard's *Jean de la lune* (1929)
Giraudoux's *Amphitryon 38* (1929)

At the Théâtre Pigalle
Giraudoux's *Judith* (1930)
Romains' *Donogoo* (1930)

At the Comédie des Champs-Elysées
Giraudoux's *Intermezzo* (1933)
Cocteau's *La Machine infernale* (1934)

At the Athénée
Giraudoux's *Tessa* (1934)
*La Guerre de Troie n'aura pas lieu* and *Supplément au Voyage de Cook* (1935)
Molière's *L'Ecole des femmes* (1936)
Giraudoux's *Electre* and *L'Impromptu de Paris* (1937)
Achard's *Le Corsaire* (1938)
Giraudoux's *Ondine* (1939)

At the Comédie Française
Corneille's *L'Illusion comique* (1936)
Giraudoux's *Cantique des cantiques* (1937)

At the Athénée
Giraudoux's *La Folle de Chaillot* (1945)
Claudel's *L'Annonce faite à Marie* (1946)
Giraudoux's *L'Apollon de Bellac* (1947)
Genet's *Les Bonnes* (1947)
Molière's *Dom Juan* (1947)
                *Tartuffe* (1950)

At the Théâtre Marigny
Molière's *Les Fourberies de Scapin* (1949)

At the Théâtre Antoine
Sartre's *Le Diable et le Bon Dieu* (1951)

Gaston Baty was given a theatre by Gémier in 1920, founded a group called "La Chimère" in 1921, and finally took over the Théâtre Montparnasse in 1930. Right from the beginning, and with Gémier's help, he opposed Copeau. Although he denied having contempt for the text of a play, Baty nevertheless made statements against what he considered useless chatter and never hesitated to cut or rewrite texts in order to subject them to his mise-en-scène. Strongly influenced by German theorists and set designers, his productions always took precedence over the acting itself. Decor, machinery, and lighting were in the foreground, for he considered the play essentially as a poetic atmosphere to be imposed by material means. At the end of his career Baty foresook real actors and devoted himself mainly to marionettes.

GASTON BATY *(1885–1952):* Outstanding Productions

Lenormand's *Le Simoun* (1920)
Claudel's *L'Annonce faite à Marie* (1921)
Pellerin's *Intimité* (1922)
Jean-Jacques Bernard's *Martine* (1922)

Eugene O'Neill's *Emperor Jones* (1923)
Gantillon's *Maya* (1924)
Strindberg's *Miss Julie* (1925)
Pellerin's *Têtes de rechange* (1926)
Elmer Rice's *The Adding Machine* (1927)
Shalom Anski's *The Dybbuk* (1927)
Pellerin's *Cri des coeurs* (1928)
Molière's *Le Malade imaginaire* (1929)

At the Théâtre Montparnasse
Brecht's *Three-Penny Opera* (1930)
Pellerin's *Terrain vague* (1931)
Baty's adaptation of Dostoyevsky's *Crime and Punishment* (1933)
Musset's *Les Caprices de Marianne* (1935)
Baty's adaptation of Flaubert's *Madame Bovary* (1936)
Racine's *Phèdre* (1940)
Shakespeare's *Macbeth* (1942)

At the Comédie Française
Labiche's *Un Chapeau de paille d'Italie* (1938)
Musset's *Le Chandelier* (1937)
Racine's *Bérénice* (1946)
Salacrou's *L'Inconnue d'Arras* (1949)

Copeau, Jouvet, Baty, and Dullin were officially consecrated in 1936, when the administrator of the Comédie Française, Edouard Bourdet, called upon them to stage both the classical and modern plays in the repertory. In 1940 Copeau himself became administrator.

*After the Cartel*

While Pitoëff died in 1939, Lugné-Poe in 1940, Copeau and Dullin in 1949, Jouvet in 1951, and Baty in 1952, new directors, many of them more or less connected with Copeau, have ensured their succession. The most eminent among them today are Jean-Louis Barrault and Jean Vilar.

An extra in Pitoëff's company, then one of Dullin's students (1931) and an actor in his company, Barrault soon reflected all the most active influences: that of Dullin and Copeau, Gordon Craig, and most particularly the mime Decroux and Antonin Artaud. His first independent production was *Autour d'une Mère,* a pantomime of William Faulkner's *As I Lay Dying.* Then, through a synthesis of theatrical symbols, in which bodily expression played a primary role, Barrault tried to recreate the fundamental Drama with plays like Cervantes' *Numance* and Knut Hamsun's *La Faim.* During Barrault's career, including his years with the Comédie Française, his direction of the Théâtre Marigny from 1946 to 1956, and of the Odéon-Théâtre de France since 1959, his style has changed with his subject matter: epico-lyrical symbolism for Claudel's works, expressionism for Gide's adaptation of Kafka's *The Trial,* sophisticated pantomime for Marivaux's comedies, and so on. Such surface eclecticism often irritated the critics. But beyond the diversity of styles there is a common basis and objective. Barrault's major contribution, an extension of the theories of Artaud and Claudel, has been an attempt to establish a vocabulary and grammar of theatrical symbols, based on the actor's vocal intonation and rhythms and on the gestures and relative positions of the body—in some ways a Western equivalent of Oriental theatre. He thus tries to express the very mystery of life, beyond the psychologism to which too many actors are still attached. A carefully calculated symbolic performance and the technical means offered by the modern stage combine to make up "total theatre" or at least to reveal the maximum of the theatricalism inherent in works as disparate as *La Vie parisienne, Oh! Les Beaux Jours,* and *Les Paravents.*

JEAN-LOUIS BARRAULT *(1910–    ):* Outstanding Productions

At the Comédie Française
Racine's *Phèdre* (1942)

Claudel's *Le Soulier de satin* (1943)
Shakespeare's *Antony and Cleopatra* (1945)

At the Théâtre Marigny
Shakespeare's *Hamlet* (1946)
Marivaux's *Les Fausses Confidences* (1946)
Prévert's *Baptiste* (1946)
Salacrou's *Les Nuits de la colère* (1946)
Gide's adaptation of Kafka's *The Trial* (1947)
Molière's *Amphitryon* (1947)
Feydeau's *Occupe-toi d'Amélie* (1948)
Camus' *L'Etat de siège* (1948)
Claudel's *Partage de midi* (1948)
Anouilh's *La Répétition* (1950)
Montherlant's *Malatesta* (1950)
Claudel's *L'Echange* (1951)
Cocteau's *Bacchus* (1951)
Claudel's *Christophe Colomb* (1953)
Giraudoux's *Pour Lucrèce* (1953)
Molière's *Le Misanthrope* (1954)
Chekhov's *The Cherry Orchard* (1954)
Racine's *Bérénice* (1955)
Giraudoux's *Intermezzo* (1955)
Aeschylus' *Oresteia* (1955)

At the Petit Théâtre Marigny
Schehadé's *La Soirée des proverbes* (1954)
Lope de Vega's *The Gardener's Dog* (1955)
Jean Vauthier's *Le Personnage combattant* (1956)

At the Théâtre Sarah Bernhardt
Schehadé's *Histoire de Vasco* (1957)

At the Théâtre du Palais Royal
Meilhac and Halévy's *La Vie parisienne* (1958)

At the Odéon-Théâtre de France
Claudel's *Tête d'or* (1959)

Anouilh's *La Petite Molière* (1959)
Ionesco's *Rhinocéros* (1960)
Giraudoux's *Judith* (1961)
Christopher Fry's *The Dark Is Light Enough* (1963)
Ionesco's *Le Piéton de l'air* (1963)
Beckett's *Oh! Les Beaux Jours* (1963)
Brendan Behan's *The Hostage* (1964)
Billetdoux's *Il Faut Passer par les Nuages* (1964)
Duras' *Des Journées entières dans les arbres* (1965)
Shakespeare's *Henry VI* (1966)
Nathalie Sarraute's *Le Mensonge* and *Le Silence* (1967)

In collaboration, with Roger Blin
Ramon del Valle-Inclán's *Divinas Palabras* (1963)
Jean-Pierre Faye's *Hommes et pierres* (1965)
Genet's *Les Paravents* (1966)

With Maurice Béjart
Flaubert's *La Tentation de Saint-Antoine* (1967)

Also a disciple of Dullin was Jean Vilar, whose beginnings were less dazzling than Barrault's. Member of an itinerant company, "La Roulotte," between 1940 and 1942, then director of two Strindberg plays in small Paris theatres, Vilar had his first great success in 1945 with Eliot's *Murder in the Cathedral* at the Vieux Colombier and was definitively established in 1947 with the Avignon Festival. As his first experiment with an outdoor stage, it led him to a type of theatre freed from the Italianate stage, set up in great open spaces, and presented to vast audiences. Rather than the outer spectacle, Vilar stressed the character—magnified or masked according to the needs of the space in which the play was performed. He considered the actor as a creator—hence the severity of the training and discipline he thought necessary. However, once the actor is really in a part, he is free to improvise or at least vary his interpretation. Out on the large stage his mission is to provoke the most intimate contact possible between the character and the thousands of spectators. Vilar, director of the Théâtre National Populaire from 1950 to 1963, sees theatre as a collective ceremony. What Copeau had achieved for an elite, he attempted "for all," with often similar principles and simplicity. And, like Copeau, he is disappointed, but his reasons are of a political and social nature, for he claims that great theatre is unattainable because of the present state of society.

JEAN VILAR *(1912–    ):* Outstanding Productions

Strindberg's *The Dance of Death* (1943)
T. S. Eliot's *Murder in the Cathedral* (1945)

In Avignon and at the TNP
Shakespeare's *Richard II* (1947)
Büchner's *Danton's Death* (1948)
Corneille's *Le Cid* (1949)
Montherlant's *Pasiphaé* (1949)
Gide's *Œdipe* (1949)
Shakespeare's *Henry IV* (1950)
Kleist's *The Prince of Homburg* (1951)
Brecht's *Mother Courage* (1951)
Molière's *L'Avare* (1952)
            *Dom Juan* (1953)
Shakespeare's *Macbeth* (1954)
Corneille's *Cinna* (1954)
Hugo's *Ruy Blas* (1954)
Claudel's *La Ville* (1955)
Hugo's *Marie Tudor* (1955)
Pirandello's *Henry IV* (1957)
Racine's *Phèdre* (1958)
Jarry's *Ubu Roi* (1958)
Musset's *Les Caprices de Marianne* (1958)
Shakespeare's *A Midsummer-Night's Dream* (1959)
Brecht's *The Resistible Rise of Arturo Ui* (1960)

Lesage's *Turcaret* (1960)
Aristophanes' *Peace* (1961)
Goldoni's *I Rusteghi* (1961)
O'Casey's *Red Roses for Me* (1961)
Giraudoux's *La Guerre de Troie n'aura pas lieu* (1962)
Robert Bolt's *A Man for All Seasons* (1963)

In collaboration, with Maurice Cazeneuve
Claudel's *L'Histoire de Tobie et de Sara* (1947)

With Gérard Philipe
Musset's *Lorenzaccio* (1952)
Pichette's *Nucléa* (1952)
Vauthier's *La Nouvelle Mandragore* (1952)

With Daniel Sorano
Molière's *Le Malade imaginaire* (1957)
      *L'Etourdi* (1959)

Jean-Louis Barrault, with the help of Madeleine Renaud, has
kept the upper hand in his Odéon-Théâtre de France, despite
attacks both from the right (when he produces Beckett or Genet)
and from the left (when he claims complete freedom for theatre
or indulges in mystical experiences or "pure theatre"). Indeed,
Barrault pays little mind to the rightist critics, and when a leftist
critic recently reproached him with: "Vous niez Brecht!" he
answered: "Je ne nie pas Brecht, mais les brechtiens m'ennuient"
(*La Table Ronde,* No. 220 [May 1966], p. 55). As for Jean Vilar,
in 1963 he left the TNP to produce "committed" plays (*Le
Dossier Oppenheimer*), operas, or adaptations of nondramatic
works. He was replaced at the TNP by Georges Wilson, who has
continued in the Vilar tradition. While he has not proved to be an
innovator, he is nevertheless responsible for first-rate productions in Paris and Avignon. Under his management, the TNP not
only has kept the balance between a classical and modern reper-
toire but has lost none of its prestige.

GEORGES WILSON *(1921–     ):* Outstanding Productions

Dürrenmatt's *Romulus the Great* (1964)
Osborne's *Luther* (1964)
Brecht's *Puntila and His Servant Matti* (1965)
Giraudoux's *La Folle de Chaillot* (1965)
Corneille's *L'Illusion comique* (1966)
O'Casey's *Purple Dust* (1966)

In collaboration, with Jean Deschamps
Vercors' *Zoo* (1963)

With Armand Gatti
Gatti's *Chant public pour deux chaises électriques* (1966)

With the Comédie Française, the TNP, and the Odéon-Théâtre de France, the Fifth Republic is subsidizing nearly all the "great" theatre in France. Moreover, the state gives moral support and financial aid to the general movement of theatrical decentralization, which began somewhat after World War II. Not only are there dramatic festivals every summer in Avignon and other provincial cities, but new companies have been organized as "Centres Dramatiques" in the provinces—the Centre Dramatique de l'Ouest, the Centre Dramatique de l'Est, the Grenier de Toulouse, the Comédie de Saint-Etienne, and the Comédie de Provence—where older directors continue to work (Jean Dasté, a student of Copeau, is with the Comédie de Saint-Etienne) and new talent has been discovered.

The most important discovery so far has been that of Roger Planchon and his Théâtre de la Cité de Villeurbanne, founded in 1957. After having produced plays by Shakespeare, Adamov, Marlowe, and Ionesco, Planchon became a leader of the Brechtian movement in France, which had begun as a result of the Berliner Ensemble's productions in Paris in 1954. Although he has done little with the plays of Brecht himself, Planchon has concentrated on bringing out the historical meaning and current value of masterworks of the past.

ROGER PLANCHON *(1931–      ):* Outstanding Productions

Shakespeare's *Henry IV* (1957)
  *Falstaff* (1957)
Molière's *George Dandin* (1958)
Brecht's *Good Woman of Setzuan* (1958)
Gogol/Adamov's *Dead Souls* (1959)
Brecht's *Good Soldier Schweik in World War II* (1961)
Molière's *Tartuffe* (1963)
Shakespeare's *Troilus and Cressida* (1964)

In collaboration, with J. Rosner
Gatti's *La Vie imaginaire de l'éboueur Auguste Geai* (1962)

In the past few years, in addition to the TNP and provincial decentralization, there has been a gradual development of theatre on the
outskirts of Paris—that is to say, in the working-class districts and
suburbs. "Houses of Culture" and "Dramatic Centers" have become hotbeds of activity, attracting a very new public to the theatre.
All such endeavors are given financial aid by the government,
chiefly at the instigation of André Malraux, and have provoked
great controversy: not only do the directors of the *secteur privé* (the
private theatres in central Paris, in contrast to the state or municipal theatres) consider them disloyal competition, but such cultural
centers are something of a paradox, since most of those aided by
the government are essentially leftist—often very far to the left.
Nevertheless, a large segment of the population that is unable to
pay the high prices of private theatres and finds little interest in
bourgeois drama now inexpensively and assiduously attends performances of Shakespeare, Molière, and modern plays.

  This new craze for "popular" theatre (which, for many, has become something of a cult) should not overshadow the work of the
independent Parisian directors who remain champions of quality—
André Barsacq (Dullin's set designer and his successor at the
Atelier), Maurice Jacquemont, and Pierre Valde, for example—
or the young directors who have so successfully introduced the

"new theatre": Georges Vitaly (Audiberti), Jean-Marie Serreau (Adamov and Ionesco), Roger Blin (Beckett and Genet), André Reybaz (Vauthier and Ghelderode), Jacques Mauclair (Ionesco), Sylvain Dhomme, and Antoine Bourseiller. In these fast-moving times some of them, such as Reybaz, have become directors at the Centres Dramatiques, while others, like Serreau or Blin, have followed their favorite playwrights onto the national stages.

From 1890 to the present the French stage has been increasingly marked by the following tendencies:

1. To coordinate all the arts of a production in order to obtain a unity of the whole on all levels.
2. To use realism in acting, yet to evolve toward an art of suggestion.
3. To establish a theatre without stars.
4. To rigorously train actors.
5. To reject the naturalistic and often the Italianate stage.
6. To use modern painters, while rejecting decorative sets in favor of functional three-dimensional decor, sometimes reduced to its simplest elements.
7. To establish companies and repertories.
8. To form writer-director teams (Giraudoux-Jouvet, Anouilh-Barsacq, Claudel-Barrault, Audiberti-Vitaly, Beckett-Blin, Genet-Blin).
9. To free theatre from commercialism.

While many of the problems remain the same, new ones have developed. For instance, the importance given to staging raises the question of the rights and limits of a director. Copeau, by affirming "the identity of any theatrical composition and the means for expressing it in space and in time," made the director as much a "creator" as the playwright. At the time of production, it is now hard to tell where the "creation" of a play stops and a betrayal of the text begins. Directors are often tyrannical, some of them systematically deform the works of the past in the name of current values or a political ideology, and nothing is helped by the attitude of those who override the plays and consider themselves great priests of a humanity whose church is the theatre.

Since, in the religious view, the objective of theatre is a kind of communion through artifice, has that communion actually been achieved? Artifice, whether the conscious use of the Italianate stage or that of new inventions, has made it possible to retheatricalize theatre, making it more unreal yet more meaningful to the spectator, and restoring its aspect of a ceremonious feast, in which the spectator is invited to participate from the depths of his being. But have the scenic reform and the consciousness of what theatre must be led to communion? And is true communion of the soul or the mind possible in the world as it is today? The answer doubtless lies outside theatre itself.

# FIRST PERFORMANCES AND IMPORTANT REVIVALS

JEAN GIRAUDOUX (*1882–1944*)

*Siegfried*

May 3, 1928, Comédie des Champs-Elysées, directed by Louis Jouvet, sets by Camille Cipra; 1952, Comédie des Champs-Elysées, directed by Raymond Rouleau.

*Amphitryon 38*

November 8, 1929, Comédie des Champs-Elysées, directed by Louis Jouvet, sets by Camille Cipra; 1957, Comédie des Champs-Elysées.

*Judith*

November 4, 1931, Théâtre Pigalle, directed by Louis Jouvet, sets by Jouvet and René Moulaert; November 24, 1961, Odéon-Théâtre de France, directed by Jean-Louis Barrault, sets by Max Ernst.

*Intermezzo*
February 27, 1933, Comédie des Champs-Elysées, directed by Louis Jouvet, sets by Léon Leyritz; March 17, 1955, Théâtre Marigny, directed by Jean-Louis Barrault, sets by Maurice Brianchon.

*Tessa* (adaptation of Margaret Kennedy)
November 14, 1934, Théâtre de l'Athénée, directed by Louis Jouvet, sets by René Moulaert; 1958, Théâtre Marigny.

*La Guerre de Troie n'aura pas lieu*
November 21, 1935, Théâtre de l'Athénée, directed by Louis Jouvet, sets by Mariano Andreu; Summer 1963, TNP (Avignon), directed by Jean Vilar, sets by André Chastel.

*Supplément au Voyage de Cook*
November 21, 1935, Théâtre de l'Athénée, directed by Louis Jouvet, set by Mariano Andreu; December 1962, Comédie Française, directed by Jacques Charon, set by François Ganeau.

*Electre*
May 13, 1937, Théâtre de l'Athénée, directed by Louis Jouvet, set by Guillaume Monin; October 28, 1959, Comédie Française, directed by Pierre Dux, set by Georges Wakhévitch.

*L'Impromptu de Paris*
December 4, 1937, Théâtre de l'Athénée, directed by Louis Jouvet, set by Guillaume Monin.

*Cantique des cantiques*
October 12, 1938, Comédie Française, directed by Louis Jouvet, set by Edouard Vuillard.

*Ondine*
May 3, 1939, Théâtre de l'Athénée, directed by Louis Jouvet, sets by Pavel Tchelitchev.

*L'Apollon de Bellac (L'Apollon de Marsac)*
June 16, 1942, Rio de Janeiro, directed by Louis Jouvet, set by

Eduardo Anahory; April 19, 1947, Théâtre de l'Athénée, directed by Louis Jouvet, set by Eduardo Anahory.

*Sodome et Gomorrhe*
October 11, 1943, Théâtre Hébertot, directed by Douking, sets by Christian Bérard.

*La Folle de Chaillot*
December 19, 1945, Théâtre de l'Athénée, directed by Louis Jouvet, sets by Christian Bérard; November 12, 1965, TNP (Palais de Chaillot), directed by Georges Wilson, sets by Jacques Le Marquet.

*Pour Lucrèce*
November 4, 1953, Théâtre Marigny, directed by Jean-Louis Barrault, sets by A. M. Cassandre; August 1963, Festival de Bellac, directed by Raymond Gérome.

### JEAN COCTEAU (*1889–1963*)

*Parade*
1916, Rome; May 18, 1917, Théâtre du Châtelet, choreography by Léonide Massine, sets and costumes by Picasso, music by Erik Satie.

*Le Bœuf sur le Toit*
February 21, 1920, Comédie des Champs-Elysées, directed by Jean Cocteau, sets by Raoul Dufy, music by Darius Milhaud.

*Les Mariés de la Tour Eiffel*
June 18, 1921, Théâtre des Champs-Elysées, choreography by Jean Cocteau, set by Irène Lagut, costumes and masks by Jean Hugo, music by "les Six."

*Antigone* (adaptation of Sophocles)
December 20, 1922, Théâtre de l'Atelier, directed by Charles Dullin, set by Picasso.

*Roméo et Juliette* (adaptation of Shakespeare)
June 2, 1924, Théâtre de la Cigale, directed by Jean Cocteau, sets by Jean Hugo.

*Orphée*
June 17, 1926, Théâtre des Arts, directed by Georges Pitoëff, set by Jean Hugo.

*La Voix humaine*
February 17, 1930, Comédie Française, set by Christian Bérard.

*La Machine infernale*
April 10, 1934, Comédie des Champs-Elysées, directed by Louis Jouvet, sets by Christian Bérard; September 1954, Théâtre des Bouffes Parisiens, directed by Jean Cocteau, sets by Christian Bérard.

*Œdipe-Roi* (adaptation of Sophocles)
June 1937, Théâtre Antoine, directed by Jean Cocteau, set by Guillaume Monin.

*Les Chevaliers de la Table Ronde*
October 14, 1937, Théâtre de l'Œuvre, directed by Jean Cocteau, sets by Jean Cocteau, costumes by Chanel; May 1966, Milly-la-Forêt, directed by Jean Rougerie, sets by Raymond Faure and Rita Bayance.

*Les Parents terribles*
November 14, 1938, Théâtre des Ambassadeurs, directed by Alice Cocéa, sets by Guillaume Monin.

*Les Monstres sacrés*
February 17, 1940, Théâtre Michel, directed by André Brulé, sets by Christian Bérard.

*Le Bel Indifférent*
1940, Théâtre des Bouffes Parisiens, set by Christian Bérard.

*La Machine à écrire*
April 29, 1941, Théâtre Hébertot, sets by Jean Marais; March 11,

1956, Comédie Française, directed by Jean Meyer, sets by Suzanne Lalique.

*Renaud et Armide*
April 1943, Comédie Française, directed by Jean Cocteau, set by Christian Bérard.

*L'Aigle à deux têtes*
November 1946, Théâtre Hébertot, sets by André Beaurepaire.

*Un Tramway nommé Désir* (adaptation of Tennessee Williams)
October 17, 1949, Théâtre Edouard VII, directed by Raymond Rouleau, set by Lila de Nobili.

*Bacchus*
November 20, 1951, Théâtre Marigny, directed by Jean Cocteau, sets by Jean Cocteau.

Major Films

*Le Sang d'un poète,* 1932, directed by Jean Cocteau.

*L'Eternel Retour,* 1944, directed by Jean Delannoy.

*Les Parents terribles,* 1948, directed by Jean Cocteau.

*Orphée,* 1950, directed by Jean Cocteau.

*Le Testament d'Orphée,* 1960, directed by Jean Cocteau.

PAUL CLAUDEL *(1868–1955)*

*L'Annonce faite à Marie*
December 22, 1912, Théâtre de l'Œuvre, directed by Lugné-Poe, sets by Jean Variot; June 10, 1946, Théâtre de l'Athénée, directed by Louis Jouvet, sets by Eduardo Anahory; March 12, 1948, Théâtre Hébertot, directed by J. Vernier; February 17, 1955, Comédie Française, directed by Julien Bertheau, sets by Georges

Wakhévitch; January 24, 1961, Théâtre de l'Œuvre, directed by Pierre Franck, sets by Pierre Simonini.

## L'Echange

January 22, 1914, Théâtre du Vieux-Colombier, directed by Jacques Copeau, sets by Doucet; November 17, 1937, Théâtre des Mathurins, directed by Georges Pitoëff, sets by Georges Pitoëff; December 12, 1951, Théâtre Marigny, directed by Jean-Louis Barrault, sets by Georges Wakhévitch.

## L'Otage

June 5, 1914, Théâtre de l'Œuvre, directed by Lugné-Poe, sets by Jean Variot; October 20, 1934, Comédie Française, directed by Emile Fabre, sets by Charlemagne; 1950, Comédie Française, directed by Henri Rollan; December 1962, Théâtre du Vieux-Colombier, directed by Bernard Jenny, sets by Pierre Simonini.

## Partage de midi

November 12, 1916, Groupe Art et Action, sets by Autant-Lara, Autant, and Girard; December 16, 1948, Théâtre Marigny, directed by Jean-Louis Barrault, sets by Félix Labisse; October 1961, Odéon-Thèâtre de France, directed by Jean-Louis Barrault.

## Tête d'or

April 25, 1924, Groupe Art et Action, directed by Mme. Autant-Lara, sets by Georges Valmier; October 21, 1959, Odéon-Théâtre de France, directed by Jean-Louis Barrault, sets by André Masson.

## Le Pain dur

October 1926, Landestheater, Oldenburg, directed by Hans Pretz; March 12, 1949, Théâtre de l'Atelier, directed by André Barsacq, sets by André Barsacq; December 1962, Théâtre du Vieux-Colombier, directed by Bernard Jenny, sets by Pierre Simonini.

## Le Père humilié

November 26, 1928, Schauspielhaus, Dresden, directed by Joseph Gielen, sets by Malinke; May 10, 1946, Théâtre des Champs-Elysées, directed by Jean Valcourt, sets by Tahard; December

1962, Théâtre du Vieux-Colombier, directed by Bernard Jenny, sets by Pierre Simonini.

*Le Repos du septième jour*
December 10, 1928, Narodowy Theatre, Warsaw, directed by Radulski, sets by Drabik; September 1965, Théâtre de l'Œuvre, directed by Pierre Franck, sets by Pierre Simonini.

*Le Livre de Christophe Colomb*
May 5, 1930, Staatsoper unter den Linden, Berlin, directed by M. Hort, sets by M. Araventinos, music by Darius Milhaud; October 1, 1953, Théâtre Marigny, directed by Jean-Louis Barrault, sets by Marc Ingrand.

*La Ville*
February 1931, Salle Patria, Brussels, directed by A. van de Velde; December 2, 1955, TNP (Palais de Chaillot), directed by Jean Vilar, set by Léon Gischia.

*Protée*
April 4, 1933, Municipal Theatre, Amsterdam, Students' Dramatic Association; May 1957, Théâtre du Tertre, directed by Serge Ligier, set by Camurati.

*Les Choéphores* (translation of Aeschylus)
March 27, 1935, Brussels.

*Jeanne au bûcher*
May 6, 1939, Théâtre Municipal d'Orléans, music by Honegger, sets by Alexandre Benois; December 18, 1950, Opéra, directed by Jan Doat, set by Yves Bonnat.

*Le Soulier de satin*
November 27, 1943, Comédie Française, directed by Jean-Louis Barrault, sets by Lucien Coutaud; October 1963, Odéon-Théâtre de France, directed by Jean-Louis Barrault, sets by Lucien Coutaud.

*La Jeune Fille Violaine*
March 1944, Salle Iéna, directed by Maurice Leroy, sets by Maurice Leroy.

*L'Histoire de Tobie et de Sara*
September 5, 1947, TNP (Avignon), directed by Maurice
Cazeneuve.

ARMAND SALACROU *(1900– )*

*Tour à terre*
December 24, 1925, Théâtre de l'Œuvre, directed by Lugné-Poe.

*Le Pont de l'Europe*
December 24, 1925, Théâtre de l'Œuvre, directed by Lugné-Poe.

*Patchouli*
January 22, 1930, Théâtre de l'Atelier, directed by Charles Dullin,
sets by Michel Duran.

*Atlas Hôtel*
April 15, 1931, Théâtre de l'Atelier, directed by Charles Dullin,
sets by G. Valako.

*Les Frénétiques*
December 5, 1934, Théâtre Daunou, directed by Raymond
Rouleau.

*Une Femme libre*
October 4, 1934, Théâtre de l'Œuvre, directed by Paulette Pax,
sets by Paulette Pax.

*L'Inconnue d'Arras*
November 22, 1935, Comédie des Champs-Elysées, directed by
Lugné-Poe, set by René Moulaert; January 13, 1949, Comédie
Française, directed by Gaston Baty.

*Un Homme comme les autres*
November 23, 1936, Théâtre de l'Œuvre, directed by Paulette
Pax, sets by Paulette Pax.

*La Terre est ronde*
November 7, 1938, Théâtre de l'Atelier, directed by Charles
Dullin, sets by André Masson.

*Histoire de rire*
December 22, 1939, Théâtre de la Madeleine, directed by Alice Cocéa.

*La Marguerite*
October 28, 1944, Théâtre Pigalle, directed by Julien Bertheau.

*Les Fiancés du Havre*
December 10, 1944, Comédie Française, directed by Pierre Dux, sets by Raoul Dufy.

*Le Soldat et la sorcière*
December 5, 1945, Théâtre Sarah-Bernhardt, directed by Charles Dullin, sets by Chapelain-Midy.

*Les Nuits de la colère*
December 12, 1946, Théâtre Marigny, directed by Jean-Louis Barrault, sets by Félix Labisse.

*L'Archipel Lenoir*
November 8, 1947, Théâtre Montparnasse, directed by Charles Dullin, set by A. M. Rodicq; March 1962, Théâtre Montparnasse, directed by Jean Mercure.

*Poof*
October 26, 1950, Théâtre Edouard VII, directed by Yves Robert, set by Serge Creuz.

*Pourquoi Pas Moi?*
October 26, 1950, Théâtre Edouard VII, directed by J. Dumesnil, set by Serge Creuz.

*Dieu le savait!*
December 2, 1950, Théâtre Saint-Georges, directed by Jean Mercure, set by Georges Wakhévitch.

*Sens interdit*
January 6, 1953, Théâtre du Quartier Latin, directed by Michel de Ré, set by Francine Gaillard-Risler.

*Les Invités du Bon Dieu*
1953, Théâtre Saint-Georges, directed by Yves Robert, set by Francine Gaillard-Risler.

*Le Miroir*
September 22, 1956, Théâtre des Ambassadeurs, directed by Henri Rollan, set by Jean-Denis Malclès.

*Une Femme trop honnête*
December 1, 1956, Théâtre Edouard VII, directed by Georges Vitaly.

*Boulevard Durand*
September 19, 1961, Centre Dramatique du Nord, and November 3, 1961, Théâtre Sarah-Bernhardt, directed by André Reybaz, sets by Raymond Renard.

*Comme les Chardons*
October 26, 1964, Comédie Française, directed by Michel Vitold, sets by Max Douy.

HENRY DE MONTHERLANT *(1893–      )*

*Pasiphaé*
December 6, 1938, Théâtre Pigalle, directed by Sylvain Itkine; Summer 1949, Avignon, directed by Jean Vilar.

*La Reine morte*
December 8, 1942, Comédie Française, directed by Pierre Dux, sets by Roland Oudot; October 1966, Comédie Française, directed by Pierre Franck, sets by Pierre Simonini.

*Fils de personne*
December 18, 1943, Théâtre Saint-Georges, directed by Pierre Dux, sets by Léon Leyritz.

*Le Maître de Santiago*
January 26, 1948, Théâtre Hébertot, directed by Paul Oettly, sets

by Mariano Andreu; February 1958, Comédie Française, directed by Henri Rollan.

*Demain il fera jour*
May 9, 1949, Théâtre Hébertot, directed by Paul Oettly.

*Celles qu'on prend dans ses bras*
October 20, 1950, Théâtre de la Madeleine, directed by Claude Sainval, set by Georges Wakhévitch.

*Malatesta*
December 19, 1950, Théâtre Marigny, directed by Jean-Louis Barrault, sets by Mariano Andreu.

*La Ville dont le Prince est un enfant*
1952, Casino de Biarritz, one scene.

*Port-Royal*
December 8, 1954, Comédie Française, directed by Jean Meyer, set by Suzanne Lalique.

*Brocéliande*
October 24, 1956, Comédie Française, directed by Jean Meyer, set by Suzanne Lalique.

*Don Juan*
November 8, 1958, Théâtre de l'Athénée, directed by Georges Vitaly, sets by Mariano Andreu.

*Le Cardinal d'Espagne*
December 18, 1960, Comédie Française, directed by Jean Mercure.

*La Guerre civile*
January 30, 1965, Théâtre de l'Œuvre, directed by Pierre Dux, sets by Georges Wakhévitch.


JEAN ANOUILH *(1910–     )*

*L'Hermine*
April 26, 1932, Théâtre de l'Œuvre, directed by Paulette Pax.

*Y'Avait un Prisonnier*
March 21, 1935, Théâtre des Ambassadeurs, set by René Moulaert.

*Le Voyageur sans bagage*
February 16, 1937, Théâtre des Mathurins, directed by Georges Pitoëff, set by Georges Pitoëff; April 6, 1950, Théâtre Montparnasse, directed by André Barsacq.

*La Sauvage*
January 10, 1938, Théâtre des Mathurins, directed by Georges Pitoëff, sets by Georges Pitoëff.

*Le Bal des voleurs*
September 17, 1938, Théâtre des Arts, directed by André Barsacq, sets by André Barsacq.

*Léocadia*
November 1940, Théâtre de la Michodière.

*Le Rendez-vous de Senlis*
February 1941, Théâtre de l'Atelier, directed by André Barsacq, sets by André Barsacq.

*Eurydice*
December 18, 1942, Théâtre de l'Atelier, directed by André Barsacq, sets by André Barsacq.

*Antigone*
February 4, 1944, Théâtre de l'Atelier, directed by André Barsacq, set by André Barsacq.

*Roméo et Jeannette*
December 3, 1946, Théâtre de l'Atelier, directed by André Barsacq, sets by André Barsacq.

*L'Invitation au château*
November 4, 1947, Théâtre de l'Atelier, directed by André Barsacq, sets by André Barsacq.

*Ardèle ou La Marguerite*
November 3, 1948, Comédie des Champs-Elysées, directed by Roland Pietri, set by Jean-Denis Malclès.

*La Répétition ou L'Amour puni*
October 26, 1950, Théâtre Marigny, directed by Jean-Louis Barrault, sets by Jean-Denis Malclès.

*Colombe*
February 11, 1951, Théâtre de l'Atelier, directed by André Barsacq, sets by André Barsacq; May 5, 1961, Festival de Bordeaux, musical adaptation by Michel Damase, directed by Roger Lalande, sets by Jean-Denis Malclès.

*La Valse des Toréadors*
January 9, 1952, Comédie des Champs-Elysées, directed by Roland Pietri, sets by Jean-Denis Malclès.

*Médée*
March 26, 1953, Théâtre de l'Atelier, directed by André Barsacq, sets by André Bakst.

*L'Alouette*
October 14, 1953, Théâtre Montparnasse, directed by Jean Anouilh, sets by Jean-Denis Malclès.

*Ornifle ou Le Courant d'air*
November 7, 1955, Comédie des Champs-Elysées, sets by Jean-Denis Malclès.

*Pauvre Bitos ou Le Dîner de têtes*
October 11, 1956, Théâtre Montparnasse, directed by Roland Pietri, sets by Jean-Denis Malclès.

*L'Hurluberlu ou Le Réactionnaire amoureux*
February 5, 1959, Comédie des Champs-Elysées, directed by Roland Pietri, sets by Jean-Denis Malclès.

*La Petite Molière*
June 14, 1959, Bordeaux; November 12, 1959, Odéon-Théâtre de France, directed by Jean-Louis Barrault, sets by Jacques Noël.

*Becket ou L'Honneur de Dieu*
October 8, 1959, Théâtre Montparnasse, directed by Jean Anouilh and Roland Pietri, sets by Jean-Denis Malclès; November 1966, Théâtre Montparnasse, directed by Jean Anouilh and Roland Pietri.

*La Grotte*
October 4, 1961, Théâtre Montparnasse, directed by Jean Anouilh and Roland Pietri, sets by Jean-Denis Malclès.

*La Foire d'empoigne*
January 11, 1962, Comédie des Champs-Elysées, directed by Jean Anouilh and Roland Pietri, sets by Jean-Denis Malclès.

*L'Orchestre*
January 11, 1962, Comédie des Champs-Elysées, directed by Jean Anouilh and Roland Pietri.

### JEAN-PAUL SARTRE *(1905–    )*

*Les Mouches*
April 1943, Théâtre de la Cité-Sarah Bernhardt, directed by Charles Dullin, sets by Adam.

*Huis Clos*
May 1944, Théâtre du Vieux-Colombier, directed by Raymond Rouleau; June 1961, Théâtre du Gymnase.

*Morts sans sépulture*
November 8, 1946, Théâtre Antoine.

*La Putain respectueuse*
November 8, 1946, Théâtre Antoine; June 1961, Théâtre du Gymnase.

*Les Mains sales*
April 2, 1948, Théâtre Antoine, directed by Pierre Valde, sets by Emile and Jean Bertin.

*Le Diable et le Bon Dieu*
June 7, 1951, Théâtre Antoine, directed by Louis Jouvet, sets by Félix Labisse.

*Kean* (adaptation of Dumas père)
November 17, 1953, Théâtre Sarah-Bernhardt, directed by Pierre Brasseur, sets by Alexandre Trauner.

*Nekrassov*
June 8, 1955, Théâtre Antoine, directed by Jean Meyer, sets by Jean-Denis Malclès.

*Les Séquestrés d'Altona*
September 23, 1959, Théâtre de la Renaissance, directed by François Darbon, sets by Yvon Henri; September 1965, Théâtre de l'Athénée.


ALBERT CAMUS *(1913–1960)*

*Le Malentendu*
1944, Théâtre des Mathurins, directed by Marcel Herrand; September 1964, Théâtre Gramont, directed by Michel Vitold.

*Caligula*
1945, Théâtre Hébertot; February 1958, Nouveau Théâtre.

*Les Justes*
December 15, 1949, Théâtre Hébertot, directed by Paul Oettly, sets by Rosnay; January 1966, Théâtre de l'Œuvre, directed by Pierre Franck, sets by Bernard Daydé.

*L'Etat de siège*
October 27, 1948, Théâtre Marigny, directed by Jean-Louis Barrault, sets by Balthus; August 1966, Théâtre de Bourgogne, directed by Roland Monod.

*Les Esprits* (adaptation of Larivey)
June 16, 1953, Château d'Angers, directed by Marcel Herrand, sets by Philippe Bonnet.

*La Dévotion à la Croix* (translation of Calderón)
June 1953, Château d'Angers, directed by Marcel Herrand.

*Requiem pour une nonne* (adaptation of Faulkner)
1956, Théâtre des Mathurins, directed by Albert Camus.

*Les Possédés* (adaptation of Dostoyevsky)
January 30, 1959, Théâtre Antoine, directed by Albert Camus, sets by Mayo.

JACQUES AUDIBERTI *(1899–1965)*

*Quoat-Quoat*
January 28, 1946, Théâtre de la Gaîté-Montparnasse, directed by André Reybaz.

*Le Mal court*
June 25, 1947, Théâtre de Poche, directed by Georges Vitaly, sets by Marie Viton; December 15, 1955, Théâtre La Bruyère, directed by Georges Vitaly, sets by Léonor Fini; November 1963, Théâtre La Bruyère, directed by Georges Vitaly.

*Les Femmes du Bœuf*
November 23, 1948, Comédie Française, directed by Jean Debucourt, set by Peynet.

*La Fête noire*
December 3, 1948, Théâtre de la Huchette, directed by Georges Vitaly, sets by André Marchand.

*L'Ampélour*
February 17, 1950, Théâtre des Noctambules.

*Pucelle*
June 1, 1950, Théâtre de la Huchette, directed by Georges Vitaly, sets by André Marchand.

*Les Naturels du Bordelais*
1953–54, Théâtre La Bruyère, directed by Georges Vitaly, sets by Roger Chancel.

*La Mégère apprivoisée* (adaptation of Shakespeare)
October 10, 1957, Théâtre de l'Athénée, directed by Georges Vitaly, sets by Léonor Fini.

*La Hobereaute*
September 20, 1958, Théâtre du Vieux-Colombier, directed by Jean Le Poulain, sets by Jacques Noël.

*L'Effet Glapion*
September 9, 1959, Théâtre La Bruyère, directed by Georges Vitaly.

*La Logeuse*
October 3, 1960, Théâtre de l'Œuvre, directed by Pierre Valde, set by Daniel Louradour.

*La Fourmi dans le corps*
May 30, 1962, Comédie Française, directed by André Barsacq, sets by Jacques Dupont.

*Pomme, pomme, pomme*
September's 1962, Théâtre La Bruyère, directed by Georges Vitaly, sets by Yves Faucheur.

*Le Cavalier seul*
January 1964, Théâtre du Cothurne, Lyons, directed by Marcel Maréchal.

*L'Opéra du monde*
October 13, 1965, Théâtre de Lutèce, directed by Marcel Maréchal, sets by Frédéric Benrath.

MICHEL DE GHELDERODE *(1898–1962)*

(For first performances in Belgium, see David Grossvogel, *The Self-Conscious Stage*.)

*La Mort du Docteur Faust*
January 27, 1928, Groupe Art et Action, directed by Mme. Autant-Lara.

*Christophe Colomb*
October 25, 1929, Groupe Art et Action, directed by Mme. Autant-Lara.

*Hop Signor!*
June 13, 1947, Théâtre de l'Œuvre, directed by Catherine Toth and André Reybaz; November 22, 1949, Théâtre des Noctambules, directed by Catherine Toth and André Reybaz.

*Escurial*
December 21, 1948, Studio des Champs-Elysées, directed by René Dupuy and Michel Vitold; July 1964, Festival du Marais (Théâtre Daniel-Sorano, Vincennes), directed by Pierre Debauche.

*Mademoiselle Jaïre*
July 4, 1949, Théâtre de l'Atelier, directed by Pierre Iglésis.

*Fastes d'enfer*
July 11, 1949, Théâtre de l'Atelier, directed by André Reybaz; October 20, 1949, Théâtre Marigny; November 22, 1949, Théâtre des Noctambules.

*Sire Halewyn*
February 17, 1950, Théâtre des Noctambules, directed by Catherine Toth and André Reybaz; July 1964, Festival du Marais (Théâtre Daniel-Sorano, Vincennes), directed by Pierre Debauche.

*Barabbas*
February 21, 1950, Théâtre de l'Œuvre, directed by Jean Le Poulain.

*La Farce des ténébreux*
November 12, 1952, Théâtre du Grand-Guignol, directed by Georges Vitaly.

*Ballade du Grand Macabre (La Grande Kermesse)*
October 12, 1953, Studio des Champs-Elysées, directed by René Dupuy, sets by Jacques Marillier.

*L'Ecole des bouffons*
October 13, 1953, Théâtre de l'Œuvre, directed by Marcel Lupovici, sets by Raymond Raynal; December 1963, Théâtre 347, directed by Marcel Lupovici.

*Magie rouge*
April 1956, Théâtre du Quartier Latin, directed by Gilles Chancrin.

*Trois Acteurs, un drame*
July 1958, Théâtre de Poche, directed by Gilles Chancrin.

*Les Aveugles*
July 1958, Théâtre de Poche, directed by Gilles Chancrin.

*Pantagleize*
1959, Comédie de l'Ouest; October 1965, Théâtre Gramont, directed by René Dupuy.

*Sortie de l'acteur*
December 4, 1963, Théâtre du Tertre.


JEAN VAUTHIER (*1910–     *)

*La Nouvelle Mandragore*
December 20, 1952, TNP (Palais de Chaillot), directed by Gérard Philipe, set by Pignon.

*Capitaine Bada*
January 10, 1952, Théâtre de Poche, directed by André Reybaz, set by René Allio.

*Le Personnage combattant*
February 6, 1956, Petit Théâtre Marigny, directed by Jean-Louis Barrault.

*Les Prodiges*
1959, Théâtre de Poche.

*Le Rêveur*
September 15, 1961, directed by Georges Vitaly, sets by Félix Labisse.

*Badadesques*
October 9, 1965, Théâtre de Lutèce, directed by Marcel Maréchal, sets by Frédéric Benrath.

## GEORGES SCHEHADÉ (*1910–      *)

*Monsieur Bob'le*
January 30, 1951, Théâtre de la Huchette, directed by Georges Vitaly, sets by Dora Maar.

*La Soirée des proverbes*
January 30, 1954, Petit Théâtre Marigny, directed by Jean-Louis Barrault, sets by Félix Labisse.

*Histoire de Vasco*
October 15, 1956, Shauspielhaus, Zurich; September 1957, Théâtre Sarah-Bernhardt, directed by Jean-Louis Barrault, sets by Jack Youngerman.

*Le Voyage*
February 17, 1961, Odéon-Théâtre de France, directed by Jean-Louis Barrault, sets by Jean-Denis Malclès.

*Les Violettes*
September 1966, Théâtre de Bourgogne, directed by Roland Monod, sets by Michel Raffaelli.

## HENRI PICHETTE (*1924–      *)

*Les Epiphanies*
December 3, 1947, Théâtre des Noctambules, directed by Georges Vitaly, sets by Matta.

*Nucléa*
May 3, 1952, TNP (Palais de Chaillot), directed by Gérard Philipe, sets by Alexander Calder.

## RENÉ DE OBALDIA (*1918–* )

*Genousie*
September 26, 1960, TNP-Récamier, directed by René Mollien, set by Raymond Guerrier.

*Impromptus à loisir*
April 7, 1961, Théâtre de Poche, directed by Arlette Reinerg, sets by Fandos.

*Le Satyre de La Villette*
March 25, 1963, Théâtre de l'Atelier, directed by André Barsacq, sets by Jacques Noël.

*Le Général inconnu*
June 11, 1964, Théâtre du Cothurne, Lyons, directed by Marcel Maréchal, set by Jacques Angéniol.

*Du Vent dans les branches de sassafras*
November 29, 1965, Théâtre Gramont, directed by René Dupuy, set by Manfred Hürrig.

## ROMAIN WEINGARTEN (*1926–* )

*Les Nourrices*
November 7, 1961, Théâtre de Lutèce, directed by Romain Weingarten, sets by Bernard Dufour.

*L'Eté*
November 1966, Théâtre de Poche, directed by Jean-François Adam, set by Jacques Noël.

### Boris Vian (1920–1959)

*L'Equarissage pour tous*
April 16, 1950, Théâtre des Noctambules.

*Les Bâtisseurs d'empire*
December 22, 1959, TNP-Récamier, directed by Jean Négroni,
sets by André Acquart.

*Le Goûter des généraux*
September 18, 1965, Théâtre de la Gaîté-Montparnasse, directed
by François Maistre, sets by François Robert.


### Fernando Arrabal (1932–      )

*Pique-nique en campagne*
April 25, 1959, Théâtre de Lutèce, directed by Jean-Marie
Serreau.

*Le Tricycle*
February 15, 1961, Théâtre de Poche, directed by Olivier Hussenot,
sets by Georges Richard; February 1964, Théâtre Daniel-Sorano,
Vincennes.

*Fando et Lis*
March 4, 1964, Théâtre de Lutèce, directed by Claude Cyriaque.

*Le Couronnement*
January 10, 1965, Théâtre Mouffetard, directed by Ivan Henriques.

*La Princesse et la communiante*
July 1966, Théâtre de Poche, directed by Jorge Lavelli.

*Le Grand Cérémonial*
April 1966, Théâtre des Mathurins, directed by Jean Négroni, sets
by Alexander Trauner.

*L'Architecte et l'Empereur d'Assyrie*
March 1967, Théâtre Montparnasse, directed by Raymond
Gérome.

### MARGUERITE DURAS (*1914–* )

*Le Square*
September 17, 1956, Studio des Champs-Elysées, directed by Claude Martin; January 15, 1965, Théâtre Daniel-Sorano, Vincennes, directed by Alain Astruc.

*Les Viaducs de la Seine-et-Oise*
February 21, 1963, Théâtre de Poche, directed by Claude Régy, sets by Jacques Dupont.

*Les Eaux et forêts*
May 14, 1965, Théâtre Mouffetard, directed by Yves Brainville, set by Jean-Marie Borga.

*La Musica*
October 6, 1965, Studio des Champs-Elysées, directed by Alain Astruc, set by José Quiroga.

*Des Journées entières dans les arbres*
December 1, 1965, Odéon-Théâtre de France, directed by Jean-Louis Barrault, sets by Joe Downing.

### ROLAND DUBILLARD (*1923–* )

*Si Camille me voyait!*
1953, Théâtre de Babylone, directed by Jean-Marie Serreau, sets by Jacques Noël.

*Naïves Hirondelles*
October 16, 1961, Théâtre de Poche, directed by Arlette Reinerg, set by Jacques Noël.

*La Maison d'os*
November 21, 1962, Théâtre de Lutèce, directed by Arlette Reinerg, set by Arlette Reinerg.

ROBERT PINGET *(1920–          )*

*Lettre morte*
March 22, 1960, TNP-Récamier, directed by Jean Martin, set by
Matias.

*Architruc*
August 5, 1962, Comédie de Paris, directed by Georges Peyrou,
set by Fandos.

*La Manivelle*
August 5, 1962, Comédie de Paris, directed by Georges Peyrou,
set by Fandos.

*L'Hypothèse*
March 7, 1966, Odéon-Théâtre de France, directed by Jean-Louis
Barrault.

CLAUDE MAURIAC *(1910–          )*

*La Conversation*
January 3, 1966, Théâtre de Lutèce, directed by Nicolas Bataille,
set by Madeleine Louys.

NATHALIE SARRAUTE *(1902–          )*

*Le Silence*
January 1967, Odéon-Théâtre de France, directed by Jean-Louis
Barrault.

*Le Mensonge*
January 1967, Odéon-Théâtre de France, directed by Jean-Louis
Barrault.

JEAN COSMOS *(1923–          )*

*Monsieur Alexandre*
June 2, 1965, Théâtre de l'Est Parisien, direceted by Guy Rétoré,
set by Bernard Guillaumot.

### ARTHUR ADAMOV (1908–    )

*L'Invasion*
November 14, 1950, Studio des Champs-Elysées, directed by Jean Vilar, set by Coussonneau.

*La Grande et la Petite Manœuvre*
November 11, 1950, Théâtre des Noctambules, directed by Jean-Marie Serreau, set by Jacques Noël.

*La Parodie*
June 5, 1952, Théâtre Lancry, directed by Roger Blin, set by Vieira da Silva.

*Le Professeur Taranne*
March 18, 1953, Théâtre de la Comédie, Lyons, directed by Roger Planchon.

*Le Sens de la marche*
March 18, 1953, Théâtre de la Comédie, Lyons, directed by Roger Planchon.

*Tous contre tous*
April 14, 1953, Théâtre de l'Œuvre, directed by Jean-Marie Serreau.

*Le Ping-Pong*
March 2, 1955, Théâtre des Noctambules, directed by Jacques Mauclair, sets by Jacques Noël.

*Paolo Paoli*
May 17, 1957, Théâtre de la Comédie, Lyons, directed by Roger Planchon, sets by René Allio.

*Les Petits Bourgeois* (translation of Gorky)
September 29, 1959, Théâtre de l'Œuvre, directed by Gregory Chmara.

*Les Ames mortes* (adaptation of Gogol)
February 12, 1960, Théâtre de la Cité, Villeurbanne, directed by
Roger Planchon, sets by René Allio.

*Le Printemps 71*
April 26, 1963, Théâtre Gérard-Philipe, Saint-Denis, directed by
Claude Martin, sets by René Allio.

### ARMAND GATTI (*1924–    *)

*Le Crapaud-buffle*
1959, TNP-Récamier, directed by Jean Négroni, sets by Jacques
Le Marquet.

*La Vie imaginaire de l'éboueur Auguste Geai*
February 16, 1962, Théâtre de la Cité, Villeurbanne, directed by
Jacques Rosner, sets by René Allio.

*La Deuxième Existence du camp de Tatenberg*
April 13, 1962, Théâtre des Célestins, Lyons, directed by Gisèle
Tavet, sets by Hubert Monloup.

*Le Poisson noir*
October 1964, Théâtre Daniel-Sorano, Vincennes, directed by
Armand Gatti, sets by Hubert Monloup.

*Chant public devant deux chaises électriques*
January 17, 1966, TNP (Palais de Chaillot), directed by Armand
Gatti, sets by Hubert Monloup.

### FRANÇOIS BILLETDOUX (*1927–    *)

*A la Nuit la unit*
May 17, 1955, Théâtre de l'Œuvre, directed by François Billetdoux,
set by Jacques Noël.

*Tchin-tchin*
January 26, 1959, Théâtre de Poche, directed by François Darbon,
sets by Francine Gaillard-Risler.

*Le Comportement des époux Bredburry*
November 30, 1960, Théâtre des Mathurins, directed by François Billetdoux, sets by Pierre Simonini.

*Va Donc chez Törpe*
September 28, 1961, Studio des Champs-Elysées, directed by Antoine Bourseiller, set by Pace.

*Pour Finalie*
April 13, 1962, Studio des Champs-Elysées, directed by Antoine Bourseiller, sets by Pace.

*Comment Va le Monde, Môssieu? Il Tourne, Môssieu!*
March 11, 1964, Théâtre de l'Ambigu, directed by Geneviève Mallarmé and François Billetdoux, sets by Jacques Noël.

*Il Faut Passer par les Nuages*
October 22, 1964, Odéon-Théâtre de France, directed by Jean-Louis Barrault, sets by René Allio.


GEORGES MICHEL *(1926–     )*

*La Promenade du dimanche*
February 27, 1966, Studio des Champs-Elysées, directed by Maurice Jacquemont and Georges Michel, sets by Alain Bourbonnais.

*L'Agression*
March 1967, TNP (Palais de Chaillot), directed by Georges Wilson.


EUGÈNE IONESCO *(1912–     )*

*La Cantatrice chauve*
May 11, 1950, Théâtre des Noctambules, directed by Nicolas Bataille.

*La Leçon*
Februray 20, 1951, Théâtre de Poche, directed by Marcel Cuvelier.

*Les Chaises*
April 22, 1952, Théâtre Lancry, directed by Sylvain Dhomme, sets by Jacques Noël.

*Victimes du devoir*
February 1953, Théâtre du Quartier Latin, directed by Jacques Mauclair, sets by René Allio; July 1965, Théâtre de Poche, directed by Antoine Bourseiller.

*La Jeune Fille à marier*
September 1, 1953, Théâtre de la Huchette, directed by Jacques Poliéri.

*Amédée ou Comment S'En Débarrasser*
April 14, 1954, Théâtre de Babylone, directed by Jean-Marie Serreau.

*Jacques ou La Soumission*
October 1955, Théâtre de la Huchette, directed by Robert Postec, sets by Jacques Noël.

*Le Tableau*
October 10, 1955, Théâtre de la Huchette, directed by Robert Postec.

*L'Impromptu de l'Alma*
Februray 20, 1956, Studio des Champs-Elysées, directed by Maurice Jacquemont, set by Paul Coupille.

*Le Nouveau Locataire*
September 10, 1957, Théâtre d'Aujourd'hui, directed by Robert Postec, sets by Siné.

*L'Avenir est dans les œufs*
1958.

*Tueur sans gages*
March 2, 1959, Théâtre Récamier, directed by José Quaglio, sets by Jacques Noël.

*Rhinocéros*
January 22, 1960, Odéon-Théâtre de France, directed by Jean-Louis Barrault, sets by Jacques Noël.

*Délire à deux*
April 1962, Studio des Champs-Elysées, directed by Antoine Bourseiller, set by Jacques Noël; March 7, 1966, Odéon-Théâtre de France, directed by Jean-Louis Barrault.

*Le Roi se meurt*
December 15, 1962, Théâtre de l'Alliance Française, directed by Jacques Mauclair, sets by Jacques Noël; December 1966, Théâtre de l'Athénée, directed by Jacques Mauclair, sets by Jacques Noël.

*Le Piéton de l'air*
February 8, 1963, Odéon-Théâtre de France, directed by Jean-Louis Barrault, sets by Jacques Noël.

*La Soif et la faim*
February 28, 1966, Comédie Française, directed by Jean-Marie Serreau, sets by Jacques Noël.

*La Lacune*
March 7, 1966, Odéon-Théâtre de France, directed by Jean-Louis Barrault, set by Jacques Noël.

*Leçons de français pour Américains*
July 1966, Théâtre de Poche, directed by Marc Dudicourt.

SAMUEL BECKETT (*1906–    *)

*En Attendant Godot*
January 5, 1953, Théâtre de Babylone, directed by Roger Blin, set by Sergio Gerstein; May 5, 1961, Odéon-Théâtre de France, di-

rected by Roger Blin; January 1966, Théâtre 347, directed by
Georges Daniel.

*Fin de partie*
April 3, 1957, Royal Court Theatre, London; April 26, 1957,
Studio des Champs-Elysées, directed by Roger Blin, set by Jacques
Noël.

*Acte sans paroles*
April 3, 1957, Royal Court Theatre, London; April 26, 1957,
Studio des Champs-Elysées, directed by Roger Blin, set by Jacques
Noël.

*La Dernière Bande*
March 25, 1960, TNP-Récamier, directed by Roger Blin; Febru-
ary 13, 1961, TNP (Palais de Chaillot), as an opera by Marcel
Mihalovici.

*Oh! Les Beaux Jours*
October 21, 1963, Odéon-Théâtre de France, directed by Roger
Blin, set by Matias.

*Comédie*
June 14, 1964, Pavillon de Marsan, directed by Jean-Marie
Serreau, set by Matias; February 28, 1966, Odéon-Théâtre de
France, directed by Jean-Marie Serreau, set by Matias.

*Va et Vient*
March 7, 1966, Odéon-Théâtre de France, directed by Jean-Louis
Barrault.

JEAN GENET (*1909–    *)

*Les Bonnes*
April 19, 1947, Théâtre de l'Athénée, directed by Louis Jouvet,
sets by Christian Bérard; 1953–54, Théâtre de la Huchette, di-
rected by Tania Balachova, sets by Michel Sarkin; May 1961,
Odéon-Théâtre de France, directed by Jean-Marie Serreau, set by
Léonor Fini.

*Haute Surveillance*
January 26, 1949, Théâtre des Mathurins, directed by Jean Genet, set by André Beaurepaire.

*Les Nègres*
October 28, 1959, Théâtre de Lutèce, directed by Roger Blin.

*Le Balcon*
May 18, 1960, Théâtre du Gymnase, directed by Peter Brook.

*Les Paravents*
April 16, 1966, Odéon-Théâtre de France, directed by Roger Blin, sets by André Acquart.

# SELECTED BIBLIOGRAPHY

I. PLAYWRIGHTS AND THEIR CRITICS

II. MODERN FRENCH THEATRE
IN GENERAL

III. THEORISTS AND DIRECTORS

# PLAYWRIGHTS AND THEIR CRITICS

JEAN GIRAUDOUX

*Théâtre complet,* 16 vols. Neuchâtel and Paris, Ides et Calendes, 1945–51.

*Les Gracques,* Paris, Grasset, 1958.

His Critics

Albérès, R.-M., *Esthétique et morale chez Giraudoux,* Paris, Nizet, 1957.

*Cahiers Renaud-Barrault,* Nos. 26 (1959), 36 (1961).

Durry, Marie-Jeanne, *L'Univers de Giraudoux,* Paris, Mercure de France, 1961.

Høst, Gunnon, *L'Œuvre de Jean Giraudoux,* Oslo, H. Aschehoug, 1942.

Houlet, Jacques, *Le Théâtre de Jean Giraudoux,* Paris, Pierre Ardent, 1945.

Inskip, Donald, *Jean Giraudoux, The Making of a Dramatist,* London and New York, Oxford University Press, 1958.

Lesage, Laurent, *Jean Giraudoux, His Life and His Works,* University Park, Pennsylvania State University Press, 1959.

————, "Jean Giraudoux, Surrealism, and the German Romantic Ideal," *Illinois Studies in Language and Literature, 36,* No. 3, Urbana, University of Illinois Press, 1952.

Magny, Claude-Edmonde, *Précieux Giraudoux,* Paris, Editions du Seuil, 1945.

May, Georges, "Jean Giraudoux: Diplomacy and Dramaturgy," *Yale French Studies,* No. 5 (1950).

*Tulane Drama Review, 3* (Summer 1959).

## JEAN COCTEAU

*Théâtre complet,* 2 vols. Paris, Grasset, 1957.

### His Critics

Dubourg, Pierre, *Dramaturgie de Jean Cocteau,* Paris, Grasset, 1954.

Fergusson, Francis, *"The Infernal Machine:* The Myth behind the Modern City," in *The Idea of a Theatre,* Princeton, Princeton University Press, 1949.

Fowlie, Wallace, *Jean Cocteau, The History of a Poet's Age,* Bloomington, Indiana University Press, 1966.

Kihm, Jean-Jacques, *Cocteau,* Paris, Gallimard, 1961.

Oxenhandler, Neal, *Scandal and Parade: The Theatre of Jean Cocteau,* New Brunswick, N.J., Rutgers University Press, 1957.

## PAUL CLAUDEL

*Théâtre,* rev. ed. 2 vols. Paris, Gallimard, 1965.

### His Critics

Bastien, Jacques, *L'Œuvre dramatique de Paul Claudel,* Reims, Bastien, 1957.

Beaumont, Ernest, *The Theme of Beatrice in the Plays of Paul Claudel,* London, Rockhill, 1957.

Berton, Jean-Claude, *Shakespeare et Claudel,* Paris, La Palatine, 1958.

Brune, Pierre, *"L'Otage" de Paul Claudel,* Paris, Archives des Lettres Modernes, 1964.

*Cahiers Paul Claudel,* Nos. 1 (1959), 2 (1960), 5 (1964), Paris, Gallimard.

*Cahiers Renaud-Barrault,* Nos. 1 (1953), 12 (1955), 25 (1958), 27 (1959).

Chiari, Joseph, *The Poetic Drama of Paul Claudel,* New York, Kennedy, 1954.

Farabet, René, *Le Jeu de l'acteur dans le théâtre de Claudel,* Paris, Les Lettres Modernes, 1960.

Peyre, Henri, "The Drama of Paul Claudel," *Thought,* 27, No. 105 (1952).


## ARMAND SALACROU

*Théâtre,* 8 vols. Paris, Gallimard, 1942–66.

### His Critics

Mignon, Paul-Louis, *Salacrou,* Paris, Gallimard, 1962.

Radine, Serge, *Anouilh, Lenormand, Salacrou: Trois Dramaturges à la recherche de leur verité,* Geneva, Trois Collines, 1951.

Van den Esh, José, *Armand Salacrou, dramaturge de l'angoisse,* Paris, Editions du Temps Présent, 1947.


## HENRY DE MONTHERLANT

*Théâtre,* Paris, Gallimard, 1954.
*Brocéliande,* Paris, Gallimard, 1956.
*Don Juan,* Paris, Gallimard, 1958.
*Le Cardinal d'Espagne,* Paris, Gallimard, 1960.
*La Guerre civile,* Paris, Gallimard, 1965.

### His Critics

Chevalley, Sylvie, ed., *Henry de Montherlant,* Paris, Comédie Française, 1960.

Laprade, Jacques de, *Le Théâtre de Montherlant,* Paris, La Jeune Parque, 1950.

Mohrt, Michel, *Montherlant, homme libre,* Paris, Gallimard, 1943.


## JEAN ANOUILH

*Pièces noires,* Paris, Calmann-Lévy, 1945.
*Nouvelles Pièces noires,* Paris, La Table Ronde, 1947.

*Pièces brillantes,* Paris, La Table Ronde, 1951.

*Pièces grinçantes,* Paris, La Table Ronde, 1956.

*L'Hurluberlu,* Paris, La Table Ronde, 1959.

*La Petite Molière,* in *L'Avant-Scène,* No. 210 (1959).

*Pièces costumées,* Paris, La Table Ronde, 1960.

*La Grotte,* Paris, La Table Ronde, 1961.

*Pièces roses,* Paris, La Table Ronde, 1961.

*L'Orchestre,* in *L'Avant-Scène,* No. 276 (1962).

### His Critics

Harvey, John, *Anouilh, A Study in Theatrics,* New Haven, Yale University Press, 1964.

Pronko, Leonard C., *The World of Jean Anouilh,* Berkeley, University of California Press, 1961.

Radine, Serge. *See* Salacrou, His Critics, above.

Vandromme, Pol, *Jean Anouilh, un auteur et ses personnages,* Paris, La Table Ronde, 1965.

## JEAN-PAUL SARTRE

*Théâtre I,* Paris, Gallimard, 1947.

*Les Mains sales,* Paris, Gallimard, 1948.

*Le Diable et le Bon Dieu,* Paris, Gallimard, 1952.

*Kean,* Paris, Gallimard, 1954.

*Nekrassov,* Paris, Gallimard, 1957.

*Les Séquestrés d'Altona,* Paris, Gallimard, 1959.

### His Critics

Albérès, R.-M., *Jean-Paul Sartre,* Paris-Brussels, Editions Universitaires, 1953.

Bentley, Eric, "From Strindberg to Jean-Paul Sartre," in *The Playwright as Thinker,* New York, Meridian, 1955.

Brombert, Victor, "Sartre and the Drama of Ensnarement," in the English Institute collection, *Ideas in the Drama,* New York, Columbia University Press, 1964.

Fergusson, Francis, "Sartre as Playwright," *Partisan Review, 16,* No. 4 (1949).

Kern, Edith, ed., *Sartre, A Collection of Critical Essays,* Englewood Cliffs, N.J., Prentice-Hall, 1962.

### ALBERT CAMUS

*Théâtre, récits, nouvelles,* Paris, Gallimard, 1962.

His Critics

Brée, Germaine, *Camus,* New Brunswick, N.J., Rutgers University Press, 1959.

————, ed., *Camus, A Collection of Critical Essays,* Englewood Cliffs, N.J., Prentice-Hall, 1962.

Reck, Rima Drell, "The Theater of Albert Camus," *Modern Drama, 4* (May 1961).

Sonnenfeld, Albert, "Albert Camus as Dramatist: The Sources of His Failure," *Tulane Drama Review, 5* (Summer 1961).

### JACQUES AUDIBERTI

*Théâtre,* 4 vols. Paris, Gallimard, 1948–61.
*Le Cavalier seul,* Paris, Gallimard, 1955.
*La Mégère apprivoisée,* Paris, Gallimard, 1957.
*L'Effet Glapion,* Paris, Gallimard, 1959.

His Critics

Deslandes, André, *Audiberti,* Paris, Gallimard, 1964.

Wellworth, George, "Jacques Audiberti: The Drama of the Savage God," *Texas Studies in Literature and Language, 4* (Autumn 1962).

### MICHEL DE GHELDERODE

*Théâtre,* 5 vols. Paris, Gallimard, 1950–57.
*Les Entretiens d'Ostende,* Paris, L'Arche, 1956.

His Critics

Grossvogel, David, *The Self-Conscious Stage in Modern French Drama,* New York, Columbia University Press, 1958.

*Tulane Drama Review, 8* (Fall 1963).

Vandromme, Pol, *Michel de Ghelderode,* Paris, Editions Universitaires, 1963.

### JEAN VAUTHIER

*Théâtre,* Paris, L'Arche, 1954.
*Le Personnage combattant,* Paris, Gallimard, 1955.

*Les Prodiges,* Paris, Gallimard, 1958.
*Bada, suivi de Badadesques,* Paris, Gallimard, 1966.

His Critics
*Cahiers Renaud-Barrault,* No. 14 (1955).

## GEORGES SCHEHADÉ

*Monsieur Bob'le,* Paris, Gallimard, 1951.
*La Soirée des proverbes,* Paris, Gallimard, 1954.
*Histoire de Vasco,* Paris, Gallimard, 1956.
*Les Violettes,* Paris, Gallimard, 1960.
*Le Voyage,* Paris, Gallimard, 1961.
*L'Emigré de Brisbane,* Paris, Gallimard, 1965.

His Critics
*Cahiers Renaud-Barrault,* Nos. 17 (1956), 34 (1961).

## HENRI PICHETTE

*Les Epiphanies,* Paris, K, 1948.
*Nucléa,* Paris, L'Arche, 1952.

## RENÉ DE OBALDIA

*Sept Impromptus à loisir,* Paris, Julliard, 1963.
*L'Air du large,* in *L'Avant-Scène,* No. 324 (1964).
*Théâtre,* Paris, Grasset, 1966.
*Du Vent dans les branches de sassafras,* in *L'Avant-Scène,* No. 350 (1966).

## ROMAIN WEINGARTEN

*L'Eté, Akara, Les Nourrices,* Paris, Christian Bourgois, 1967.

## BORIS VIAN

*Théâtre,* Paris, Pauvert, 1965.

His Critics
Baudin, Henri, *Boris Vian: La Poursuite de la vie totale,* Paris, Editions du Centurion, 1966.

Noakes, David, *Boris Vian*, Paris, Editions Universitaires, 1965.
Vree, Freddy de, *Boris Vian*, Paris, Le Terrain Vague, 1965.

### FERNANDO ARRABAL

*Théâtre*, 3 vols. Paris, Julliard, 1958–65.
*Théâtre panique*, Paris, Christian Bourgois, 1967.

### MARGUERITE DURAS

*Les Viaducs de la Seine-et-Oise*, Paris, Gallimard, 1960.
*Théâtre I*, Paris, Gallimard, 1965.
*Des Journées entières dans les arbres*, in *L'Avant-Scène*, No. 348–49
  (1966).

Her Critics
*Cahiers Renaud-Barrault*, No. 52 (1965).

### ROLAND DUBILLARD

*Naïves Hirondelles, suivi de Si Camille me voyait*, Paris, Gallimard,
  1962.
*La Maison d'os*, Paris, Gallimard, 1966.

### JEAN TARDIEU

*Théâtre de chambre*, Paris, Gallimard, 1955.
*Poèmes à jouer*, Paris, Gallimard, 1960.

### ROBERT PINGET

*Lettre morte*, Paris, Editions de Minuit, 1959.
*La Manivelle*, Paris, Editions de Minuit, 1960.
*Ici ou Ailleurs, Architruc, L'Hypothèse*, Paris, Editions de Minuit,
  1961.

### CLAUDE MAURIAC

*La Conversation*, Paris, Grasset, 1964.

### NATHALIE SARRAUTE

*Le Silence, Le Mensonge*, Paris, Gallimard, 1967.

### ARTHUR ADAMOV

*Théâtre*, 3 vols. Paris, Gallimard, 1953–66.
*Théâtre de société*, Paris, Les Editeurs français réunis, 1958.
*Les Ames mortes*, Paris, Gallimard, 1959.
*Le Printemps 71*, Paris, Gallimard, 1961.
*Ici et Maintenant*, Paris, Gallimard, 1964.

### ARMAND GATTI

*Théâtre*, 4 vols. Paris, Editions du Seuil, 1959–66.
*V comme Vietnam*, Paris, Editions du Seuil, 1967.

### FRANÇOIS BILLETDOUX

*Théâtre*, 2 vols. Paris, Editions du Seuil, 1961–64.

### EUGÈNE IONESCO

*Théâtre*, 4 vols. Paris, Gallimard, 1954–66.
*Notes et contre-notes*, Paris, Gallimard, 1962.

His Critics
Benmussa, Simone, *Ionesco*, Paris, Seghers, 1966.
Bonnefoy, Claude, *Entretiens avec Eugène Ionesco*, Paris, Pierre Belfond, 1966.
Burke, Kenneth, "Dramatic Form—And," *Tulane Drama Review, 10* (Summer 1966).
*Cahiers Renaud-Barrault*, Nos. 29 (1960), 42 (1963), 53 (1966).
Coe, Richard N., *Eugène Ionesco,* New York, Grove Press, 1961.
Lamont, Rosette, "The Metaphysical Farce: Beckett and Ionesco," *French Review, 32* (February 1959).
Pronko, Leonard, "The Anti-Spiritual Victory in the Theatre of Ionesco," *Modern Drama, 2* (May 1959).
———, *Eugène Ionesco,* New York and London, Columbia University Press, 1965.

### SAMUEL BECKETT

*En Attendant Godot*, Paris, Editions de Minuit, 1952.
*Fin de partie, Acte sans paroles*, Paris, Editions de Minuit, 1957.

*La Dernière Bande, suivi de Cendres,* Paris, Editions de Minuit, 1959.
*Oh! Les Beaux Jours,* Paris, Editions de Minuit, 1963.
*Comédie et actes divers,* Paris, Editions de Minuit, 1966.

### His Critics
*Cahiers Renaud-Barrault,* No. 44 (1963).
Champigny, Robert, "Interpretation of *En Attendant Godot,*" *PMLA,* 75, No. 3 (1960).
Cohn, Ruby, *Samuel Beckett, The Comic Gamut,* New Brunswick, N.J., Rutgers University Press, 1962.
Harvey, Lawrence, "Art and the Existential in *En Attendant Godot,*" *PMLA,* 75, No. 1 (1960).
Kenner, Hugh, *Samuel Beckett, A Critical Study,* New York, Grove Press, 1962.
Kern, Edith, "Drama Stripped for Inaction: Beckett's *Godot,*" *Yale French Studies,* No. 14 (Winter 1954–55).
Lamont, Rosette. *See* Ionesco, His Critics, above.
Leventhal, A. J., "Mr. Beckett's *En Attendant Godot,*" *Dublin Magazine* (April–June 1954).
Mayoux, Jean-Jacques, "Le Théâtre de Samuel Beckett," *Etudes Anglaises, 10,* No. 4 (Paris, 1957).
Mélèse, Pierre, *Beckett,* Paris, Seghers, 1966.
*Perspective, 11* (Autumn 1959).
*Revue des Lettres Modernes,* No. 100 (1962).
Tindall, William York, *Samuel Beckett,* New York and London, Columbia University Press, 1964.
Torrance, Robert M., "Modes of Being and Time in the World of *Godot,*" *Modern Language Quarterly,* 28 (March 1967).

## JEAN GENET

*Haute Surveillance,* Paris, Gallimard, 1949.
*Le Balcon,* Décines, L'Arbalète, 1956.
*Les Bonnes,* in *L'Atelier d'Alberto Giacometti,* Décines, L'Arbalète, 1958.
*Les Nègres,* Décines, Barbezat, 1960.
*Les Paravents,* Décines, Barbezat, 1961.

His Critics

Brustein, Robert, "Antonin Artaud and Jean Genet: The Theatre of Cruelty," in *The Theatre of Revolt,* Boston, Little, Brown, 1964.

Driver, Tom, *Jean Genet,* New York and London, Columbia University Press, 1966.

Goldmann, Lucien, "Le Théâtre de Genet et ses études sociologiques," *Cahiers Renaud-Barrault,* No. 57 (1966).

McMahon, Joseph, *The Imagination of Jean Genet,* New Haven, Yale University Press, 1963.

Magnan, Jean-Marie, *Essai sur Jean Genet,* Paris, Seghers, 1966.

Nugent, Robert, "Sculpture into Drama: Giacometti's Influence on Genet," *Drama Survey, 3* (February 1964).

Sartre, Jean-Paul, *Saint Genet, comédien et martyr,* Paris, Gallimard, 1952; *Saint Genet: Actor and Martyr,* trans. Bernard Frechtman, New York, Braziller, 1963.

*Tulane Drama Review,* 7 (Spring 1963).

Zimbardo, Rose A., "Genet's Black Mass," *Modern Drama, 8* (December 1965).

# II

# MODERN FRENCH THEATRE IN GENERAL

*Aspects of Drama and the Theatre,* Kathleen Robinson Lectures, Sidney, Sidney University Press, 1965.

Beigbeder, Marc, *Le Théâtre en France depuis la Libération,* Paris, Bordas, 1959.

Bernay, Jacques G., and Reinhard Kuhn, *Panorama du théâtre nouveau* (anthology), 4 vols. New York, Appleton-Century-Crofts, 1967.

Brée, Germaine, "The New Theatre of France," *Portfolio and Art News Annual,* No. 3 (1960).

*Cahiers Renaud-Barrault,* Nos. 46 ("Billetdoux, Jean-Pierre Faye, Robert Pinget, Romain Weingarten," 1964), 53 ("Ionesco, Beckett, Pinget," 1966), 54 ("Répertoire contemporain," 1966).

Cohn, Ruby, "Four Stages of the Absurdist Hero," *Drama Survey,* 4 (Winter 1965).

Corvin, Michel, *Le Théâtre nouveau en France,* Paris, Presses Universitaires de France, 1963.

*L'Esprit Créateur* ("New Directions in French Drama"), 2 (Winter 1962).

Esslin, Martin, *The Theatre of the Absurd,* New York, Doubleday Anchor, 1961.

Fowlie, Wallace, *Dionysus in Paris, A Guide to French Contemporary Theatre,* New York, Meridian, 1959.

Grossvogel, David, *The Blasphemers: The Theatre of Brecht, Ionesco, Beckett, Genet,* Ithaca, Cornell University Press, 1965.

Pronko, Leonard C., *Avant-Garde: The Experimental Theatre in France,* Berkeley and Los Angeles, University of California Press, 1962.

Pucciani, Oreste F., *The French Theatre since 1930* (anthology), Boston, Ginn, 1954.

Serreau, Geneviève, *Histoire du nouveau théâtre,* Paris, Gallimard, 1966.

Simon, Pierre-Henri, *Théâtre et destin,* Paris, Armand Colin, 1959.

Surer, Paul, *Le Théâtre français contemporain,* Paris, Société d'Edition et d'Enseignement Supérieur, 1964.

*Yale French Studies,* Nos. 5 ("The Modern Theatre and Its Background," 1950), 14 ("Motley: Today's French Theatre," 1954–55), 29 ("The New Dramatists," 1962).

# III

# THEORISTS AND DIRECTORS

## BOOKS

Artaud, Antonin, *Œuvres complètes,* 6 vols. Paris, Gallimard, 1956–
65; from Vol. 4, *The Theatre and Its Double,* trans. Mary Caroline
Richards, New York, Grove Press, 1958.

————, *Lettres d'Antonin Artaud à Jean-Louis Barrault,* Paris, Bordas,
1952.

Baecque, André de, *Le Théâtre d'aujourd'hui,* Paris, Seghers, 1964.

Barrault, Jean-Louis, *Réflexions sur le théâtre,* Paris, Vautrain, 1949.

————, *Nouvelles Réflexions sur le théâtre,* Paris, Flammarion, 1959.

Baty, Gaston, *Le Masque et l'encensoir, introduction à une esthétique
du théâtre,* Paris, Bloud et Gay, 1926.

———— and René Chavance, *La Vie de l'art théâtral des origines à nos
jours,* Paris, Plon, 1932.

Bentley, Eric, *In Search of Theatre,* New York, Knopf, 1953.

Blanchart, Paul, *Gaston Baty,* Paris, Nouvelle Revue Critique, 1939.

————, *Histoire de la mise en scène,* Paris, Presses Universitaires de
France, 1953.

Boll, André, *La Mise en Scène contemporaine, son évolution,* Paris,
Nouvelle Revue Critique, 1944.

*Cahiers Renaud-Barrault,* No. 22–23 ("Artaud et le théâtre de notre temps," 1958).

Chancerel, Léon, *Jean-Louis Barrault,* Paris, Presses Littéraires de France, 1953.

Cogniat, Raymond, *Gaston Baty,* Paris, Presses Littéraires de France, 1953.

———, *Cinquante Ans de spectacles en France: Les Décorateurs de théâtre,* Paris, Librairie Théâtrale, 1955.

Copeau, Jacques, *Souvenirs du Vieux Colombier,* Paris, Nouvelles Editions Latines, 1931.

Dhomme, Sylvain, *La Mise en Scène d'Antoine à Brecht,* Paris, Fernand Nathan, 1960.

Dullin, Charles, *Souvenirs et notes de travail d'un acteur,* Paris, Odette Lieutier, 1946.

*Encyclopédie du Théâtre contemporain,* ed. Gilles Quéant, 2 vols. Paris, Publications de France, 1957.

*Europe* ("Le Théâtre en France"), No. 396–97 (1962).

Frank, André, *Georges Pitoëff,* Paris, L'Arche, 1958.

Gassner, John, *Form and Idea in Modern Theatre,* New York, Dryden Press, 1956; rev. ed. *Directions in Modern Theatre and Drama,* New York, Holt, Rinehart and Winston, 1965.

Gouhier, Henri, *L'Essence du théâtre,* Paris, Aubier, 1943.

———, *Le Théâtre et l'existence,* Paris, Aubier, 1952.

———, *L'Œuvre théâtrale,* Paris, Flammarion, 1958.

Hort, Jean, *Les Théâtres du Cartel,* Geneva, Skira, 1944.

Jouvet, Louis, *Réflexions du comédien,* Paris, Librairie Théâtrale, 1952.

———, *Témoignages sur le théâtre,* Paris, Flammarion, 1952.

Knapp, Bettina, *Louis Jouvet, Man of the Theatre,* New York, Columbia University Press, 1957.

Lenormand, Henri-René, *Les Pitoëff, souvenirs,* Paris, Odette Lieutier, 1943.

Lerminier, Georges, *Jacques Copeau,* Paris, Presses Littéraires de France, 1953.

Mignon, Paul-Louis, *Le Théâtre d'aujourd'hui de A jusqu'à Z,* Paris, Editions Michel Brient, 1966.

Pitoëff, Georges, *Notre Théâtre,* Paris, Messages, 1949.

Robichez, Jacques, *Le Symbolisme au théâtre: Lugné-Poe et les débuts de l'Œuvre*, Paris, L'Arche, 1957.

Rouché, Jacques, *L'Art théâtral moderne*, rev. ed. Paris, Bloud et Gay, 1924.

Sarment, Jean, *Charles Dullin*, Paris, Calmann-Lévy, 1950.

Touchard, Pierre-Aimé, *Dionysos, apologie pour le théâtre*, Paris, Editions du Seuil, 1949.

Valogne, Catherine, *Jean Vilar*, Paris, Presses Littéraires de France, 1954.

Veinstein, André, *La Mise en Scène théâtrale et sa condition esthétique*, Paris, Flammarion, 1955.

Vilar, Jean, *De la Tradition théâtrale*, Paris, L'Arche, 1955.

## PERIODICALS

*L'Avant-Scène*
*Bref* (TNP)
*Cahiers Renaud-Barrault*
*Le Théâtre dans le monde* (UNESCO)
*Théâtre populaire*

# INDEX